CONFEDERATE GENERALS

Jefferson Davis and the Confederate Generals depicts many of the South's most colorful military leaders, including (*left to right*) A. P. Hill, John Bell Hood, Davis, J. E. B. Stuart, Stonewall Jackson, Robert E. Lee, James Longstreet, Joseph Johnston, P. G. T. Beauregard, and Jubal Early. A portrait of Robert Toombs hangs on the wall. *David J. Eicher Collection*

CONFEDERATE GENERALS

Life Portraits

GEORGE CANTOR

TAYLOR TRADE PUBLISHING
DALLAS, TEXAS

For my brother, Mike, who walked with me on my first Civil War battlefield.

Designed by David Timmons

Published by Taylor Publishing Company
1550 West Mockingbird Lane
Dallas, Texas 75235
www.taylorpub.com

Library of Congress Cataloging-in-Publication Data

Cantor, George, 1941–
Confederate generals : life portraits / George Cantor.
p. cm.
Includes bibliographical references and index.
ISBN 0-87833-179-4
1. Generals—Confederate States of America—Portraits. 2. Generals—Confederate States of America—Biography. 3. Confederate States of America. Army—Portraits. 4. Confederate States of America. Army—Biography. 5. United States—History—Civil War, 1861–1865—Portraits. I. Title.

E467 .C36 2000
973.7'42'0922—dc21 00-042592

10 9 8 7 6 5 4 3 2 1

Printed in the United States of America

CONTENTS

Introduction vii

THE LEGENDS
- Robert E. Lee 3
- Thomas J. "Stonewall" Jackson 16
- Joseph E. Johnston 30
- James Longstreet 43

THE CAVALRYMEN
- James Ewell Brown Stuart 57
- Nathan Bedford Forrest 69
- John Hunt Morgan 79

THE WESTERN COMMANDERS
- Albert Sidney Johnston 91
- John Bell Hood 102
- Patrick Cleburne 113

THE DIFFICULT MEN
- Jubal A. Early 125
- Braxton Bragg 137
- Robert A. Toombs 148

THE ECCENTRICS
- Pierre Gustave Toutant Beauregard 161
- Leonidas Polk 173
- George E. Pickett 183

Bibliography 194

Index 196

INTRODUCTION

Very early in the research for this book, I stood in the living room of the Hunt-Morgan House in Lexington, Kentucky, making polite small talk with the guide who had just shown me through the place.

Since this was the home of John Hunt Morgan, the conversation naturally turned to Confederate cavalry leaders. The guide mentioned that even though he worked at Morgan's home, his favorite Confederate leader was Nathan Bedford Forrest.

I agreed with his choice, I said, except for that nasty business about his helping to found the Ku Klux Klan. Instantly, the guide's smile froze.

"There was never any proof of that," he said tersely. And that ended the conversation.

That was my introduction to the War Between the States as it enters its third century. In so many Southern hearts and minds the war and its leading personalities are issues as hot and immediate as...well, which flag flies over the state capitol.

As I write these words, 135 years after the stillness at Appomattox, a controversy rages about South Carolina's use of the Confederate flag. Most white Southerners insist the flag is a precious portion of their heritage and belongs at the seat of state government. African-Americans respond by marching with signs that read: "Your heritage is our racism." The dispute even spilled over into the primary election campaigns for the U.S. presidency forcing each candidate to take a stand.

It is the war that will not go away. World War I is half a century closer to us in time and can even be viewed in motion in the film archives. Yet to most Americans its issues and leaders are vague and unfamiliar. But the names and battles of the Civil War are as close to us as breathing.

Abraham Lincoln is still regarded as the greatest U.S. president because of his leadership during the war.

The echoes of "There stands Jackson like a stone wall" and "Lee to the rear!" still ring like chimes in the night.

Pickett's Charge has passed into the fabric of the language as the symbol of a valiant but doomed effort. Amateur historians join in heated debates over James Longstreet's role at Gettysburg, Joseph E. Johnston's strategy in Georgia, and Jefferson Davis's competence as a leader, arguing as if it had all just been on the evening network news.

The Civil War is so deeply engrained in the American experience, and its roots reach so deeply into our history, that it remains, overwhelmingly, the dominant feature in the landscape of the past.

As I learned in my research, you cannot discuss the Mexican War, the Spanish-American War, or World War I without also touching on some aspect of the Civil War. It was part of the western expansion. Of the campaigns against the Indians. The culture of the U.S. Military Academy. Patterns of immigration from Europe. Religious belief. The specter of the Jim Crow laws that followed.

The very topography of the land, down to hills and streams that are barely blips on a map but whose names have been magnified by the blood that was spilled there, carry its memory.

Growing up in the North, my sympathies naturally went with the Bluecoats in all the old movies and the popular histories. But as I learned more about the Confederate military leaders in the course of writing this book, the one thing that impressed me was what a remarkable group of individuals they were. Their actual lives were stranger by far than anything Hollywood ever contrived.

I only wish there had been room for more than the 16 leaders included in this book. I sincerely regret the omission of the birdlike Richard Ewell. Of Ambrose P. Hill, haunted by the legend of Stonewall Jackson, the man he replaced in command. Of John Pemberton, the Philadelphian who fought for the South and was accused of treachery when he had to surrender

Vicksburg. Of Joseph Wheeler, who lived long enough to charge up San Juan Hill with Teddy Roosevelt in 1898 and famously cried out: "We've got the Yankees on the run, boys."

But those who remain in these pages are striking enough. The high-spirited gallantry of Stuart and Morgan. The ferocious Forrest and how he understood psychological warfare better than any West Point general. The stalwart Cleburne, who found a home in the South but never truly understood it.

The shattered wreck that was Pickett after Gettysburg. The bitter debate between Longstreet and Early in the 30 years following the war. The fire-eating politician Toombs who foresaw that the war would end the world he knew.

You can still feel their presence in the land they fought for.

Political analyst Michael Barone wrote that the Civil War remained the major dividing point in domestic politics right up to the election of Franklin D. Roosevelt in 1932.

I believe he is wrong. It really has never gone away. The war is always there, its emotions just an inch below the surface. I learned that much in John Hunt Morgan's house.

George Cantor
March 2000

The Legends

ROBERT E. LEE

"That he was the greatest man this country has produced I have no doubt. And the proudest thing in my life is that I have seen, talked with and shaken hands with him."

Rev. W. Strother Jones, a former student at Washington College, quoted in the book General Robert E. Lee After Appomattox, 1922

To fully understand Robert E. Lee it is necessary to journey to Stratford Hall, ancestral home to four generations of Lees, on the bluffs above the Potomac River, in the northern neck of Virginia. In the ancient bricks of this distinguished plantation house, birthplace of Robert E. Lee, is the sense of permanence and position that bound the family to the soil of this state.

In the midst of the Civil War, as he allowed his mind to wander briefly to happier days, he mused about it dreamily in a letter to his wife.

"In the absence of a home," he wrote, "I wish I could purchase Stratford. That is the only place I could go to…that would inspire me with feelings of pleasure and local love. You and the girls could remain there in quiet. It is a poor place but we could make enough cornbread and bacon for our support and the girls could weave us clothes. I wonder if it is for sale and for how much."

He had left almost half a century before, forced to depart because his father's weakness for land speculation had depleted the family fortune. But this place, which symbolized so much of what it meant to be a Lee of Virginia, still haunted his dreams.

Stratford Hall was built by his great grandfather, Thomas Lee, in the 1730s. By that time, the Lees already had been in Virginia almost 100 years. They had cleared the wilderness, helped to govern the young colony, signed the Declaration of Independence, and fought beside George Washington during the Revolution. When Lee was born here in 1807, the house already echoed with the greatness of the past.

A visit to Stratford Hall somehow makes the terrible decision that Lee was forced to make in 1861 more intelligible. One can grasp how his loyalty to Virginia, the land possessed by his ancestors and which in turn possessed them, overrode his sense of obligation to the Union his forebears helped create.

He disapproved of secession and felt slavery was a curse. Yet when offered the post that would have placed him in command of the Union army, he did not hesitate to refuse it.

"I have not been able to make up my mind to raise my hand against my relatives, my children, my home," he wrote to his sister. "…Save in defense of my native state, with the sincere hope that my poor services may never be needed, I hope I may never be called on to draw my sword."

Stratford Hall is located just a few miles down the Potomac from the birthplace of Washington, the public figure Lee admired above all others. It was his father, Light Horse Harry Lee, one of the most trusted officers on Washington's staff, who delivered the eulogy that came to symbolize his place in America's national life: "First in war, first in peace and first in the hearts of his countrymen."

Lee would marry the daughter of Washington's stepson, George Washington Parke Custis. Through her he inherited the pillared Arlington mansion that overlooks Washington, D.C., from its hilltop across the Potomac. This was the other home, besides Stratford, that he was forced to give up.

The mansion was taken by federal troops after the Lees fled and later was seized by the government for nonpayment of taxes. A settlement was later made with Lee's descendants, but by that time the property had become Arlington National Cemetery.

Then as now the view of the capital from here is

Both gentleman and soldier, Robert E. Lee represented the quintessential Confederate general. ***Library of Congress***

magnificent. President John F. Kennedy visited the place a few weeks before his death in 1963 and told a companion that it was such a beautiful sight "I could stay here forever." His grave is situated just below the house.

It was in this house that Lee paced through a sleepless night over his decision to resign from the U.S. Army. He left here for Richmond to assume command of Virginia's troops on April 22, 1861, and never returned. That is why in the previously quoted letter to his wife, written eight months later, he referred to the family's "absence of a home." Both of the places he loved most had been lost, and for a man with such a keen sense of place, the losses were irreparable.

When he lived at Arlington, he occasionally would take the short ride to Alexandria and walk by the house where he had lived as a young boy, after the family had given up Stratford Hall. Once the occupants of the dwelling on Orinoco Street were startled to see him peering over their garden wall. He apologized and explained that he just wanted to see how some of his favorite trees were blooming.

His residence in Alexandria, the place Washington considered his hometown, deepened his sense of admiration for the first president. Washington's dignity, sense of gravity, ability to inspire others, and frugality were qualities that Lee deliberately sought to emulate. The Custis family had acquired many articles associated with Washington and placed them in the Arlington house. Lee lived among them for years, which must have strongly reinforced his sense of identification.

It was his father, however, who provided the most direct link to the great general. Light Horse Harry had fought brilliantly throughout the Revolution as a cavalry leader reporting directly to Washington.

After the war, he was elected to three one-year terms as governor of Virginia. Washington chose him personally to command the force that put down the Whiskey Rebellion of 1794 in western Pennsylvania. Lee's ability to do it without casualties enhanced his popularity, and he was elected to Congress in 1799.

But this brilliant man also had a weakness. It only became apparent after his marriage to a distant cousin, Matilda Lee, which allowed him to come into possession of Stratford Hall. Matilda died in 1790, and three years later Harry married Ann Carter, a member of another of Virginia's most illustrious families. Robert was the fifth child of this marriage. There were six children altogether growing up at Stratford.

The cost of supporting this large family in a style deemed proper to their standing was more than Harry Lee could handle. A poor manager, he invested heavily in bad land deals and was humiliated by a term in debtor's prison in 1808. While incarcerated, he spent the time writing a history of the southern campaigns of the Revolutionary War, regarded for most of the nineteenth century as the standard text.

He could never get out from under the burden of accumulated debt, however, and in 1811, when Robert was four years old, the family had to leave Stratford for the modest house in Alexandria. It was a point of pride with Robert as an adult that he managed his money wisely. When asked by a young mother for the most important quality she could teach her child, he responded, "Self denial."

Even after the move, trouble followed Harry. While defending a friend who published a federalist newspaper in Baltimore, he was beaten by a mob and suffered injuries that broke his health. He went to the West Indies to try to recover, but on the voyage home his strength gave out, and he died in Georgia in 1818.

During his father's absence and after his death, Robert was forced to take on responsibilities far beyond the usual scope of a child. His mother would later describe him as "a son and daughter to me." He not only became the man of the house but also a loving companion to his mother, whom misfortune had turned into an invalid.

As he grew through his teenage years, it became obvious that the family lacked the means to send him to college. For the son of such a distinguished line to enter trade was unthinkable. So Secretary of War John Calhoun, a sympathetic fellow Southerner, arranged an appointment to West Point.

Lee entered the Academy in 1825, and his maturity quickly became evident. In his four years at West Point, he was never given a demerit, and he consistently excelled at his classes. His nickname, in fact, was the Marble Model. But he was not the austere goody-goody the name implies and was among the most popular cadets.

He graduated second in his class and had his choice of assignments. As with most top students in that era, he picked the engineers and for the next 17 years was given a variety of assignments across the country. He was sent as an assistant to work on the construction of Fort Pulaski, near Savannah, Georgia, and Fort Monroe, near Hampton, Virginia.

After a three-year stint in Washington, he went to the Midwest: first to help settle a boundary dispute between Ohio and Michigan that had almost led to a farcical war in 1835, and then to supervise harbor construction in St. Louis. Then it was back east to Fort Hamilton, in New York City.

By this time he was 39 years old. He had taken time out during his assignment in Virginia to marry Mary Ann Randolph Custis, a bright and attractive young woman whose other suitors had included Sam Houston. They were distant cousins who had known each other since childhood, and Mary Ann had long ago developed "an attachment" to the handsome Lee.

The wedding was held in the mansion at Arlington on June 30, 1831. Those who were there remembered it years later as "a piece of Virginia life pleasant to recall." As his army was driven back into the fortifications at Petersburg on their anniversary in 1864, Robert would write Mary Ann: "Do you recollect what a happy day thirty three years ago this was? How many hopes and pleasures it gave birth to."

The couple had seven children, and while Mary Ann usually accompanied her husband to his various postings, she always returned to Arlington to give birth. He managed to obtain furloughs that enabled him to be in Arlington to spend 24 of the 30 Christmases of their married life before the start of the war.

The turning point in Lee's military career, as with so many other Civil War leaders, was the outbreak of hostilities with Mexico in 1846. His performance in the Mexican War was acclaimed by his commanders, especially Winfield Scott. Lee discovered in himself a genius for reconnaissance work, and he developed the firm conviction that the critical advantage always belongs to the general who knows the territory best.

Stratford Hall, the Lee ancestral home, loomed large in Lee's memory. *National Archives and Records Division*

At Cerro Gordo, Lee found a path around the left flank of well-fortified Mexican batteries. In the final advance on Mexico City, he discovered a crossing of the great lava field of Pedregal, which acted as a natural barrier to the capital. Later, during the climactic struggle at Chapultepec Castle, in September 1847, he was slightly wounded and won a promotion to brevet colonel.

Many historians have tried to trace how the things Lee learned in Mexico were applied two decades later in Virginia. But conflicting lessons can be drawn from the same events.

He did come to understand the importance of turning movements, as at Cerro Gordo. But he also learned from Scott that there comes a time to be audacious and hit the enemy where he least expects it, as at Chapultepec.

The greatest lesson he learned was the reality of war: how it is fought on the ground and how a commander must handle his staff. That was invaluable and could be obtained in no other place. Moreover, he had come under the eye of the watchful Scott, established as the army's ranking general. He called Lee "the very best soldier I ever saw in the field."

After the Lees fled Arlington mansion in the wake of his decision to join the Confederacy, federal troops occupied the building. The property later became Arlington National Cemetery. ***National Archives and Records Division***

After the war, however, it was back to the mundane world of engineering jobs. The next one was closer to home, however, in Baltimore, which mitigated some of the tedium involved in the assignment.

In 1852, to his surprise, he was named superintendent of the Military Academy. He was not eager to take the posting because he did not feel himself qualified to direct the education of young men.

During his last years, when he was president of what was to become Washington and Lee University, he expressed regret at not having learned more of the Classics. He felt that a military education alone did not prepare men adequately for the other roles they would be called upon to fill in life. So his three years at West Point were spent in reforming the curriculum and raising academic standards.

His eldest son, George Washington Custis Lee, graduated first in his class at the Academy in 1854. His nephew, Fitzhugh Lee, also earned a degree during Lee's tenure there, although standing only 45th in a class of 49.

At one point, Lee ordered a court-martial of his nephew who had been caught visiting an off-limits establishment. He narrowly avoided being expelled, but after his discipline was served, Fitz led a unanimous pledge by his class to refrain from any further offenses and was treated warmly by Lee.

His tenure at the Academy also gave Lee the chance to know many young officers who would soon serve under him, including the cavalry leader Jeb Stuart.

Henry "Light Horse Harry" Lee, Lee's father, served as an officer under George Washington and later as a governor of Virginia. ***Independence National Historical Park***

In 1855, a former Mexican War associate, Jefferson Davis, now secretary of war, responded to repeated requests by transferring Lee to his first field command, with the Second Cavalry. This was one of the army's elite units, assigned to the western frontier. Out of its ranks would come several of the leading officers in the coming war, including its commander, Albert Sidney Johnston.

As it turned out, however, this also became an

Lee married Mary Ann Randolph Custis in June 1831. ***Library of Congress***

unsatisfying experience for Lee. Much of his time was taken up sitting on courts-martial, which he disliked, and he would spend only half of the next three years on active duty.

His reputation for fairness and his belief that punishment properly meted out could be a form of kindness made him invaluable for this legal work. It also may have given him an insight into the minds of failed soldiers and some idea about what it would take to inspire them.

During this time he also was working out his own ideas about slavery and the possibility of secession.

"There are few, I believe, in this enlightened age, who will not acknowledge that slavery as an institution is a moral and political evil," he wrote in a personal letter in 1856. "…I believe it is a greater evil to the white than to the black race … Their emancipation will sooner result from the mild and melting influences of Christianity than from the storms and tempests of controversy."

In that same year, he prayed that the new president, James Buchanan, "will be able to extinguish fanaticism both North and South, cultivate love for the country and Union and restore harmony between the different sections."

His father-in-law passed away in 1857, leaving a vague and convoluted will, and Lee was called upon over the next two years to settle the large estate. Moreover, arthritis had turned his wife into a chronic invalid. He received a series of furloughs while sorting it all out and in his depressed state considered leaving the army to become a full-time planter.

His finances were not good and, he wrote at the time, "the necessity I have daily for money has made me, I fear, parsimonious." He also confessed a sense of having advanced as far as he could go in his chosen profession.

He was now 50 years old and still a handsome man, with a full head of dark hair. He also wore a brown mustache. As with Lincoln, the beard that would become his most distinguishing feature was not grown until the war began. Observers noted that he had a burly upper torso and thick neck while his legs were rather short and slender. Although he stood five foot ten, his build gave him almost a misshapen appearance.

In the fall of 1859, Lee was surprised to find his former student, Stuart, at his front door carrying sealed orders for him. The cavalry leader happened to be in Washington visiting the Patent Office when the report of John Brown's raid on Harpers Ferry came in (although at this time it was not yet known that Brown was in command of it).

It speaks to Lee's standing in the army that he was chosen to lead the Marines who were sent to put down this attack. He did so quickly with minimal loss of life. "If war comes," said the admiring Scott, now general-in-chief, "it would be cheap for our country to insure Lee's life for $5 million a year."

Lee hadn't liked what he had seen and firmly believed that Brown deserved hanging as a "fanatic or madman." It disturbed him that Brown's trial and death created a furor in the North, and he was troubled by the deepening sense of national conflict.

During the Mexican War, Lee learned valuable military lessons, such as the flanking movement employed at Cerro Gordo. ***Library of Congress***

In 1852, Colonel Lee found himself superintendent of the United States Military Academy at West Point. ***West Point Museum Collection, United States Military Academy***

He returned to his unit in Texas in February 1860 and watched helplessly from a distance as the thing he feared most slowly took shape. Everyone in power seemed unable to avert it. He had hoped wistfully that the Democrats would unite to oppose Lincoln, but in a letter to the future General Earl Van Dorn, he pointed out, "Politicians, I fear, are too selfish to become martyrs."

"As far as I can judge from the papers we are between a state of anarchy and civil war," he wrote to his wife. "May God avert us from both.... I fear mankind for years will not be sufficiently Christianized to bear the absence of restraint and force."

To his daughter, he added: "If the bond of the Union can only be maintained by the sword & bayonet, instead of brotherly love & friendship, & and if strife and civil war are to take the place of mutual aid & commerce, its existence will lose all interest with me."

He was convinced that "Secession is nothing but revolution." He had no sympathy for those who wished to dissolve the government made by Washington, his model of the great man.

Yet how could he assist in the invasion of his home state? To Lee this would be a sacrifice of honor, a betrayal of his heritage. That far he was unwilling to go, even to save the Union.

In February 1861, he was summoned to Washington by Scott. Texas already had seceded, and there was some question whether Lee, still an officer in the U.S. Army, would be arrested before he could leave the state. "Has it come so soon to this," he sadly remarked to Mrs. Caroline Darrow, a unionist he met in San Antonio.

Historian Bruce Catton remarked on the irony that would have deprived the Confederacy of its greatest leader had the hotheads in Texas had their way. "Subsequent history could have been substantially different," he says in concise understatement.

But Lee was allowed to leave and arrived in Washington on March 1, still hoping for a compromise that would keep Virginia in the Union. He met with Scott for three hours on March 5 and expressed his unwillingness to fight against his native state. Scott, who still hoped that he would stay with the Union, placed him on holding orders to keep him close by.

Scott was also a native of Virginia. He had been secretly approached himself by a delegate from that state to be offered the command of its armed forces. He refused to listen. Unlike Lee, he had resolved the conflict in his mind by convincing himself that he intended to act only in defense.

Moreover, Scott detested Davis, whom he called "a Judas [who] would not have sold the Savior for 30 shillings, but for the successorship to Pontius Pilate he would have betrayed Christ and the apostles and the whole Christian Church."

Scott offered Lee a promotion to colonel of the First U.S. Cavalry on March 16, and Lee accepted. However, he now was telling neighbors that he might "resign and go to planting corn."

On April 17, Virginia's constitutional convention, meeting in secret, voted for secession. The following day Lee was again called to Washington and formally offered command of the Northern army by Francis P. Blair, one of the power brokers in the Republican administration. He was told the offer came directly from Lincoln.

Once more Lee reviewed the reasons he had to decline. He then walked over to Scott's office for a final meeting with his old friend. Scott told him that his position had become a contradiction and that he either had to resign or be prepared to follow any orders given to him.

Virginia already had sent troops against the federal arsenal at Harpers Ferry, the same place Lee had been called upon to defend for the Union only 18 months before. On April 19, the news of Virginia's secession came out, and Lee knew that his time for delaying the inevitable had expired.

There followed a night of pacing and prayer. His own family was deeply divided. His sons Custis and Rooney spoke bitterly against secession, and Lee's sister, Ann, was married to a dedicated unionist. A visitor to Arlington on this day described the house "as if there had been a death in it."

Shortly after midnight he walked from his bedroom with his letter of resignation in hand.

"You can scarcely conceive the struggle it has cost Robert to resign," his wife wrote to a friend. "To contend against the flag he has so long honored, disapproving, as we both do, the course of the North & South."

Two days later, he left for Richmond, and on April 23, when he was offered the command of Virginia's troops by the governor, he accepted. He never returned to Arlington but would, as he put it, "share the misery of the people of my native state."

More than 13 months would pass before he assumed command of what would become the Army of Northern Virginia. In the first weeks of the war, it almost appeared as if he had made a mistake in taking the assignment.

His title was military advisor to the president with the rank of general. But exactly what his duties were to be was imprecise. He was put to work fortifying river and coastal defenses and then sent to the western part of the state in September to recapture what would soon become West Virginia from the Union.

But at Cheat Mountain he was unable to dislodge a federal force. Hampered by terrible weather and four brigadiers who refused to cooperate, he returned to Richmond with a somewhat blemished reputation. He was regarded in public estimation, in fact, as far inferior in leadership qualities to both Davis and P. G. T. Beauregard, the hero of Fort Sumter and Manassas.

Davis sent him off to South Carolina to strengthen coastal defenses and he did not return to Virginia until March 1862. Although Davis insisted that he recognized Lee's talents, there was no place to send him. His old commander, Albert Sidney Johnston, was in command in the west, and Joseph E. Johnston led the army of Virginia.

General Winfield Scott called Lee "the very best soldier I ever saw in the field." He tried to keep Lee loyal to the Union, but Lee's obligation to Virginia was too strong. ***Library of Congress***

Within months both would be out of the picture, with A. S. Johnston killed at Shiloh in April and J. E. Johnston severely wounded in the Peninsula Campaign, while blocking General George McClellan's advance on Richmond from the southeast. On the day after Johnston was wounded, June 1, 1862, Lee assumed command of Virginia's Confederate forces.

He had never directed a battlefield command before. He would almost always face a numerically superior enemy, which was also better supplied. Yet in the next 13 months he conducted a series of campaigns that have passed into military legend and graced him with a reputation for invincibility.

While other Confederate generals complained of the unfavorable conditions under which they were asked to fight, Lee accepted it as a given and went on to fashion his strategy from that point. He was convinced that his army could handle anything. But one of the main reasons for his two thrusts into the North, which culminated in the battles of Antietam and Gettysburg,

Lee's children opposed secession, but followed their father's example. Custis (*left*) served as an aide to Jefferson Davis, later assisting with the defense of Richmond. Rooney (*right*) rode with J. E. B. Stuart in the cavalry. ***National Archives and Records Division***

was to obtain desperately needed food and equipment for his men.

"There were never such men in an army before," he told General John Bell Hood. "They will go anywhere and do anything if properly led. But there is the difficulty—proper commanders. Where can they be obtained?"

It was a question that would haunt him throughout the war. But the men he led idolized him with an attitude bordering on worship.

"I've heard of God," was the often quoted remark of one Confederate soldier. "But I've seen General Lee."

His primary biographer, Douglas Southall Freeman, attributes this to his "fortitude and character…in contrast with the dissipation, smallness, indiscipline and selfishness" of other Confederate leaders. He continues:

"In case after case, Lee patiently assuaged the victims of hurt pride, stimulated the discouraged, appealed to the better nature of wavering men and by force of his own righteousness more than by the exercise of his authority reconciled bitter differences or induced personal enemies to work together…

"In the hearts of Lee's subordinates were all the explosive qualities that existed elsewhere, but the General himself possessed the combination of tact, understanding, prestige, firmness and personal character necessary to prevent the explosion."

He needed all of those qualities to contend with the South's commander-in-chief. Historian Bernard DeVoto wrote, "The only military strategist that Lee could not defeat was Davis."

Although the Confederate president was in over his head when it came to planning strategy, he fancied himself a great military leader. He did have a West Point background, after all, and had served as secretary of war. Lee, while recognizing Davis's shortcomings, deferred to him without question because he was raised in the tradition of civilian control of the army.

He regarded Davis's interference as simply one more burden he had to overcome, as with the greater numbers and superior supplies of the enemy. Historian Clifford Dowdey writes, however, that Davis seemed unconscious of the "thoughtless wastes that he exacted of Lee's time, energies, and talents.

"So Lee had to fight two wars—the open fight against the avowed enemy and the tacit fight to achieve his ends through the constituted authority."

A large part of the problem lay in the fact that Davis was convinced that winning the war meant holding territory. Lee understood, on the other hand, that victory depended on breaking the opposition's will to fight. Maintaining control of any given piece of land was irrelevant to that end.

Once Davis tied Lee to the defense of Richmond and its rail connections to the outside, says Dowdey, the cause was hopeless. The South could not possibly win a war of siege.

On the other hand, Lee could never conceive of the war in terms that were wider than Virginia. Less gifted subordinates—James Longstreet and Beauregard—understood that the war had to be viewed as a single piece, with movements in the west affecting Union actions in Virginia. They repeatedly urged an invasion of Kentucky to draw pressure away from the South's more strategic locations.

But Lee could never bring himself to part with the men needed to undertake such a campaign. He had come into the Confederacy on account of Virginia, and that is where his focus always remained.

He also relied heavily on personal reconnaissance, a holdover from his experience in the Mexican War. So he was reluctant to agree to any campaign over territory that he could not see for himself.

It is acknowledged without question that Lee is one of the greatest military leaders America ever produced. In his ability to meticulously prepare defenses, but then suddenly strike audaciously at a numerically superior enemy, there has never been an equal.

He seemed to have the uncanny ability to place himself inside the heads of the opposing generals and anticipate their moves. To gauge the strength and weaknesses of his own forces and those arrayed against him. To know the precise moment when a desperate risk had the best chance of success.

Lee continued to suffer severe criticism in the Southern press and political circles in Richmond throughout the war. Especially after Gettysburg, he was second-guessed often. None of the mythic qualities had yet surrounded him. That would come only after the final defeat. In 1864, he was a still a man and not a marble statue, regarded as just one of many important Confederate leaders.

But the loyalty of the soldiers never wavered. "His power to inspire confidence," writes Freeman, "and to create morale was due to his record of victories, his inflexible justice, his attention to detail, his great aptitude for organization, his imperturbable presence in battle, his regard for his men and the quality of his military material."

The most famous instance of this came at The Wilderness, in May 1864, when an uncharacteristically emotional Lee tried to personally lead a counterattack across open fields. The Texas brigade of General John Gregg refused to go forward if he did not get out of harm's way.

"Lee to the rear," came the chant down the entire gray line. "Go back, General Lee, go back," some of them began to call. "We won't go unless you go back."

Soon it became a shouted chorus: "Lee to the rear! Lee to the rear!" It took several moments before Lee

Though considered early on inferior to favorite commanders like P. G. T. Beauregard, Lee eventually eclipsed all other Confederate generals. *Library of Congress*

Such was the regard for Lee that when he tried to lead a counterattack at The Wilderness, a chant went up demanding "Lee to the rear!" *David J. Eicher Collection*

On April 9, 1865, Lee met General Ulysses S. Grant at the Wilmer McLean House to surrender his army. *National Archives and Records Division*

Following his meeting with Grant, Lee departed to return to his lines. *Battles and Leaders of the Civil War*

seemed aware of what was going on and turned his horse, Traveler, around.

"I thought him at that moment the grandest specimen of manhood I ever beheld," Shelby Foote quotes an anonymous Texan as writing. "He looked as though he ought to have been, and was, the monarch of the world."

It may have been the most extraordinary demonstration of affection by ordinary troops for a general in American history. Only the gruff Longstreet seemed unmoved by the episode. He joked that Lee had seemed to go "off his balance" and that if he intended to lead the troops, Longstreet would go off to a safer place "because it was not comfortable here."

Ironically, Longstreet was seriously wounded later in the battle, depriving Lee of his most able subordinate for most of the balance of the war.

Even at the very end, with no realistic hope remaining, Lee managed to extricate himself from the surrounding Union force at Richmond and continue the fight on the retreat west to Appomattox. But even the greatest of leaders must at last bow to the inevitable.

"There is nothing left for me to do but to go and see General Grant," he said finally, "and I would rather die a thousand deaths."

Lee was now the white-bearded, hollow-eyed old man of the familiar photographs. He seemed to have aged 20 years in the last four. He was frequently ill during the war, the precursor to the heart disease that would take his life in five more years.

The two men had met once before, while serving in Mexico, and Grant, in an effort to break the tension reminded Lee of that. "I know I met you on that occasion and I have often thought of it," Lee responded. He then quickly put aside any further effort at small talk.

"I suppose, General Grant, that the object of our present meeting is fully understood. I asked to see you to ascertain upon what terms you would receive the surrender of my army."

Grant outlined his terms, and Lee found them generous. "This will have the best possible effect on the men," he said. He shook hands with Grant, walked to the door, and, while standing on the porch waiting for Traveler to be brought up, twice pounded his gloved fist with great force into his open palm.

Then on this Palm Sunday morning, April 9, 1865, he prepared to return to his family in Richmond.

Lee was now 58 years old. He had no means of support. His property had been taken away. Although he had been given generous terms of parole, there were serious questions as to how he could support himself. He didn't have long to wait for an answer.

Less than four months after the surrender at Appomattox, the board of trustees of Washington College met, in the Shenandoah Valley town of Lexington, Virginia. It was trying to decide the place's future. It had been wrecked in the war, and by the board's own description the college was "a broken down place."

But a friend of one of its members, Colonel Bolivar Christian, had been admonished by Lee's daughter, Mary, that "while the Southern people were willing and ready to give her father everything that he might need, no offer had ever been made by which he could earn a living for himself and his family."

The board voted Lee in as president by unanimous

Days after the surrender, Lee posed for this photo in a Confederate uniform, despite his having signed a parole. *Library of Congress*

acclamation. Then there was an embarrassed silence, as if the board realized that the leadership of their college would hardly be the sort of job that a man who was called the greatest figure in the South would consider.

Nonetheless, they sent him the proposal and to their surprise received his acceptance within three weeks. Lee already had been offered administrative jobs by the University of the South and the University of Virginia, but had turned down the first because it was denominational and the second because it was state-supported.

Washington College, however, was a private institution. Moreover, it had been endowed originally by Lee's greatest hero, George Washington. His son, Captain Robert E. Lee, writing in 1901, said that his father had accepted because of his positive experience as superintendent at West Point. He also saw "the opportunity for starting almost from the beginning and for

This postwar image of Lee astride his horse Traveler became a popular symbol of the Lost Cause during Reconstruction. ***Library of Congress***

helping, by his experience and example, the youth of his country to become good and useful citizens."

He rode to Lexington alone on Traveler in September, a four-day journey from Richmond, and took up his duties immediately. The school then consisted of a faculty of five and an enrollment of less than 100. On the strength of his reputation, he built up its endowment and quadrupled its enrollment over the next five years. He also inspired the faculty to turn out young men whose professional training was "softened" by the liberal arts and who were "finished" Christians.

Lee felt so strongly about that last point that he insisted a new chapel was to be built before a new house for him. He moved, instead, into the home once occupied by Stonewall Jackson, when he was a math professor at the adjoining Virginia Military Institute.

Lee traveled tirelessly to promote and raise funds for the school, and it took a toll on his health. He was stricken with what was probably a heart attack on September 28, 1870, and died two weeks later in Lexington. His last words were "Strike the tent."

Lee was buried in the chapel he had ordered built on the campus. Shortly afterwards the name of the school was changed to Washington and Lee University.

At one time he thought of writing a history of his wartime campaigns, but he came to feel that it was more important to look ahead instead of back. His speeches in the postwar years were filled with exhortations for Southerners to be good citizens, repair their part of the country, and accept the outcome of the war.

When Lee visited Washington, D.C., in 1869 and paid a courtesy call on President Grant, he spoke of the railroad he hoped would be built through Lexington. "You and I, General," said Grant, "have more to do with destroying railroads than building them." Lee was not amused and left after a few more minutes of awkward conversation. The destruction of the war was something he chose not to dwell upon.

Nonetheless, after his death, when Lee had attained near deification in the South, he became a symbol of all that was good and noble about the Lost Cause. His name also was invoked to justify all manner of resistance to Reconstruction and, in the following century, to defend Jim Crow and segregation. It is difficult to imagine that he would have approved of that.

His onetime top assistant, Longstreet, was castigated in the South in the 1870s when he dared question Lee's tactics at Gettysburg. Even a century after his death, generals and presidents could criticize Lee only at their peril.

In 1957, President Dwight D. Eisenhower accompanied Britain's Field Marshal Viscount Montgomery on a walking tour of the Gettysburg battlefield, near Ike's farmhouse retreat.

With the press in tow, the two famous generals offered the opinion that Lee should have tried to turn the Union left instead of ordering Pickett's Charge and that he deserved to be "sacked" for the mistake. The outcry in the South was so severe that Eisenhower had to apologize a few days later, after being reminded that the two World War II generals hadn't done so well, either, at the Battle of the Bulge.

In 1975, 110 years after his original application, Lee's citizenship was restored by Congress. The original papers had not been properly notarized and when they were resubmitted they were lost for more than a century somewhere in the federal bureaucracy.

Even here, however, there was not total accord. A few Congressmen insisted on holding out for a blanket forgiveness of all Vietnam draft resisters if Lee were given his pardon. That motion was voted down, 407–10, and Robert E. Lee became an American citizen again.

A few months after the surrender, Lee became president of Washington College. Following his death, the institution was renamed Washington and Lee University. *Library of Congress*

After his death in 1870, Lee was mourned at Arlington, his former home. *Library of Congress*

THOMAS J. "STONEWALL" JACKSON

"Surely General Jackson will recover. God will not take him from us now when we need him so much."

Robert E. Lee, May 9, 1863, the day before Jackson's death

To die at the height of one's fame and accomplishments may be the kindest gift posterity can offer any individual.

So many other great figures of the Civil War went through the gall of defeat or the tarnishing of their achievements through later failure. In the case of U. S. Grant, his two terms as president of the United States have come down as, perhaps, the most incompetent and corrupt administration in American history.

But Jackson remains for eternity "The Mighty Stonewall," unconquered and unsullied, the greatest military leader this country ever produced. His campaigns are still studied for the near perfection of their execution. The Shenandoah Valley, Second Manassas, Chancellorsville are pored over by military historians as pinnacles of the art of war.

Deeply religious, an inspirational leader to his men, a loving husband and, too briefly, a father, Jackson comes down through the decades as a man who approached the ideal.

His ability to disappear, and then suddenly turn up miles from where he was supposed to be, with his army at the very rear of the enemy, was incomparable. The few failures in his record, such as his performance during the Peninsula Campaign of 1862, are so baffling that the reasons behind them are still argued furiously.

His utter ferocity in battle, compared by historian Douglas Southall Freeman to a "reincarnated Joshua," is regarded with awe. "He lived by the New Testament and fought by the Old," added Freeman.

His men called him "Old Blue Light" for the unearthly gleam that came into his eyes in the midst of battle. His stern Presbyterianism, indeed, seemed to belong more to the era of the great religious wars than the War Between the States.

"We must do more than defeat their armies," he told an aide after the Battle of Fredericksburg. "We must destroy them." When the bravery of opposing troops was pointed out to him, Jackson responded: "Shoot them all. I don't want them to be brave."

Out of an earnest conviction that he fought at God's side, Jackson was the most fearsome of the Confederate leaders. One of his chief aides, General Richard Ewell, was convinced that the man was slightly insane.

His odd quirks carried into personal life, too. His students at Virginia Military Institute (VMI) referred to him as "Tom Fool," because of his classroom manner and insistence that his way was the only way to solve a given problem.

Occasionally, say the guides at his former home in Lexington, Virginia, he would leave his study and come into the living room to be with his wife, Anna. But he would sit with his face to the wall, a signal that he was deep in thought and not to be disturbed. Only when he turned around to face the room was he fully ready to rejoin her.

Yet on his deathbed he told her, "My darling, you are very much loved. You are one of the most precious little wives in the world."

Some say that even more than the defeat at Gettysburg, the death of Jackson marks the true turning point of the war. Because if he had been living, they insist, Gettysburg would not have been a defeat.

As he lay dying, the *Richmond Whig* editorialized that his recovery was assured because he had been sent by God to lead the Southern cause. "He is no accidental manifestation of the powers of faith and courage," the newspaper said. "He came not by chance in this day and to this generation. He was born for a purpose and not until that purpose is fulfilled will his great soul take flight."

The journey to such an exalted place in the hearts of his countrymen began in modest circumstances, in what would later become West Virginia. His forebears were Scotch-Irish and, like so many of that group who came to America in the middle of the eighteenth century, they made their way west into the Appalachians. Some of the Jacksons prospered there, but his father, Jonathan, was not among them.

Jonathan Jackson opened a law practice in the rough-hewn town of Clarksburg in 1817, shortly after his marriage to Julia Beckwith Neale, of Parkersburg. Thomas was their third child, born in 1824 and named for his maternal grandfather. He would add the middle name Jonathan as an adult to honor his father.

Jonathan Jackson was a good lawyer but a terrible businessman. He extended credit to too many clients, and when he died during a typhus epidemic, when Thomas was two years old, the family was left destitute. His mother remarried, but four years later she passed away of complications following childbirth.

The surviving children had to be dispersed among various relatives. Thomas was sent to his uncle, Cummins Jackson, on his farm and mill near Weston, West Virginia. This upbringing turned out to be a boyhood idyll out of Huck Finn's dreams. It was open country, and the Jacksons had horses to race and foxes to hunt. The household, run by a group of bachelor uncles, was cheerfully chaotic.

It was, however, a life that was short on schooling, but somewhere along the line Jackson acquired a taste for learning. He walked to a nearby country school and, while not regarded as especially quick-witted, he studied assiduously. As a 16-year-old he even served two terms as a teacher.

Learning led to religion, and he began attending Methodist services, much to the disapproval of his fun-loving uncles. Although he would never stray for long from his Presbyterian faith, he did give some thought at this time to becoming a Methodist minister. Perhaps to put such ambitions aside, Cummins got his nephew a job as constable. This involved riding the court circuit to serve papers and collect debts, rather responsible work for a 17-year-old. But Jackson did it well.

Thomas J. "Stonewall" Jackson outshone Lee in popularity in the early part of the war. His name resounded in both the South and North. ***Library of Congress***

He had convinced himself, however, that the only way he would get ahead was through a college education. Upon learning that an appointment to West Point was open in his congressional district, he prevailed upon Cummins to use his political connections to land it for him. This was done, and Jackson arrived at the Military Academy in 1842.

He wore country clothes, which marked him immediately as something of a rube. He also was woefully unprepared for the course of study. For much of his first year, there was every indication that he would have to drop out. His name stood near the bottom of The Immortals, the ironic name for the tail end of the class.

After the death of his parents, Jackson lived on his uncle's farm near Weston, West Virginia. ***Library of Congress***

Recitation was painful for him, and he also picked up 15 demerits for lapses in conduct. He was referred to sarcastically as The General, as in General Andrew Jackson. No one seriously believed that he ever actually would earn that rank or anything close to it.

But he refused to accept that judgment. Applying himself to study with a fearsome single-mindedness, he gradually climbed in the rankings. By the end of his four years at the Academy, he stood 17th in the class. The story went that if he had been given one more year he would have ranked first. The man who did wind up at the very bottom of his class of 1846 was George E. Pickett.

There was a price to this purposefulness, however. In later years, Jackson said he could not recall ever speaking to a woman during his entire time at West Point.

The Mexican War was already on at the time of his graduation, and the newly minted Second Lieutenant Jackson was sent to join the artillery of General Winfield Scott at the Vera Cruz landing. In his 15 months in Mexico he was brevetted to captain and then to major for gallantry on the battlefield.

At the storming of Chapultepec Castle, the war's climactic battle, he stayed with his gun even after coming under raking fire from the Mexican defenders. On a day when several future Civil War generals won notice for valor, Jackson's bravery was regarded as of the highest order.

When asked if he felt fear during the engagement, the young officer replied that he seemed to have "a more perfect command of my faculties in the midst of fighting." But years later, while teaching at VMI and asked by a student whether he had felt fear on that day, Jackson responded: "Very much afraid, Mr. Murfee. Very much afraid."

His time in Mexico also seemed to heighten his religious awareness. Observing the ritual of the Catholic Church for the first time, he began to question and write to relatives about his own convictions. A few years later, he decided to become baptized as an Episcopalian. But he returned, eventually, to the Presbyterian Church as a rite more amenable to his own stark system of belief.

With the end of the war, however, the realities of army life began wearing on him. He was sent to Fort Columbus and Fort Lawson, both in the New York City area, and also did a stint of court-martial duty at the Carlisle Barracks, in Pennsylvania.

He accepted a transfer to Fort Meade, Florida, in 1851 and, for a time, service in this exotic place seemed to satisfy him. But Jackson quarreled with a superior officer, Major William French, and found himself confined to quarters. He retaliated by filing charges against French for conduct unbecoming an officer and, in an escalation of the stakes, "moral degeneracy."

Jackson had entered an especially zealous phase of his Christian growth and felt bound to expose hypocrisy wherever he found it. The incident did credit to neither man, and all charges were dismissed as unworthy of serious consideration. French refused to back down and came off the worse of the two, losing his command and being transferred to another Florida post.

But the affair had soured Jackson on the army, and when a position opened unexpectedly at VMI, professor of natural philosophy and artillery tactics, he rushed to apply. Eventually, he was chosen over some formidable competition, including future Union generals George McClellan and William S. Rosecrans.

His chief advocate at VMI was another general in the making: a Confederate one, Daniel Harvey Hill. He remembered Jackson from Mexico, but, more important, he did not want anyone from the North considered for the job. So Jackson turned in his resignation from the army in early 1852 and, at the age of 28, headed for an academic career in Lexington.

It was not an altogether successful career. Although just 10 to 12 years older than the young men in his classes, Jackson was regarded as something of a fuddy-duddy, a dry lecturer who seldom departed from the textbook and whose classes were excruciatingly dull. He also did not welcome the give-and-take of classroom argument.

The cadets made fun of him behind his back, mocking his theories on healthy eating, good posture, and hydrotherapy. He had a habit of raising his arm bolt upright from time to time because he thought the blood flow was improved when it was stretched out to full length.

In later years, Jackson's soldiers regarded the gesture as a benediction that he was invoking upon them. At VMI, however, it was just regarded as another of old "Tom Fool's" peculiarities.

While he made his living in the classroom, his passion was the Presbyterian Church and the work he performed in its behalf. He was especially interested in running a religious school for the children of black slaves.

It was through the church that he came to know Eleanor Junkin. Her father was a minister and the president of Washington College, which was also located in Lexington. (It was the school that Lee would head after the war.) Jackson and Eleanor were married in September 1853, and began a domestic life filled with religious study and educational travel.

Her twin sister accompanied the newlyweds on a trip to Quebec City, and many years later she recalled Jackson standing on the Plains of Abraham, the place General James Wolfe had died a heroic death a century before in the battle that secured Canada for Great Britain.

"To die as he died," said Jackson prophetically, "who would not die content."

After just 14 months of this happy marriage, however, Eleanor went into premature labor after a taxing stagecoach ride and died in childbirth. The baby did not survive.

"I cannot realize that ... my wife will no more cheer the rugged and dark way of life," he wrote her sister, who was so shaken that she had to move to Philadelphia to be with relatives. "The thought rushes in upon me that it is insupportable, insupportable."

He threw himself with redoubled effort into religious work to ease his grief and became a director of a small savings bank. In the summer of 1856, he took a leave and went on a tour of Europe by himself, concentrating on the continent's great works of art.

When he returned home, he seemed refreshed, optimistic. His friend Hill had moved to Davidson College, in North Carolina. There he renewed his acquaintance with Mary Anna Morrison, whom Jackson had met in Lexington. As was his late wife, she too was the daughter of a Presbyterian minister who was also a college president.

Following graduation from West Point, Jackson made his way south to fight in the Mexican War. *U.S. Army Military History Institute*

The two met again when Jackson visited Hill, a friendship was developed through the mail, and in 1857 they were married. Once more he settled down in satisfaction to a domestic routine. But again his happiness was marred when another infant daughter died, this time at the age of three months.

He tried traveling once more as a shield against despair, taking Anna along to several spas in an effort to combine a trip that would revive her spirits and his health. The stomach problems that would trouble him throughout his life had returned in force and Jackson was convinced that his liver was failing as well.

In the fall of 1859, he was sent to Charles Town with the VMI corps of cadets, assigned by the governor to act as a guard at the hanging of John Brown. He was posted at the foot of the scaffold and wrote his wife that he had offered a prayer for Brown's soul at the moment of execution.

Jackson had little sympathy for Brown and was no opponent of slavery. He felt it was part of the Divine order, and it was not for him to question the design of Providence. He owned some slaves himself but felt that humane treatment was an imperative.

Jackson joined the artillery of General Winfield Scott's army as it landed at Vera Cruz. ***Library of Congress***

As did any reasonably informed individual of the time, he saw the approaching storm that would soon engulf the country. But Jackson regarded war as "the sum of all evils" and felt that a crisis could be avoided if inflammatory debates about states' rights were avoided. Failing that, he suggested to his minister that a day of prayer whereby "all the Christian people in the land could be induced to unite … and avert so great an evil."

But in the spring of 1861, when VMI cadets tore down an American flag in Lexington and narrowly avoided a confrontation with the state militia, Jackson addressed the corps to commend them. "The time for war has not yet come," he said, "but it will come, and that soon. When it does come, my advice is to draw the sword and throw away the scabbard."

The time came for Jackson on April 21. He was ordered to Richmond with the institute's upper classmen. But when he arrived at the capital, he was treated as a nonentity. Having no other use for him, Virginia made Jackson a major in the Engineering Corps, a field in which he had almost no experience. Within three months, however, his name would be known throughout the country.

Jackson was promoted to colonel and sent to Harpers Ferry, John Brown's goal just 16 months before, at the end of April. His job was turning raw Virginia volunteers into a fighting corps. He was so adept at it that by mid June he was made a brigadier general under General Joseph E. Johnston, newly appointed commander of Confederate forces in Virginia.

Jackson immediately demonstrated to his new superior that he was not one to trifle with. He refused a formal transfer of command until Johnston produced the proper documentation. Rather than taking offense, Johnston was impressed by Jackson's respect for the legitimacy of authority and correct military standards and marked him as a leader.

In July, he accompanied Johnston on the move from Harpers Ferry to join General P. G. T. Beauregard's army at Manassas, a strategic rail junction just west of Washington, D.C. The first major encounter of the war was shaping up here, and Beauregard's plan called for Jackson to be held in reserve. But the battle soon found him.

The troops on both sides were still too green to execute the best-laid plans, and Beauregard's overly complicated orders were far from the best. The fight turned into a confused melee, a series of individual combats. But it soon became apparent that the danger was on the Confederate left. Federal forces were crossing a stone bridge there and threatening to flank it.

As Southern forces were driven back by this assault, Jackson's brigade was drawn up to form a defensive line at the crest of Henry Hill. Jackson had posted them behind the brow of the hill, so that oncoming troops would be forced to clear the entire elevation before getting an open shot at them.

Beauregard was in the process of shifting his entire army, and if the line at Henry Hill did not hold, there was a strong threat of his being engulfed. Several shattered brigades were in full retreat as their officers tried desperately to rally them.

"General, the day is going against us," one of his officers cried to Jackson. "If you think so, sir," he responded gruffly, "you had better not say anything about it."

Among those attempting to halt the retreat was the mounted General Barnard Bee. He had been one year ahead of Jackson at West Point, and the two men knew each other well. What happened next has passed into the very fabric of Americana. Standing in his stirrups, Bee hollered to his men and motioned towards Jackson.

"Look! There is Jackson standing like a stone wall."

What he said next is open to debate. Most often it is rendered as: "Rally behind the Virginians." In some cases, it is more flowery: "Let us determine to die here and we will conquer."

An instant later Bee was knocked from the saddle with a wound that resulted in his death on the following day. But his contribution to the lore of this conflict was immeasurable.

The line anchored by Jackson did hold and, with the immediate danger past, Beauregard was able to rally his forces and carry the day. As the routed Federals hastened back to safety, Jackson told the surgeon who was dressing a wound to his finger, "Give me ten thousand men, and I will be in Washington tomorrow."

But the Confederate army was exhausted, and the war was not to end quite as easily as that. The report of the battle that appeared in the *Charleston Mercury*, however, made Jackson an instant hero. In later years, he insisted that Bee's words were meant to apply to his men, who were henceforth known as the Stonewall Brigade. But the Jackson legend had begun to build.

In a letter to his wife, written immediately after the battle, he expressed content that Beauregard and Johnston should get the credit for the victory. "But I am thankful to my ever kind Heavenly Father that He makes me content to await His own good time and pleasure for commendation—knowing that all things work together for my good."

It is a strange sentiment from one who always insisted that he was not interested in fame or "commendation." But it is also quite human.

In October, he was promoted to major general. In a mere six months, Jackson had gone from "Tom Fool," the unknown professor, to Stonewall, a critical component of the Confederate army. In the following month, he was sent to familiar territory, the Shenandoah Valley, where the legend was to be burnished to an even higher gloss.

The lull after First Manassas lasted nine months. By the spring of 1862, it became apparent that federal forces were planning a major assault on Richmond. It was essential that Jackson occupy as many Union troops as possible in the Shenandoah. If they were tied down there, they could not link up with McClellan and overwhelm Johnston's army protecting the Confederate capital.

The campaign did not begin well. Jackson had taken the town of Romney, in West Virginia, in January, and left Brigadier General W. W. Loring in charge there. He then returned to the more centrally located base at Winchester, Virginia.

Loring resented the assignment to what he regarded as a backwater and sent a letter of complaint to the War Department. Secretary of War Judah P. Benjamin responded by ordering Jackson to bring Loring back to Winchester. Jackson complied and then turned in his resignation, with the statement that "with such interference in my command, I cannot expect to be of much service in the field."

Johnston and the governor of Virginia, John Letcher, quickly moved to smooth things over and Benjamin backed down, stating that his orders were "mere suggestions."

But in March there was some question whether confidence in Jackson had been misplaced. Union troop withdrawals from the Shenandoah Valley had started, and Jackson was told to do what he could to hold the remaining forces there. He ended up attacking a far larger Union force at Kernstown on March 23 and was driven off with heavy losses.

There were now whispers in Richmond that this Jackson was a reckless incompetent. Coupled with the Loring incident, severe doubts were raised about his leadership abilities.

But the hopeless attack at Kernstown paid major dividends. Jackson's aggressiveness startled the Union command. It now assumed that his resources were much greater than was previously thought. Otherwise, how could he dare attack a 9,000 man federal force? The Valley provided a clear invasion route to Washington, D.C., which was lightly defended because of the troops sent against Richmond. All of this made the Northern command highly nervous.

So the corps of General Nathaniel Banks, which already was on the way to McClellan, was sent back to the Valley, and still other troops were transported to West Virginia to counter Jackson. He had suffered a tactical defeat but won a major strategic victory.

From the middle of April on, Jackson was under the command of Lee for the first time. Lee had known him since the Mexican War, had observed his actions closely, and believed he was the man for what needed to be done in the Shenandoah.

He outlined three options to Jackson for tying up the Union forces aligned against him and concluded, "The blow, wherever struck, must, to be successful, be sudden and heavy."

Jackson met Daniel Harvey Hill during the Mexican War. Later, they became friends and Confederate comrades-in-arms. ***Library of Congress***

Jackson continued his army career after the Mexican War, but eventually left to teach at the Virginia Military Institute. ***U.S. Army Military History Institute***

It was a pattern the two men followed for the next 13 months. Lee would broadly outline the military necessities and leave it to Jackson to accomplish them by the most effective means. Lee never found another general who could work with him in that way.

Jackson, secretive by nature, absorbed Lee's orders and without further consultations began putting them into effect. With 9,000 men under his direct command, he faced three federal armies totaling 60,000 men. Banks, with the largest force in the Valley, was confident that he was in control of the situation. Then on May 5 Jackson disappeared.

He turned up three days later near McDowell, Virginia, opposite a federal force coming at him from West Virginia. It was under the command of the famed western explorer, John C. Fremont. Although outnumbered, the Union troops went on the attack and inflicted 500 casualties, twice the number they incurred.

But, eventually, Jackson drove them back and pursued them west into the mountains for a few days. He had no intention of engaging in another battle. He just wanted to take Fremont out of the Valley, and he had done exactly that.

Now he turned his attention to Banks, who still had no idea where his adversary was. Unfortunately for Banks, Jackson used screening cavalry and intervening mountain ridges to slip behind him, join an 8,000-man force under General Richard Ewell, and gather his strength for a hammer blow.

It landed at Front Royal on May 23. First the small force protecting Banks's rear was destroyed; then the main body of the army itself was shattered at Winchester, two days later. A soundly defeated Banks retreated back across the Potomac while Jackson's men cheerfully helped themselves to the supplies his army had abandoned in its flight.

Now two opposing forces had been taken off the board. Jackson's men began proudly referring to themselves as the "foot cavalry," infantry that could march with incomparable speed and turn up where least expected.

With the situation outside Richmond coming to a boil, the Union command was forced to recall 20,000 more men to deal with Jackson. No one knew where he would turn up next. He might even decide to march on Washington.

Fremont was ordered to head back into the Shenandoah and get behind Jackson from the south, while Brigadier General James Shields was sent to seal off the other end of the Valley. But Fremont could not move across the muddy mountain roads quickly enough to close the trap. Jackson, by marching 40 miles in 36 hours, remained ahead of both of them, heading south.

The two Union armies in pursuit were separated by Massanutten Mountain. The trick was to prevent them from converging.

On June 8, Ewell was dispatched to take on Fremont's force. At the Battle of Cross Keys, Fremont was pushed back once more. Meanwhile, Jackson turned his attention to Shields at Port Republic and opened battle there on the following day. This was a much tougher fight. But with the outcome in doubt, Ewell, who had slipped away from Fremont's front during the night, came up and hit the Union left with two regiments. That decided the matter.

With the retreat of Shields, Jackson had defeated three separate armies in the space of a month and prevented 60,000 men from joining McClellan. The Shenandoah Valley campaign is regarded by many historians, according to *the Dictionary of American Biography*, as "the most remarkable display of strategic science, based on accurate reasoning, correct anticipation of the enemy's plans, rapid marches and judicious disposition of an inferior force in all American military history."

Jackson was now poised either to continue the campaign in the Valley or to join Lee at Richmond for the counteroffensive against McClellan. "I think the sooner Jackson can move this way, the better," Lee suggested to Jefferson Davis. "We may strike them here before they are ready there."

Davis concurred, and Jackson moved east for the start of the Seven Days Battles of June 1862. But it was here that something went terribly wrong. Jackson turned out to be the biggest disappointment of the weeklong engagement.

He arrived several hours late on June 26. General Ambrose P. Hill, who was supposed to move in concert with Jackson across the Chickahominy River, decided he couldn't wait any longer and started the advance without him. That also put the rest of Lee's offensive plan into motion without the critical component of Jackson.

He had been slowed in the mountains and also by road barricades put up by Union engineers. When he finally got to the launching area, instead of taking up his assigned position, Jackson reported to headquarters. By the time his men entered the fight, it was 12 hours later than anticipated.

The Battle of Mechanicsville was costly in terms of Confederate casualties, with 1,484 losses compared to McClellan's 361. Jackson's arrival did convince the Union general, however, that his position now was untenable, and he began the retreat back to his waiting fleet for evacuation.

On the following day, Jackson again came up late at Gaines Mill when he went down the wrong road. On June 29, at the critical battle at Frayser's Farm, where Lee thought he had the chance to destroy McClellan's army, Jackson failed to assist General James Longstreet at the critical hour, and the chance was lost.

Finally, at White Oak Swamp, by failing to ford a stream and move on a weak position, he allowed a retreating federal force to elude him, and, instead, entered into a pointless artillery duel with his adversary.

That made four failures in five days, and Lee, for the only time, was exasperated with Jackson. "Yes, [McClellan] will get away," he snapped to General Jubal A. Early, "because I cannot have my orders carried out."

What can explain this performance by the most reliable of Lee's lieutenants? Most historians believe that Jackson was simply mentally and physically exhausted by the stress of conducting the Shenandoah campaign and then immediately covering the distance to join Lee at Richmond.

Promoted to colonel, Jackson went to Harpers Ferry in 1861 to train Confederate recruits. Shortly thereafter, he was made brigadier general under Joseph E. Johnston. ***National Archives and Records Division***

On the night before Frayser's Farm, he fell asleep in the middle of supper. Other times, he was observed sitting outside his tent, staring at the ground. At one point, he turned to his staff and said: "Gentlemen, let us at once to bed and rise with the dawn and see if tomorrow we cannot do something."

"Worked beyond the limit of his iron endurance," writes Frank E. Vandiver, in *Mighty Stonewall*, "Jackson did not realize that he had lost contact with reality. It had become obvious to his staff ... that he was in a stupor possibly caused by pent-up fatigue, unhealthy and unfamiliar climate and the confusion of foreign geography."

There are also suggestions that he simply could not adapt to fighting in swampland, but needed open vistas to employ the expansive vision that showed him at his best. He would soon have the opportunity to display it again.

With McClellan disposed of, Lee now intended to start a counteroffensive. It was designed to carry the war into the North, resupply his army, and convince public opinion that the Union simply could not win. On July 13, barely two weeks after the repeated blunders at the Seven Days, Lee sent Jackson north as the advance guard of this invasion to attack forces under Major General John Pope.

Realizing that Pope had divided his forces, Jackson fell upon the smaller army, numbering about 12,000 men, at Cedar Mountain, near Culpeper, Virginia. Although he had 22,000 men under his command, Jackson was in for a hard fight. At one point, the Stonewall Brigade was pushed back, and Jackson him-

At First Manassas, Jackson earned his nickname during his unflinching stand "like a stone wall" on Henry Hill. *Museum of the Confederacy, Richmond, Virginia. Photo by Katherine Wetzel*

self came to the front to rally his men, waving a sheathed sword and a battle flag while Union bullets sang past his ears.

As inspirational as his actions were, it was his superior numbers that carried the day. Jackson later called it "the most successful of [my] exploits." But Robert Krick, in an article on the fight in *The Civil War Battlefield Guide*, says that was "a judgment surely based on the excitement of an adrenaline-laced personal involvement rather than any sense of tactical or strategic prowess."

Now that Jackson had made his presence known, the last of the Union pressure on Richmond was lifted, and Lee was free to join him at the end of August. The plan he conceived when they combined was among the most daring of his career. Disregarding all standard military doctrine, he divided his force in the face of a numerically superior enemy.

But he had measured Pope and found him wanting. So he did not hesitate to detach Jackson and send him on a swift flanking movement—50 miles in 40 hours—to get behind the Union general. Pope had no idea where Jackson was when he suddenly swept in from the west to capture the federal supply station at Manassas Junction.

The small Union force there was routed, and Jackson's men enthusiastically helped themselves to goods intended for the Northern army. What they couldn't cart away, they burned.

An infuriated Pope now knew exactly where Jackson was, however, and was determined, in his words, to "bag" him. But this also was part of Lee's plan. Jackson had campaigned brilliantly in the Shenandoah by using rapid movements. Now he would have to hold his position against Pope's frontal assault, while the rest of Lee's army came up on the Union rear.

Jackson had stationed himself just a few miles from the old Manassas battlefield, where he had won his nickname 13 months before. On August 28, Pope threw everything he had at him. These were among the best soldiers in the Union army, part of McDowell's Iron Brigade, and the two sides fought to a bloody standoff, with one-third of the men on both sides killed or wounded.

Pope went at Jackson again on the following day, but the attacks were poorly coordinated and poorly reinforced. The Confederates were able to repair the breaches in their line before Union forces could take advantage of them. On August 30, Pope attacked again, piling into Jackson's entrenched army with such force that Jackson finally sent word to Lee that he had to have help if he was to hold on.

But Pope's attack had exposed his entire left flank, and it was at this moment that Longstreet sent 30,000 men swooping down on him. Pope never saw the blow coming and, indeed, Longstreet had delayed it until the battle developed in just this way.

Pope was routed and sent into retreat to Washington. In less than a week, he was relieved of command. While Second Manassas had resulted in 8,350 casualties for Lee, he was now poised to continue his movement north, and his faith in Jackson's abilities for independent command was completely restored.

"Old Jack" had now acquired an aura of invincibility in the army. His battered cap, grimy old uniform, and ugly oversized boots became marks of endearment. His habit of awakening several times and praying in the night before a battle was well known. He would refuse to play cards and was rigorous in his observance of the Sabbath. According to one story, he would not mail a letter if he knew it would travel on a Sunday.

He was not the easiest of men for his subordinates. On the march north from Manassas, he became displeased at the lack of discipline shown by troops of Ambrose P. Hill. He criticized Hill in front of members of his staff. The outraged Hill took out his sword, handed it to Jackson hilt first, and told him that if he intended to take command of his troops he might as well take his sword, too.

Jackson placed Hill under arrest, and for the next several days Hill marched in the rear of his own men.

Jackson's passion for secrecy upset the officers who served under him. He told them that his plans were kept "under my hat" and that was all they needed to know. But when orders did come, they were sometimes unfathomable. "I never saw one of Jackson's couriers approach," said Ewell, "without expecting an order to assault the North Pole."

Jackson, himself, was absolutely loyal to Lee and said that he "would follow him blindfolded."

Lee now sent him back to Harpers Ferry, which he captured on September 15, taking more than 12,000 prisoners. A *New York Times* correspondent who saw him there wrote that the general wore a uniform "which any northern beggar would consider an insult to have offered him." His men, he added, looked even worse. "Ireland in her worst straits could present no parallel," said the man from the *Times.*

In the Shenandoah Valley, Jackson directed his most brilliant campaign, tying up thousands of federal troops with his fast marches and surprise attacks. *U.S. Army Military History Institute*

While in Winchester in 1862, Jackson sat for the photograph from which numerous later images were drawn. *National Archives and Records Division*

But they could fight. "My men have sometimes failed to take a position," Jackson stated, "but to defend one, never!"

He almost had to change that boast at Antietam, the horrific battle that blunted Lee's northern advance in Maryland. Jackson was posted on the Confederate left at a Dunker church and endured a powerful artillery assault from General Joseph Hooker. The infantry charge that followed nearly did sweep Jackson's corps from its position. Only the arrival of John Bell Hood's Texans turned the impetus of the fight around and sent Hooker into retreat.

The battle ended in a stalemate, however, and Lee was now faced with the necessity of getting back to the Rappahannock River in Virginia to hold that line against a Northern advance. On the way, Jackson was given word that he had been promoted to lieutenant general, with command of the Second Corps of the Army of Northern Virginia.

In observance of this auspicious event, Jeb Stuart, a personal favorite of Jackson's, presented him with the gift of a handsome new uniform, complete with gold braid. When Jackson put it on to please Stuart, it caused a sensation throughout the army. It was so out of character with Jackson's usual demeanor that its appearance was cheered wildly by his men, and it provided the gruffly humorous Longstreet with no end of amusement.

Even as he prepared for the work ahead, the Battle of Fredericksburg, on December 13, Longstreet could not resist a gentle jibe at Jackson. "General," he asked, "do not all those multitudes of Federals frighten you?"

The grim Jackson, looking far older than his 38 years, answered without a trace of levity. "We shall see very soon," he said, "whether I shall not frighten them."

As it turned out, the Union soldiers had good reason for fear. This was one of the bloodiest days of the war, with Longstreet and Jackson masterfully entrenched on Marye's Heights, and the incompetent General Ambrose Burnside sending wave after wave of men in a hopeless assault on the position. There were 12,600 Union casualties during the battle, and almost two-thirds of them came at Marye's Heights. Burnside, like Pope before him, was thoroughly whipped and soon out of a job.

Jackson made numerous errors during the Seven Days Battles. At Gaines Mill, he arrived late after heading down the wrong road. *National Archives and Records Division*

"They went as they came," Jackson wrote his wife, "in the night. They suffered heavily as far as the battle went but it did not go far enough to satisfy me."

Both Jackson and Lee were angered at looting by Union soldiers and heavy damage to civilian property in the town of Fredericksburg. "What can we do?" asked a staff officer in helpless rage. "Do?" replied Jackson. "Why, shoot them." The warrior could barely restrain his eagerness to put his words into action.

But the winter lull in fighting had begun. It gave Jackson, who had been campaigning almost without halt for nine months, time to restore himself. Most important, he could enjoy a reunion with his wife and meet, for the first time, his infant daughter, Julia, who had been born in November. He even moved from his tent into a nearby house, which had been offered for the comfort of his family, for the occasion.

On April 29, the visit abruptly ended. The sound of guns indicated that Hooker had begun his long-awaited offensive to cross the Rappahannock. The family said goodbye, not to see each other again until Jackson was on his deathbed.

Hooker intended to turn Lee's flank and drive him out of the Fredericksburg line. He accomplished that, but Lee retreated to the west and reformed his front at the edge of an area known as The Wilderness. It was a dark tangle of forests and ravines, impenetrable to the pioneer settlers of the area and supposedly impassable for an army.

Hooker established his furthest position at a crossroads settlement called Chancellorsville and prepared to occupy the high ground at Zoan Church, the only elevation for miles around.

Lee was outnumbered by a factor of two and a half to one. But he was opposed by a general who did not have the ability to react when the enemy failed to respond according to plan. "I've got Lee just where I want him," Hooker bragged. "He must fight me on my own ground." But Lee refused to cooperate.

Again he audaciously split his outnumbered force, sending Jackson on May 1 to clear the Federals from Zoan ridge. He encountered only weak resistance. Rather than seizing his advantage here, Hooker had chosen, instead, to entrench at Chancellorsville, leaving his right flank exposed. It was a fatal error.

The two Confederate generals now hatched their boldest plan. Meeting at a campfire that evening, they pored over maps of the area, heard Stuart's scouting reports, and discussed what must be done. "Show me what to do, and I will do it," Jackson said.

Lee would hold Hooker's force of 70,000 men with just 14,000 of his own, and make a show of retreating south. Meanwhile, Jackson would get to the Union rear by marching his corps, 30,000 strong, 12 miles through The Wilderness on roads that were barely lines on a

Jackson made a swift flanking maneuver to surprise General John Pope and capture the federal supply station at Manassas Junction. ***Library of Congress***

Jackson had this photo made just prior to the action at Chancellorsville that cost him his life. ***National Archives and Records Division***

Near Chancellorsville, Jackson and Lee met one last time to discuss strategy for the following day's battle. *Battles and Leaders of the Civil War*

While returning to his line, Jackson was fired upon by nervous Confederates. *Library of Congress*

map. They came out at the Orange Turnpike, where Hooker was most vulnerable.

He was doubly vulnerable because the troops on this wing were highly disgruntled. They were predominantly of German origin and had enlisted to fight under one of their own, General Franz Sigel. He had fought in the unsuccessful Revolution of 1848 in Germany, as had many of the soldiers he commanded. But Sigel was inept, his corps had fought poorly, and he resigned under criticism in February.

His replacement, General Oliver O. Howard, did not connect with his German-speaking troops. His XI Corps was not ready for what Jackson was about to throw at them. There was probably no unit in the army that could have been.

Cavalry General Fitzhugh Lee was by Jackson's side when he first saw the totally unsuspecting federal army in front of him.

"His eyes burned with a brilliant glow, lighting his sad face," Lee wrote years later. "His expression was one of intense interest; his face was colored slightly with the paint of the approaching battle and radiant in the success of his flank movement."

Jackson had begun his march at 8 A.M., about four hours later than originally planned. It was now 5:15 P.M., and 90 minutes of daylight remained. Jackson judged that would be sufficient.

His corps came out of The Wilderness, screaming the rebel yell and driving the confused and unprepared soldiers under Howard before them. "Darkness was upon us," one of them would write later, "and Jackson was on us and fear was on us."

The victory at Chancellorsville is usually described as the most brilliant feat of generalship in the war, the culmination of Jackson's genius and the Confederacy's most inspiring hour. But Jackson was not content to let the victory rest. He wanted to cut off the Union escape route at the United States Ford of the Rappahannock.

It was now dark, but Jackson had the opportunity in his grasp and would not be put off. He rode to a forward position that his own pickets had just claimed in a hard fight with Pennsylvania troops. When they saw riders approaching, they assumed it was federal cavalry and opened fire.

"Cease fire!" hollered Jackson's officers. "You are firing into your own men."

Thinking that this was a trick, the entire Confederate line opened up at the horsemen. Jackson was hit three times, twice in his left arm and once in the palm of his right hand, which had been raised to shield his face from low branches.

The loss of blood and pain were great, and Jackson quickly lapsed into shock. He was carried to the rear in a litter, in the midst of an artillery duel, and was dropped once en route. Finally, an ambulance was located to take him to a medical station where an anesthetic was given to him and his arm was amputated.

Lee would remark, "General Jackson has lost his left arm but I have lost my right one."

It was thought that the wounds, although severe, could be treated and that Jackson would fight again after a period of recuperation. "Any victory is dearly bought which deprives us of the services of General Jackson even for a short time," Lee had added.

Jackson was transported to Guinea Station, located

well behind the Confederate lines, after Lee concluded the sweeping victory at Chancellorsville. It also was convenient to the railroad to Richmond. An office on the Thomas Chandler plantation was converted into a sick room, and arrangements were made for his comfort.

He had chatted amiably about Hooker's battle plan on the 25-mile ambulance ride from the hospital, and for several days he gained strength. His wounds seemed to be healing. But unknown to his physician, Jackson had contracted pneumonia. While his external wounds were well tended, the disease was destroying him.

On May 7, he took a turn for the worse and morphine was administered to ease the pain. His wife and Julia arrived that afternoon, only to find their reunion had turned into a death watch, as Jackson drifted in and out of consciousness and delirium.

On May 10, a Sunday, Anna Jackson was told that the end was a few hours away. With perfect calm, her husband accepted the inevitable. "It is the Lord's day; my wish is fulfilled," he said. "I have always desired to die on Sunday."

At 3 P.M., in his final delirium, he began issuing orders to the absent Ambrose P. Hill and one of his majors. Pausing in mid-sentence, he smiled and said: "Let us cross over the river and rest under the shade of the trees."

Then the man who had not permitted one of his letters to travel on the Sabbath left on a final Sunday journey.

Jackson's death plunged the South into deepest mourning. He had become the greatest hero of the war, eclipsing even Lee for a time.

During the early months of 1863, the two generals had studied plans for an invasion of Pennsylvania. They weighed the possibility of capturing and destroying the state's anthracite coal mines, damaging the North's industrial capacity. That invasion would proceed in just a few weeks. But Jackson was not there and its result would extinguish the South's best hope.

Jackson's grave became a popular attraction after the war. An image of Lee visiting his fallen friend made for potent Lost Cause imagery. *Library of Congress*

JOSEPH E. JOHNSTON

"I have had nearly all the Southern generals in high command in front of me, and Joe Johnston gave me more anxiety than any of the others. I was never half so anxious about Lee."

U. S. Grant, quoted in Around the World with General Grant, *by A. R. Young*

He was the commanding general at the first great battle of the Civil War, and he was the commanding general at the last one. He was the only man to head both the eastern and western Confederate armies. Both his subordinates and his opponents admired him as a master of military skill.

And yet Joseph Eggleston Johnston won no decisive victory. He wasted much of his energy in a bitter, and, ultimately, pointless feud with Jefferson Davis that lasted long after the war was over and the Confederacy dissolved. His most recent biographer, Craig L. Symonds, describes him as "an enigma—idealized by a few, vilified or dismissed by many others, ignored by most."

He was adored by his men and detested by his superiors. He went through the entire war lamenting the circumstances in which he was forced to command. Outnumbered in the field and undercut by Davis and his cabinet, he never quite found himself in the right place under conditions that suited him.

When given the chance to take command of the Army of Tennessee at a critical moment, his sense of honor prevented him from seizing the day. His greatest skill was, in fact, avoiding battle, a quality that made him suspect in the eyes of Davis and Secretary of War Judah P. Benjamin. His enemies in Richmond scorned him as "Retreatin' Johnston," and he made highly placed enemies easily.

"Love was not easily destroyed in his heart," wrote historian Douglas Southall Freeman. "Hate once inflamed always was cherished."

He was called "The Gamecock," because of his small size and combative nature. He looks out from the old photographs, with neatly trimmed military beard, high forehead, and direct gaze. His bearing is aristocratic, the perfect image of a military man who takes words like "honor" very seriously and highly personally.

Johnston was Old Virginia, fully as much as Robert E. Lee, the man most often held up as the example of all things Johnston aspired to but could not attain. Their fathers served in the same unit in the American Revolution. He was, in fact, named for Peter Johnston's squad commander in that war, Joseph Eggleston. His mother was a niece of Patrick Henry.

Peter Johnston was a jurist and a man who evidently welcomed challenges. Although assigned to a comfortable circuit in central Virginia, he arranged to move, instead, to the village of Abingdon, on the state's far western frontier. It was there, at a rural estate called Cherry Grove, that Joseph was born in 1807.

He was educated at the local academy founded by his father. Although he had six older brothers, it was clear that the senior Johnston saw something in the boy. Maybe it was the way he kept asking him to retell the stories of his war exploits, pressing him for the smallest details. When Joseph was eight years old, Peter presented the boy with his military sword, a treasure Joseph carried with him for the rest of his career.

Inevitably, he was sent off to the U.S. Military Academy in 1825, and there he found himself in the same class as Lee, with whom he maintained a distant friendship.

While bothered by poor eyesight, Johnston was an outstanding student and graduated thirteenth in the class (but well behind Lee's second ranking). He chose the artillery as his branch of service, and in the next few years his assignments hovered at the fringe of several historic events—Nat Turner's Rebellion in Virginia, the Black Hawk War in Illinois, and the Nullification Crisis in South Carolina.

In none of these did he see action, although Nullification did give him some bad moments. South Carolina was so affronted by the tariff backed by President Andrew Jackson in 1832 that it declared the act of Congress void, interposing the power of the state before the federal government.

Three of Johnston's brothers were living in South Carolina and were members of the state militia, which would have opposed Johnston's troops. But the situation was defused by a compromise, and, to his relief, Johnston never had to make a decision on the issue.

It wasn't until four years later that he first came under hostile fire. He was sent to Florida to serve on the staff of General Winfield Scott in the Second Seminole War, a brutal affair in which U.S. troops were sent into the Everglades to track down an elusive and dangerous foe.

Johnston had welcomed the assignment as an opportunity for advancement. But after two demoralizing years of chasing the Seminole to no good purpose, he had enough. Johnston resigned his commission to become a civil engineer. The only job he could find, however, sent him right back to Florida in 1837 as a civilian employee of a military topographical expedition.

Ironically, it was in this situation that he first was called upon to exercise his skills as a soldier. His surveying party came under attack by the Seminole near the Jupiter River. Several American officers were cut down by rifle fire, and Johnston was creased by a bullet across the scalp, a wound clearly evident in later years on his receding hairline.

Despite a panicked flight by several of the untrained recruits, Johnston rescued the party by organizing a retreat that held off the Indians for five hours. He was the last man back to the boats and managed to save all but five members of the expedition.

He had conducted himself with valor, and the experience changed his mind about a military career. Johnston accepted a new commission as second lieutenant, U.S. Engineers.

One of his first assignments was to map the Canadian border along lakes Huron and Superior, in Michigan. Accompanying him on the expedition was Lieutenant Robert McLane, who had fought beside him on the retreat in Seminole country.

Johnston was now a man in his mid 30s, almost past marrying age. While he was drawn to family life, his career gave him few opportunities to meet a suitable wife. A voracious reader, he sought companionship in his books. But when he accompanied McLane home to Maryland during Christmas, 1840, he met his friend's younger sister, Lydia.

Prior to Lee's taking command of the Army of Northern Virginia, Joseph E. Johnston was the South's leading military figure. ***National Archives and Records Division***

She was 15 years younger than he and, while not regarded as a beauty, was known for her quiet wit and intelligence. Johnston was immediately attracted, and after a lengthy courtship, the two were married in 1845. They were well matched intellectually and, while they would have no children, the couple became surrogate parents over the years to a variety of nephews and friends.

In little more than a year, Johnston would get another and stronger taste of combat. Promoted to lieutenant colonel, he was sent to join his former commander, Scott, at Vera Cruz. The American landing here in March 1847 began the final phase of the Mexican War, the overland expedition to take Mexico City.

A few days before the landing, Johnston was sent out on the cruiser *Petrita* to scout the coastline. On the vessel with him were Lee, George Meade, George McClellan, and P. G. T. Beauregard. The ship came under fire from shore batteries, but all 11 salvos missed the mark. Some historians wonder playfully how the course of the Civil War would have been changed if one of them had hit.

In the weeks to come, however, the enemy's aim improved. Johnston was wounded twice at Cerro Gordo, and while leading the culminating assault at the fortress of Chapultepec, he was hit three more times.

"Johnston is a great soldier," was Scott's often quoted assessment, "but he has an unfortunate knack for getting himself shot in nearly every engagement." There would be other wounds to come. One of his aides in the Civil War would tell Southern diarist Mary Boykin Chesnut, "No man exposes himself more recklessly to danger than General Johnston, and no one strives harder to keep others out of it."

After the Mexican War, Johnston returned to the Topographical Engineers. After an assortment of postings, he and Lydia in 1858 happily found themselves in Washington, D.C. She and Varina Howell Davis, wife of the future Confederate president, became inseparable companions, "pointed out as the cleverest women in the United States," wrote Mrs. Chesnut.

Johnston rose to brigadier general in the Quartermasters Corps, and at the age of 54, he was securely situated in the peacetime military establishment. But when Virginia seceded in the spring of 1861, he knew the course he would follow, despite the cost.

"It is ruin in every sense of the word," Johnston told Secretary of War Simon Cameron in turning in his resignation. "But I must go."

When friends urged Lydia Johnston to convince her husband to stay with the Union, she shook her head. "My husband cannot stay in an army which is about to invade his country." When they begged her to keep him out of the Confederate Army nonetheless, she responded sadly, "But how is Joe Johnston to live? He has no private fortune or no profession but that of arms."

Johnston also knew that as the highest-ranking officer to join the Confederate Army, he was in line to become top field commander for the South, a role he confidently expected to fill when the organization of the army was completed. In the meantime, he was sent off to Harpers Ferry as a brigadier general, in July 1861, and ordered to carry on operations in the northern part of the Shenandoah Valley.

His troops quickly came to admire their lean, erect commander. "He sat his steed like a part of the animal," wrote one of his officers, W. G. Cobb, "and there was that about him which impressed us all with the idea that he was at home with the management of an army as well as of a horse."

But Johnston did not care for the disposition of forces at Harpers Ferry. Many of his men were ill. They were also inadequately equipped in his view and confronted by a larger federal force. In the first of many such maneuvers in this war, Johnston slipped away behind a cavalry screen, confounding an opponent who had no idea where he had gone. He had, in fact, gone to Manassas by railroad, linking up with Beauregard to fight the first major battle of the war.

While Johnston was the superior officer, he graciously stepped aside when he learned that Beauregard already had drawn up a battle plan. Johnston, instead, took an observer's position on the Confederate right. With mounting concern, however, he watched the deterioration of the situation on the left, where federal forces had a numerical advantage.

"The battle is there," he, at last, told Beauregard. "I am going."

With Beauregard right behind him, Johnston arrived in time to stabilize and rally the Southerners, restoring order to the sagging Confederate line. The counterattack organized here drove the Union forces from the field and resulted in the unexpected victory at Bull Run.

While Davis had not been altogether happy over Johnston's retreat from Harpers Ferry, Bull Run made the general a hero in Virginia. Johnston confidently awaited the word from Richmond that would give him the command position he anticipated.

But on August 31, 1861, Davis sent down the list of men who had been made full generals. Johnston's name was fourth, behind Adjutant General Samuel Cooper; Davis's good friend Albert Sidney Johnston, and Lee. Joseph E. Johnston still retained the field command of the army in Virginia, but he could not contain his outrage. This was more than a slight; it was a betrayal.

He wrote Davis a vehement protest, kept it for two days, and then mailed it anyhow. "It seeks to tarnish my fair fame as a soldier and a man," he wrote, "earned by more than thirty years of laborious and perilous service." It went on in this vein for six pages, and when Davis received it, he was enraged.

This was his full response. "Sir: I have just received and read your letter of the 12th instant. Its language is, as you say, unusual; its arguments and statements utterly one-sided and its insinuations as unfounded as they are unbecoming. I am, Jeff'n Davis."

There was never any question of cordial relations between the two men again. Their personalities were too much alike, each too eager to find and take offense. The hatred between them only deepened as the war went on, with damaging results for the Confederate cause.

Johnston served on General Winfield Scott's staff during the Second Seminole War. *Library of Congress*

Nonetheless, Johnston remained in command of the army and stayed put at Manassas, holding the railroad crossing and the battlefield, just as the Union army had left it.

His Richmond critics soon began accusing him of inaction in failing to pursue the retreating Federals all the way to Washington, although that was never seriously considered as a possibility by any Confederate officer in the field. They also said that Johnston was ignoring the fact that he was no longer in the army of a powerful nation, but of a new country with limited resources.

"He was wantonly wasteful of supplies," writes historian Clifford Dowdey, "just as though he had an inexhaustible flow at his beck and call. He gave up ground with the same abandon, always with the most logical military reasons.... He lacked the larger vision of correlative action and the will to strike boldly for success. He made war as he might play chess, without stakes."

But it might also be argued that Johnston understood better than anyone in Richmond that he was fighting a war in which holding territory was meaningless. It made no difference how much land was given up, as long as the army was preserved and prepared to deal a deadly blow to a careless or overextended invader. That became the basic point of conflict between Johnston and Davis, one that was never adequately resolved.

Moreover, he soon found himself on the wrong side of Benjamin, a powerful intellect who was wholly devoted to Davis. The secretary of war managed to get Beauregard transferred to the west, convincing him that it would be for his own good to be independent of Johnston, although neither general had requested it.

He also insisted on Johnston carrying out a Davis directive to reorganize the army so that troops from the same state served in the same units. Davis thought this would raise morale, but Johnston felt it was a dangerous undertaking in the face of an enemy force that was gathering strength and now outnumbered him three to one.

Johnston felt he was being treated as an adversary. The loss of Beauregard and other officers, he said, had "crippled the army" and impaired its discipline. Early in 1862, he was called to Richmond for confidential discussions with Davis and his cabinet on withdrawing the army to a more secure line of defense. By the time he returned to his hotel, he found that news of the proposed withdrawal had arrived ahead of him.

Johnston was badly shaken by this breach of security and decided he could not trust the men around Davis. That resulted in the general employing a certain vagueness in all the plans he relayed to Richmond for the rest of the war, adding to the general air of distrust between him and Davis.

By March, Johnston had become aware of General McClellan's plan to advance on Richmond from the southeast, after landing troops on the peninsula between the James and York rivers. With Davis protesting every step of the way, Johnston made the decision to abandon guns and a meat packing plant near Manassas and fall back to a defensive line at Yorktown, interposing himself between the Union army and the capital.

The army passed through Richmond in April, parading in front of thunderously cheering crowds before moving into position at Yorktown. But Davis had no sooner accepted the logic of the move than Johnston decided that this line, too, was untenable and ordered a retreat to the outer reaches of Richmond itself.

Only a direct order from Davis, on the advice of Lee, kept him at Yorktown. Lee, who had assumed command of all Southern armies within Virginia, wanted to fight as far from the center as possible, while Johnston, writes Symonds, "believed in engaging the enemy in force, even if he had to give ground to achieve it."

Johnston acceded to their demand. But on May 1, with McClellan aligned before him and opening up with his siege guns, Johnston gave the order to retreat. Davis was flabbergasted, not the first time he would be confounded by the strategy of this general.

"I determined to retire because we can do nothing here," Johnston responded in explanation. "The enemy will give us no chance to win. We must lose. By delay we may insure the loss of Richmond, too."

General James Longstreet, who regarded Johnston as the finest general in America and constantly sought to serve under him again during the course of the war, covered the retreat with a brilliant delaying action at Williamsburg. At one point, Johnston even pitched in, wading into a mudhole and helping his men pull a 12-pound cannon out of the muck. "Our battery used to swear by Old Joe," said one artilleryman who had witnessed the act.

The army was safe, but Davis was fuming at the withdrawal to the capital. He wanted action or at least a start on his pet plan to reorganize the army by states. Johnston ignored him, concentrated his forces, and waited for the right moment to deal the overextended McClellan a crushing blow.

On May 31, the opportunity came. In his advance on Richmond, McClellan split his forces on either side of the Chickahominy River. Johnston quickly drew up a plan that would strike at the smaller of the two forces in overwhelming numbers and destroy it.

It depended on Longstreet, Daniel Harvey Hill, and Benjamin Huger coordinating their movements to converge together on the march from Richmond to the point of attack. But Longstreet chose to take his brigades over another route and got them all tangled up with Huger's. The resulting confusion never allowed Johnston to concentrate enough manpower to break through the federal lines.

Afterwards, he blamed himself for giving verbal

Johnston received several wounds during the Mexican War, two at Cerro Gordo. ***Library of Congress***

orders that were too imprecise. Moreover, the forces that did get to the right place on time had to fight through fields flooded by a torrential downpour.

While Hill's attack scored an initial breakthrough, a Union force under General Edwin Sumner was able to cross the Chickahominy in time to halt the Confederate advance at Fair Oaks (the name under which the battle was known to the Union side). The fight ended in a stalemate, although it was billed in the South as a victory. For Johnston, however, the result was personally disastrous.

As he rode to Fair Oaks to view the fighting, he advised a colonel on his staff that it was no use trying to dodge in the saddle "because once you hear them the bullets have passed." No sooner had he spoke than he was hit by rifle fire in the shoulder and then by shrapnel in the chest.

The first wound was minor, but the second knocked him from the saddle unconscious. As members of his staff carried him on a litter for medical help, Davis and Lee, who had come out from Richmond to watch the course of the battle, came riding up. When Johnston came to, the first person he saw was Davis, which must have given the general quite a turn.

But the president was gracious and offered Johnston his hand. The general accepted it and then made a horrifying discovery. "My sword," he said. "My father wore it in the Revolutionary War and I would not lose it for $10,000. Will someone please go back and get it for me?"

The request was honored, and Johnston was carried to the rear and into five months of recuperation.

The battle wound down the following day, whereupon Lee was named commanding general of the renamed Army of Northern Virginia.

Anger at Johnston for the confusion during the attack was set aside when the severity of his wounds was learned. Otherwise, some historians say, he may have been removed from command anyhow and subjected to an investigation.

Johnston's first biographer, Bradley Johnson, insisted that if he hadn't been wounded, the general would have extracted a victory at Seven Pines. However, that is an opinion shared by few.

During his long convalescence in Richmond, Johnston did everything he could to shield Longstreet from blame for his role in the battle, even going so far as to request rewriting of official reports. Symonds writes that Johnston, in his own mind, felt that his verbal orders may have been at fault, but that in protecting Longstreet he was also taking some of the blame from himself.

By November 1862, he decided that he was ready to return to action. But Lee had ended the threat to Richmond, won several major victories, and was in firm

In April 1861, the Confederate government made Johnston a brigadier general and sent him to Harpers Ferry. ***Library of Congress***

control of the Virginia campaign. Davis, however, was eager to send Johnston to the western theater to coordinate the actions of the two Confederate armies there: Braxton Bragg's in Tennessee and John Pemberton's in Mississippi.

During his recuperation, Johnston had made important political connections, especially among those who hated Davis. They were convinced that his appointment was the answer to the dangerous situation in the west.

"Gentlemen," said Senator William Lowndes Yancey, of Alabama, in a toast at a farewell dinner for him, "let us drink to the only man who can save the Confederacy, General Joseph E. Johnston."

The general rose from his chair and nodded to Yancey. "The man you describe is already in the field—in the person of General Robert E. Lee," he responded. "I will drink to his health."

Johnston already had his doubts about the actual power he could employ, and he feared that an arrangement in which he would be in command of two widely separated armies was unworkable. Besides, as always, he would be at a severe numerical disadvantage.

When he arrived at Chattanooga to take over the new job, his depression only deepened. "Nobody ever assumed a command under more unfavorable circumstances," he wrote to a friend. It was a refrain that could be the theme of his career.

Lydia Johnston shared her husband's outlook. "How ill and weary I feel in this desolate land," she wrote to a friend in Virginia. "How dreary it all looks & how little prospect there is of my poor husband doing ought than lose his army. Truly a forlorn hope it is."

The news of his protégé Longstreet's great success

After watching General P. G. T. Beauregard's battle plan at Manassas deteriorate, Johnston took command and turned the engagement into a Confederate victory. ***Library of Congress***

at Fredericksburg that fall failed to lift his spirits. "What luck some people have," Johnston said. "Nobody will ever come to attack me in such a place."

He left on an inspection tour of the critical fortress at Vicksburg, and what he found there concerned him even more. He felt its entrenchments were totally inadequate, "the usual defect of Confederate engineering." Moreover, Pemberton was in complete agreement with Davis that Vicksburg had to be defended at all costs, even if that put his army at risk.

Johnston told Davis afterwards that the command structure—he called it a "nominal geographic command"—was impossible. While Lee's army, on which this model was based, had just one purpose in front of it, the western armies faced wholly different adversaries and objectives.

Davis told him that's exactly why he had been sent there: he was the only man who could deal with it and there was nothing in his orders to prevent him transferring troops from one army to the other. That only made Johnston, who hated to interfere with decisions made by his subordinates, feel even worse.

But when the chance came to replace Bragg and assume actual leadership of the Army of Tennessee, he could not bring himself to do it. Several of that army's generals were in open revolt against Bragg in early 1863. They questioned his competence and implored Davis to replace him.

Davis wanted Johnston for the job, and it was the post Johnston wanted, too. But it was his responsibility to file the report that would have led to Bragg's removal, and he could not bring himself to do that. According to his sense of honor, that would have meant using his authority to advance his own self-interest, and such an act was unworthy. Johnston even went out of his way to praise Bragg's positive attributes.

To his critics, however, all this meant that Johnston lacked the decisiveness to seize the moment. So Bragg stayed, and Johnston continued to fret.

His mental outlook was also affecting his health. His wounds began bothering him in early spring, just as U. S. Grant began to make his move against Vicksburg. He had run past the fortresses' guns on the Mississippi River, landed south of the city in Louisiana, crossed back into Mississippi, and then began moving on Vicksburg from the land side.

By the time Johnston could get to Jackson, Mississippi, on May 13, 1863, with a small force of 6,000, Grant had managed to interpose his army between Pemberton and the reinforcements. He then wheeled east to drive Johnston out of Jackson, sleeping in the same hotel room the Confederate general had occupied on the previous night.

Johnston ordered Pemberton to come up on Grant's rear and attack. But Pemberton refused, calling the order "suicidal." Moreover, he understood that with such a move Johnston meant to abandon Vicksburg, and his orders from Davis had been to hold the city. By his understanding, that was supposed to be the point of the entire campaign.

He, instead, started falling back to the west and was caught and badly mauled by Grant at Champion Hill. Pemberton had no alternative now but a retreat into Vicksburg.

On May 17, Johnston ordered its evacuation. "If you are invested at Vicksburg," he relayed to him, "you must ultimately surrender. Under such circumstances, instead of losing both troops and place we must, if possible save the troops."

Pemberton refused to move, however, and the siege of Vicksburg, which fell seven weeks later, was a Confederate catastrophe.

Johnston came under fire for not replacing Pemberton, although by the time that became necessary, he could no longer reach Pemberton. Davis, whose orders had been the main influence on Pemberton's decisions, insisted that Johnston had not moved aggressively enough. "We lost because of a lack of provisions inside and a general outside who wouldn't fight," he said bitterly.

Against his wishes, Johnston maintained a defensive line at Yorktown. ***National Archives and Records Division***

Johnston expected primary rank in the Confederate military, but Jefferson Davis placed him fourth. The slight caused a permanent rift between the men. ***Library of Congress***

Despite urgings from Richmond, however, Johnston knew that an attack on Grant would have been futile and would only have resulted in unnecessary casualties. Mississippi was Davis's home state, however, and he regarded its loss as a personal affront.

Through the end of May, Johnston had informed Pemberton that "I am too weak to save Vicksburg.... It will be impossible to extricate you unless you co-operate and we make mutually supporting movements. Communicate your plans and suggestions, if possible."

But Pemberton's only plan was to hold on, and that was impossible. "Their principal faith seems to be in Providence and Joe Johnston," Grant wrote William T. Sherman on June 25. Nine days later neither had come through, and Vicksburg surrendered. Pemberton had lost his army but Johnston, at least, had survived to fight another day.

He also won the respect of Sherman, who was aligned opposite him for most of the Vicksburg campaign. "I think we are doing well out here," he told Grant, "but won't brag till Johnston clears out.... If he moves across the Pearl River and makes good speed, I will let him go."

Sherman's regard for him would continue to grow through the war's final hours. Pemberton, however, never forgave Johnston for what he came to regard as a betrayal. Shelby Foote writes that when the two men met after Pemberton's parole, he correctly saluted but refused to take Johnston's hand. The two never met again.

During the fighting at Fair Oaks, Johnston was wounded in the shoulder and chest. His recuperation took five months. ***Library of Congress***

Now Johnston only had to deal with one army, Bragg's, and that one was foundering. Bragg had allowed the Union army to break out of Chattanooga. He had antagonized Longstreet, and many of his subordinates were in open rebellion. Once more Johnston was in line to take over the command. This time the burden of making that decision was taken from him.

In a meeting of Bragg's staff with Davis, with Bragg seated in the room, Longstreet spoke the unpleasant truth. "Bragg could be of greater service elsewhere than at the head of the Army of Tennessee," he said. But when Longstreet suggested Johnston as his successor, Davis froze. He said that he was "not minded to accept that solution to the premise."

But the political pressure from Johnston's friends, especially Senator Louis T. Wigfall of Texas, was irresistible. In December 1863, Johnston got the job.

The next federal objective was Atlanta, and Johnston was charged with reorganizing the army to stop such a move and then to attack. But the offensive was not in Johnston's game plan. In his view, Davis and his cabinet had learned nothing from Vicksburg. In trying to protect territory, they had lost an army. He would not allow that to happen again.

"I can see no other mode of taking the offensive here than to beat the enemy when he advances and then move forward," he informed Richmond. Then he set about introducing himself personally to as many of the troops as he could. "I do not believe there was a soldier in his army but would gladly have died for him," one private wrote many years later.

But that was precisely the point. Johnston did not ask them to die. Of all the leading Southern generals in this war, he was the most reluctant to spend lives. His strategic philosophy mandated that the army must be saved at all cost.

Davis was driven wild as Johnston began his retreat to the south, leaving nothing behind for Sherman to use, taking few losses, but surrendering territory by the week. Sherman was too smart to do Johnston the favor of attacking him directly, and as the Confederates withdrew to each new position, he would flank them and force a further retreat.

Johnston had an army of 45,000 men and was facing a force of 110,000, with almost twice the number of heavy guns. By the end of June, he had fallen back to Kennesaw Mountain, only 691 feet high but commanding a view of Sherman's entire force. This was a place Johnston could hold and goad the Union general into attacking.

On June 27, Sherman obliged. The assault cost him 3,000 casualties, about three times the number suffered by Johnston. But his superiority in manpower again was far too large for Johnston to hold the position. Once more he had to fall back, closer to Atlanta, to a prepared defensive works near Smyrna.

The campaign had turned into a chess match between two masters. Johnston kept his army together against overwhelming odds and remained as a barrier between Sherman and Atlanta. Sherman, however, kept his communications and supply lines open, never leaving himself vulnerable to being cut off from his base, as Johnston had hoped.

His ability to utilize his advantage in material and organization, the two great resources available to the North, made him an unstoppable opponent. Yet Johnston's skillful retreats left him unable to deliver the death blow.

Johnston requested an additional 5,000 cavalry and planned to attack Sherman's supply lines, forcing the federal army into a frontal assault. But his time was running out. Convinced that Johnston had no plan to hold Sherman out of Atlanta, and receiving only hazy communications from the general, an exasperated Davis ordered him once more to take the offensive.

"I know that Mr. Davis thinks he can do a great many things other men would hesitate to attempt," was Johnston's response in a bitter letter to Senator Wigfall. "For instance, he tried to do what God failed to do. He tried to make a soldier of Braxton Bragg, and you know the result."

A few days later, on July 17, Johnston was informed that he was relieved of command. But the most relieved man in Georgia when he heard the news was Sherman.

"At this critical moment," he said, "the Confederate Government rendered us most valuable service."

When Johnston's successor, John Bell Hood, went on the offensive, Sherman smashed his army, entered Atlanta, and began his famous March to the Sea.

Johnston retired to Macon and then to Columbia, South Carolina. The clamor to replace him, meanwhile, had been replaced by finger-pointing for the massive failure of Hood. Davis was blamed and so was Bragg, for engineering the shift behind the scenes. Johnston increasingly appeared to be the injured party, and his strategy, after Hood's blunders, was accepted as the right one.

Among those who were convinced that Johnston belonged in the field was Lee. Finally, in February 1865, with Southern hopes dwindling to invisibility, a highly reluctant Davis once more summoned Johnston and placed him in command of the remnant of his former army, which over the previous seven months had been forced to retreat into North Carolina.

It was an announcement made with ill grace. Davis expressed the hope that Johnston's "defects" would be remedied "by the control of the general-in-chief." For

Though Johnston ordered the evacuation of Vicksburg, General John Pemberton stubbornly remained until it fell into Union hands. *Library of Congress*

In the West, Johnston continued to incur Davis's wrath but earned the wary respect of Union General Ulysses S. Grant. *National Archives and Records Division*

General William T. Sherman attacked Johnston's far smaller force at Kennesaw Mountain, but he lost 3,000 troops in the process. Johnston retreated with a third that number lost. *Library of Congress*

his part, Johnston once more sounded the familiar refrain that there was little he could do. He had been handed a dwindling force, no staff, and no tactical advantage.

He also understood that the cause was now hopeless and his primary task would be "to obtain fair terms of peace." There was still a forlorn hope that if somehow Lee could break out of Grant's encirclement at Richmond, the two Confederate armies would link up. Then they might threaten to prolong the war enough to gain more favorable terms for peace.

But those hopes dwindled as the iron noose around Richmond was drawn ever tighter and Johnston was pressed once more by Sherman. The engineering skills of Sherman's army were a source of wonder to the Confederates. "Sherman's men march with a rifle in one hand and a spade in the other," was the saying.

Johnston himself said privately that the relentless advance of his old adversary proved to him that "there had been no such army in existence since the days of Julius Caesar."

On March 19, 1865, the two forces clashed for the final time. Sherman had convinced himself that he need not fear an attack because "Johnston was a logical man who behaved logically." But in this last, desperate blow, Johnston put aside all his theories and went on the attack at the Battle of Bentonville, near Goldsboro, North Carolina.

At one point, the Union left crumpled under this furious assault. Some of the finest military minds on the Confederate side were assisting Johnston, and the battle plan they drew up, using the swampy terrain to protect their own flanks, was impeccable. All they lacked were the men to carry it out.

The Army of Tennessee had shriveled to 21,000. Sherman had a two-to-one advantage, and another Union force was driving inland from the coast to link up with him. Bentonville was fought in an effort to prevent that, but the federal numerical edge was simply too great. By the second day of the fight, Sherman's force had increased to 60,000 men, and Johnston had no alternative but to withdraw.

It was the last time Confederate troops ever successfully took the offensive. In a few weeks, news came that Richmond had fallen. Johnston suspended all penalties for desertion and prepared for the inevitable end.

Davis had escaped from the capital, however, and on April 12, three days after Lee's surrender at Appomattox, the president met with Johnston and his staff and urged a continuation of the fight. He wanted to raise an army of deserters and draft dodgers. They listened to Davis in disbelief. Foote describes the meeting as "being closeted with a dreamy madman."

Johnston clashed with Sherman a final time at the Battle of Bentonville. Sherman's numerical advantage, however, inevitably forced Johnston's withdrawal. *Library of Congress*

Finally asked to give his views, Johnston replied: "My views are, sir, that our people are tired of the war, feel themselves whipped and will not fight."

Having heard the generals, Davis wearily consented to Johnston's plan to seek terms and then continued his flight south.

On April 17, a meeting between Johnston and Sherman was arranged at the Bennett Farm, a few miles west of Durham. It was the first time the two men had ever met face to face, although no two opposing generals in the war knew each other better.

They exchanged greetings affably. Sherman then asked if he could speak to Johnston in private. When the two men were alone, he showed Johnston a telegram he had received earlier that morning. It informed him that Abraham Lincoln had been assassinated.

Johnston was stunned. Sherman wrote later that "large beads of perspiration came out on his forehead and he did not attempt to conceal his distress." Johnston sensed that this ended any chance of a liberal peace and told Sherman that it "was the greatest possible calamity to the South." Sherman answered that he blamed neither him nor Lee, but he could "not say as much for Jeff Davis and men of that stripe."

They met again on the following day and concluded an armistice. Johnston insisted on surrendering all Confederate armies still in the field, although Sherman didn't believe he was empowered to accept such a sweeping proposal. It was, however, an expansive document that restored the constitutional rights of Southerners and would have formed the basis for a generous peace.

But it was too late. Lincoln's death had changed everything. The Republican leadership was in no mood for reconciliation, and the draft was rejected out of hand. On April 26, the two generals met for a final time. With very little choice other than to sign the more restrictive document, which offered no promise of rights to the South, Johnston affixed his signature and the war ended.

"I made this convention to spare the blood of this gallant little army," Johnston telegraphed the governors of the southern states. "To prevent further sufferings of our people by the devastation from invading armies and to avoid the crime of waging a hopeless war."

On May 4, he said farewell to his troops and then, at last, went home.

Lydia Johnston had said at the start of the war that her husband had no other occupation but that of arms. But now there were no more arms to bear. Johnston was 58 years old and had to begin a new life.

He moved to Savannah and entered the insurance business. He prospered at it. His name was golden in the South, and by the early 1870s he had 120 agents working for him. With his livelihood assured, Johnston moved to Richmond and turned his attention to settling some old scores with Davis. It was a bad miscalculation.

Johnston met Sherman at the Bennett Farm on April 17, 1865 to discuss terms for surrender. ***Library of Congress***

In the wake of President Abraham Lincoln's assassination, federal government officials rejected Sherman's generous peace terms. Johnston signed a new surrender document of April 26. ***Library of Congress***

Davis had become a beloved symbol in the South, but the old warrior was convinced that his policies had harmed the Confederacy in general and Johnston in particular. His book *Narrative of Military Operations Directed During the Late War Between the States* appeared in 1874. It did not do well—and with a title like that, no wonder.

He insisted on refighting Seven Pines and defend-

During Reconstruction, Lee and Johnston became icons of the Lost Cause. *Library of Congress*

ing his strategy at Vicksburg and on the retreat through Georgia. But his sharp criticisms of Davis were received with scorn, and his old adversaries, Bragg and Hood, answered Johnston with angry blasts. Hood, who was tired of hearing how he had failed as Johnston's successor, accused him of ruining the army before he ever got control.

To make matters worse, when Davis's autobiography appeared, his references to Johnston were mild, making the general appear to be ungracious and boorish.

"A number of Johnston's corrections are petty," concludes Symonds, "and the cumulative effect is to make the author himself appear petty." His reputation took a terrible beating, and even those who had been neutral in the quarrel began to side with Davis, if only for the more dignified way in which he conducted himself.

Still, Johnston was elected to serve a single term in Congress from Virginia, and in 1885, with Democrats once more in control of the White House, he was appointed commissioner of railroads.

With the death of Lydia in 1887, however, much of the fire went out of the man. He threw himself into work, making vigorous inspection of the railroads under his supervision. But when Grover Cleveland lost the 1888 election, Johnston was out of a job.

In retirement, with the war he had fought from start to finish over for a generation, his popularity again began to rise. He was elated by an emotional reception he received in Atlanta in 1890, when hundreds of men he once commanded ran into the street to take up the traces of the carriage in which he was riding and pull it cheering through the city. Johnston wept at the sight.

The following month he went to Richmond to help with the unveiling of the equestrian statue of his old comrade, Lee, and again was cheered exuberantly by massive crowds. When Sherman passed away in 1891, Johnston was invited to New York as an honorary pallbearer.

It was a dismal February day, with a cold rain falling. As Johnston stood at the grave, bystanders urged the old man to put on his hat so that his head would not be soaked. "If Sherman were standing in my place and I were in his," he responded, "he would not put on his hat."

He did become ill from the day's exertions, and his condition worsened throughout March. Too weak to fight off the infection, he died in his Washington home on March 21 at the age of 84. Several Union generals joined the mourners at his funeral. He was buried in Baltimore, at the side of his beloved Lydia.

An enigma he may have been to history. But the men he led had no questions about his greatness. One of them, a private from Tennessee, was quoted by Symonds. "We privates loved you," he said, upon hearing of Johnston's death, "because you made us love ourselves."

JAMES LONGSTREET

"Thing is, if anything bad happens now, they all blame it on you. I seen it comin.' They can't blame General Lee. Not no more. So they all take it out on you. You got to watch yourself, General."

Capt. Thomas J. Goree, of Longstreet's staff,
in the novel The Killer Angels *by Michael Shaara*

Through four hard years of his life, James Longstreet fought the Union army. For the last 37 years of his life, he fought the Confederates, who were far less merciful and much less forgiving.

During the Civil War and immediately thereafter, he was praised as one of the South's most effective fighting generals. He was Robert E. Lee's "Old War Horse," the one general the top commander could always rely upon, and the closest to him personally. He was Old Pete, the Bull of the Woods, loved by his men and his subordinates, regarded as one of the true military geniuses the war produced.

But after the war, he made the two greatest mistakes of his life: he became a Republican, and he dared to criticize Lee's generalship.

As one recent study of his life phrased it, Longstreet became "Lee's Tarnished Lieutenant." He was transformed into a traitor to the Southern cause, a man who turned to the hated enemy for political comfort and appointments. More than that, he was demonized as the man who lost the war. A small group of former military leaders and writers decided that it was Longstreet's actions on the second and third days of the Battle of Gettysburg that had given away that victory to the North, and with it any chance of an ultimate Confederate triumph.

When he tried to defend himself in speeches and magazine articles, he came across as defiling the memory of Lee, who was transformed into a Southern saint following his death in 1870. Never a diplomatic man, Longstreet got himself in deeper and deeper the more he protested.

Although feelings moderated towards the end of his life and he was warmly greeted at the few Confederate reunions he attended, Longstreet bore the blame for Gettysburg long after his death. His second wife, Helen Dortch Longstreet, carried on the campaign to clear his name until her own death in 1962—99 years after the battle that had besmirched her husband's reputation.

But the weight of historical judgment was too much to overcome. "He did not possess the qualities necessary to successful independent command, and his skill in strategy was not great," was the dismissive judgment of Douglas Southall Freeman, preeminent Southern military historian of the first half of the twentieth century.

Only in the 1970s did a few revisionist historians begin to reexamine the record and make a case that Longstreet had done all he could in an offensive that was the greatest blunder of Lee's career.

One of his biographers, William G. Piston, also makes the interesting point that Longstreet's reputation remained damaged for so long because he had no state that rushed to defend him. Most Confederate states adopted a highly parochial attitude towards the conduct of the war, praising generals who were favorite sons and ignoring or disparaging all others.

Virginia took the lead in this phenomenon, and because this is where the seat of the Confederate government was located, its outlook was most influential in shaping Southern views. The reputations of Virgini-

Respected for his sharp military mind and his tenacious leadership, James Longstreet nonetheless lost favor with the Southern public in the postwar years when he criticized Lee. ***Lloyd Ostendorf Collection***

ans such as Lee, Stonewall Jackson, and J. E. B. Stuart were magnified, both during and after the war.

But Longstreet had been born in South Carolina, grew up in Georgia, and was appointed to the U.S. Military Academy, through a technicality, as representing Alabama. Moreover, his forebears came from New Jersey and were thought to be of Dutch descent. None of this gave him the sort of loyal constituency that would defend him when he was personally attacked.

Part of the difficulty in assessing Longstreet's life is the lack of personal documentation that survived his death. Most of it was destroyed in a fire at his home, near Gainesville, Georgia, in 1889.

It is known that he was born on a plantation belonging to his grandparents, near Edgefield, South Carolina, in 1821, but moved as an infant to his father's farm near Gainesville. This city at the edge of the Blue Ridge Mountains now sits adjacent to a man-made lake and is a weekend resort for Atlanta residents. But in Longstreet's youth it was still deep in the back country, and he grew up far from the haunts of Georgia gentility.

When his father died in 1833, he went to live with his uncle, Augustus Baldwin Longstreet. For the rest of his life the general looked upon him as a second father. He owned a prosperous cotton plantation outside Augusta, Georgia, but was also gathering a reputation as one of Georgia's outstanding intellects. Augustus wrote extensively and would become president of Emory College and the University of Mississippi.

It was while living here that the younger Longstreet was introduced to the gracious part of the Southern antebellum world. Augustus, although he became a Methodist minister, also was known to enjoy a game of cards and a touch of whiskey. James was similarly inclined.

He aspired to West Point but upon seeking an appointment found that Georgia's allotment had already been used up. But his mother, who had remar-

For years, Longstreet received the blame for the Confederate defeat at Gettysburg. Only much later did historians clear his name. ***National Archives and Records Division***

ried and moved to Alabama, managed to win his admission from that state.

When Longstreet arrived in 1838, the Military Academy was filled with men who would achieve greatness in the war. He roomed with future Union general William S. Rosecrans and was a close friend of U. S. Grant, who would later marry one of Longstreet's cousins.

He was not an especially distinguished scholar, graduating 54th in his class of 62 in 1842. After brief postings to the Jefferson Barracks, in St. Louis, and then to Louisiana and Florida, Lieutenant Longstreet was sent to join the Eighth Infantry in the Mexican War.

As a staff officer concerned primarily with logistics, he developed a detailed knowledge of how an army moves and sustains itself, qualities that would be put to use in later years. In September 1847, he joined General Winfield Scott's expedition against Mexico City and volunteered for combat.

The deciding battle of the war was fought at Chapultepec Castle, the hilltop fortress guarding the approach to the Mexican capital. In most capsule summaries of American history, this war is treated as something of a walkover, an unequal struggle that Mexico never had a chance of winning. In reality, many of the battles were closely run affairs, and Scott's strategy called for high-risk frontal assaults on well-defended positions.

"Casualties at Resaca de la Palma were so high that four riddled companies had to be disbanded and the survivors transferred to other units," writes historian Robert Leckie. "At Molino del Rey, half of the regiment's officers were casualties. At Churubusco so many men fell [Scott] was barely able to maintain his attack."

Chapultepec was another bitterly fought engagement. The defenders of the castle, many of whom were cadets from Mexico's military academy, are still regarded as national heroes. The Americans had to climb a nearly vertical slope through deadly musket fire to storm the stronghold. Longstreet, who bore the colors, was wounded in the attack and later promoted to brevet major for his actions.

Leckie feels that it was in these attacks that Longstreet began developing his theories of defensive warfare, the necessity of "maneuvering the enemy into making the frontal assault." These were theories 50 years ahead of their time, and many of his ideas were not put into effect until long after his death. They were also the fundamental cause for his historic disagreement with Lee.

Longstreet returned to the Jefferson Barracks after the war and married Maria Louisa Garland, the daughter of Brigadier General John Garland. He had met her on his first tour of duty there six years before, and their marriage, although touched by terrible tragedy, would last for 41 years.

Longstreet was wounded in action as he bore the colors during the attack on Chapultepec Castle. ***Library of Congress***

It was also an advantageous match for Longstreet's career. Through Garland's influence, he was given a succession of desirable postings. During a stint as commandant at Fort Bliss, Texas, he led a 240-man expedition against the Mescalero Apache. It never made contact with the enemy but was the largest force under Longstreet's command until the Civil War. Most of his time, however, was spent deepening his knowledge of the army's channels of supply, invaluable nuts and bolts training.

In 1858, he transferred to the paymaster's department. He was, by all accounts, a devoted husband and father and wanted to have a more settled life for his growing family. That is where the eve of war found Major Longstreet, stationed at Albuquerque as paymaster for the New Mexico Territory.

He remained there until the firing on Fort Sumter made war inevitable. He turned in his resignation on June 1, 1861, and headed for Texas, then Virginia, to seek a post with the Confederate Army. According to Freeman, what Longstreet had in mind was paymaster, the same job he was carrying out in the U.S. Army. He was 40 years old and had "abandoned his aspiration for military glory." He repeated that statement in his own memoirs.

Piston insists, however, that he wanted to command a company from Texas, which he had come to think of as home because of his army service there. Jefferson Davis, desperate to find any leaders with military experience, made him a brigadier general.

Following the Mexican War, Longstreet married Louisa Garland. In 1862, the couple lost three of their children to scarlet fever. ***Library of Congress***

He was sent off to help guard the important rail junction at Manassas and was embroiled in the first action of that fight. He drove off a Union reconnaissance force on July 18, three days before the major engagement at Bull Run. Commanding the Fourth Brigade, he fought well in this first battle of the war and was in position to press an assault on the retreating Union forces late in the afternoon.

A superior officer, General Milledge L. Bonham, on the mistaken assumption that the Federals were gathering for a counterattack, stopped his advance, although no order for a halt had come down from the commanding general, Pierre G. T. Beauregard.

An infuriated Longstreet, writes Freeman, rode off alone, dismounted "and exploded in his wrath. He had pulled off his hat, had thrown it on the ground and with bitter words for Bonham had stamped in a white rage."

It was an uncharacteristic outburst for Longstreet, a man described most often with the word stolid—or, as a later era would call it, unflappable. His performance at Bull Run, maintaining organization in a highly disordered fight, won him promotion to Major General, at the urging of General Joseph E. Johnston, in October 1861.

At this time in his life, he was growing slightly deaf. His full beard, broad shoulders, and height of just under six feet gave him a commanding appearance. Although his conversation could be gruff and his answers short, in part because of his hearing problem, he was also known as a convivial companion at cards or a drink.

His chief of staff, Gilbert Moxley Sorrel, who would later become a brigadier general, described him as "a soldier every inch and very handsome, tall and well proportioned, strong and active, a superb horseman ... eyes glint steel blue, deep and piercing."

Capt. Thomas J. Goree, a more plainspoken Texan, wrote to relatives that "those not well acquainted with him think him short and crabbed, and he does appear so except in three places; 1st when in the presence of ladies, 2nd at the table; and 3rd on the field of battle. At any one of these places he has a complacent smile on his countenance and seems to be one of the happiest men in the world."

But in January 1862, with his military career brightly ascending, he was stricken by the darkest of tragedy. Scarlet fever was sweeping Richmond. He was summoned there with the urgent message that all four of his children had been afflicted. Three of them died within days, and much of the laughter left Longstreet's life. He gave up cards and whiskey, joined the Episcopal Church, and devoted his full energies to being a soldier.

The long lull in fighting came to a welcome end for him in May 1862. General George McClellan landed an invading Union army on the Virginia peninsula between the James and York rivers and began to move on Richmond. Longstreet fought several brilliant delaying actions against McClellan's numerically superior force, enabling Johnston to withdraw and form defensive lines around the capital.

But all his success was almost undone at Seven Pines. McClellan had divided his army along the Chickahominy River, 10 miles southeast of Richmond. Upon learning this, Johnston ordered a coordinated attack on May 31, with Longstreet in command of the right wing.

According to most accounts of the battle, Longstreet took it upon himself to change the line of march, moving from his designated route along the Nine Mile Road and onto the Williamsburg Road. This put him on the same route being used by Major General Benjamin Huger, and the two forces became hopelessly tangled up.

While the generals haggled over who had received his commission first and thus had priority on the road, hours ticked away. But while Longstreet won the debate, his force now was nowhere near where Johnston wanted it to be. The attack at Seven Pines lacked the numbers needed at the point of critical thrust, and Huger's men never got into the fight at all. McClellan escaped the trap, and Johnston had to retreat back to Richmond.

Johnston generously attributed Longstreet's actions to a mistake arising from a verbal misunderstanding. Still, Longstreet's willingness to change a superior's orders as he saw fit has been interpreted by many military historians as a disturbing harbinger of trouble ahead.

But in the next phase of the Peninsula Campaign, after Lee succeeded Johnston as commanding general, Longstreet performed flawlessly. In the overall Confederate victory that repelled McClellan's invasion, he quickly won Lee's confidence as one of his most able subordinates. It was then that Lee first came to refer to him as "my war horse."

Lee quickly arranged for the generals above Longstreet in rank to be transferred. By July, Longstreet and Stonewall Jackson were the two senior major generals, with Longstreet in charge of five divisions.

In August, the reorganized army began moving north, towards the old battlefield of Manassas, where it had fought 13 months before. The return engagement would end in a sweeping victory but also would bring Longstreet further criticism for delays in executing orders.

Lee had received information that the Union force which now opposed him, commanded by General John Pope, was going to be massively reinforced by McClellan, who was preparing to advance south from Washington, D.C. Lee felt that he had to strike first. In a gamble that went counter to all accepted principles of war, he divided his already outnumbered army and sent Jackson on a rapid movement to turn Pope's right flank.

Pope was brimming with confidence, an attribute Lee felt he could use to his advantage. Never one to disparage an opponent, Lee could not resist a dig when he learned that Pope was accustomed to sending off urgent bulletins dated "Headquarters in the saddle." "General Pope has his headquarters," said Lee, "where his hindquarters should be."

So Jackson was sent out to provoke Pope into doing something rash. He succeeded with a raid that destroyed the Union supply base at Manassas. The infuriated Pope, knowing that he had a vast numerical advantage, said that he would "bag" Jackson and turned his full attention to pounding him.

So intent was he on destroying Jackson that he neglected to notice the rest of the Confederate force, headed by Lee and Longstreet coming up on his left. By August 29, Pope was poised between the two jaws of a pincer.

As Jackson's force stood up to the continued battering, Lee three times urged Longstreet to throw in his men. On each occasion, Longstreet demurred. First because his entire 30,000 man force had not yet assembled. Then because he felt an adequate reconnaissance had not been made and he had no idea where McClellan was. Finally, because it was too late in the day.

Longstreet's actions are still the focus of debate among historians. Leckie said that the delays cost Lee the "magic moment." Mark Mayo Boatner III was convinced that Longstreet "deprived his commander of a great victory by not attacking as soon as he fell in on Jackson's flank."

Freeman wrote that Longstreet's reasoning was "certainly defensible and may be valid, but his general attitude showed for the first time that though he was vigorous and effective when his judgment approved the plans of his superior, he was slow to yield his own opinions and equally slow to move when he thought

On the way to Seven Pines, Longstreet rerouted his troops, which became entangled with those under General Benjamin Huger. The delay allowed General George McClellan to escape the Confederate trap. ***Library of Congress***

Longstreet attacked the troops of General John Pope (above) at Second Manassas. His advance on August 30, 1862 (top), routed the Union forces. *National Archives and Records Division/Library of Congress*

his commander's course was wrong. This was to become the greatest defect of his military character."

Since Second Manassas ended as an unqualified Confederate victory, one has the sense that these criticisms were only intended to lay an ex post facto foundation for the attack on Longstreet's subsequent actions at Gettysburg.

Longstreet explained later that on the first day at Second Manassas Lee was "urging nothing less than a piecemeal attack on an unknown force over unknown ground." While it would have been Lee's prerogative to overrule his subordinate, tellingly he did not.

The following day, when Longstreet was ready to close the trap, he did it superbly. Ordering an artillery assault on the still unsuspecting Pope and then counterattacking with his infantry, he shattered the Union lines and turned the assault on Jackson into a rout.

Pope was badly beaten and within weeks was transferred out of Virginia to the campaign against the Sioux in Minnesota. Still, because he was able to extricate himself from the pincers without losing his army, Longstreet's delays supposedly tarnished an overwhelming victory.

Nonetheless, Lee's confidence in him was, if anything, enhanced. Even though Longstreet expressed doubts about carrying on this northern probe into Maryland, a campaign that ended in the bloody standoff at Antietam, he fought well there. In October he was promoted to lieutenant general in command of the First Corps of the Army of Northern Virginia, an unlikely trajectory for a man who had acquired a reputation for disregarding orders.

He was certainly acquiring a reputation, however, as a tireless campaigner. He always had the advantage over an opponent because he apparently needed no sleep. The men who served under him began regarding Longstreet's inexhaustible pool of energy with awe as an almost supernatural trait.

He was also known as a leader deeply concerned over his men's well-being. Asked why he was taking the time to dig his gun emplacements so deep, Longstreet replied, "If we only save a finger of a man, that's good enough."

Within a few weeks, he was able to demonstrate his grasp of defensive tactics. Ambrose Burnside had taken over as major general of the Army of the Potomac. Eager to show his aggressiveness, he tried to beat Lee across the Rappahannock River and get between him and Richmond.

But Lee reached the river first, at Fredericksburg, Virginia, and ordered Longstreet to defend the opposite heights. He devised a system of entrenchments that would become a model of defensive warfare, with traverse ditches cut through to reduce the chances of shrapnel penetration from the sides. It was essentially the same design that would be used half a century later along the Western Front of World War I in Belgium and France.

Lee's battle plan called for Longstreet to hold the heights against an all-out Union assault, and then to throw Jackson onto the federal flanks. Everything depended on the strength of Longstreet's defenses, and Lee expressed his concern.

"General," responded Longstreet, "if you put every man on the other side of the Potomac on that field to approach me over the same line, and give me plenty of ammunition, I will kill them all before they reach my line."

Brigadier General E. P. Alexander, his chief of

artillery, added to that assessment. "We cover that ground so well," he said, "that we will comb it as with a fine-tooth comb. A chicken could not live on that field when we open on it."

Longstreet was so confident in his position, he even chided Jackson at a meeting before the battle. "Jackson," he asked, with a nod towards the troops intended to be held back for the counterattack. "What are you going to do with all those people over there."

"Sir," said an unsmiling Jackson, "we will give them the bayonet." No one could tell Stonewall that he would play a diminished role in any battle.

Burnside's assault began on the morning of December 13. Marked by incredible bravery by the Union soldiers trying to reach an impregnable enemy uphill through a 150-yard wide rain of fire, the battle became a bloodbath. It was while observing this scene that Lee made his often quoted remark: "It is well that war is so terrible. We should grow too fond of it."

Burnside's army escaped destruction, but it suffered 12,600 casualties, almost two and a half times the number incurred by the Southern forces.

The result of this battle fully convinced Longstreet that in this war the side seizing the defensive advantage could not be defeated. It would require a superiority in numbers by the attacking force that was almost impossible to establish. All of his thinking now rested on that assumption, and he would soon find himself at odds with Lee on this very basic philosophy of conducting the war.

The two men also differed on overall strategy. To Lee, who fought as a Virginian and whose staff was filled with men loyal primarily to that state, the critical point of the war was to ensure victory there. Longstreet, however, felt the war would be won or lost in the west. Early in 1863, he suggested that his corps be detached to join the Army of Tennessee. The resulting numerical advantage would then lift the Union threats to the vital rail center at Chattanooga and the river fortress at Vicksburg.

Longstreet also had in mind succeeding General Braxton Bragg, who was a favorite of President Jefferson Davis but was widely thought of within the army as an incompetent. Instead, in February, he was sent to southeastern Virginia to secure supply routes from North Carolina, a state that was becoming the critical manufacturing depot for the Confederacy.

It was an independent command and while the work was important, it was fairly routine. His attempts to capture federal positions at Suffolk, Virginia, were repulsed. To his critics, the campaign indicated a failure of strategic imagination and, indeed, Lee sent him several messages wondering just what it was he was up to. After two and a half inconclusive months, Longstreet was ordered to rejoin Lee in May 1863.

Longstreet differed with Lee on overall strategy for the war. While Lee looked to secure victories in his native Virginia, Longstreet viewed the West as the critical theater. ***Library of Congress***

Within days, fate would impel him down the road that would mark the rest of his life.

Jackson had fallen in the great Confederate victory at Chancellorsville. There was no question now of Longstreet's going west. He was the unquestioned first among Lee's lieutenants, and it was on him the general would rely for the planned great drive into Pennsylvania.

Lee felt the war's momentum was entirely with him, and he now sought the great battle on Union soil that would destroy the North's will to continue. Longstreet agreed with the overall aim. He was under the impression, however, that Lee had agreed that this campaign would be carried on with an offensive strategy and defensive tactics.

Freeman calls this a "mistaken understanding" and Boatner "an erroneous impression." Writing years later, Longstreet felt that he and Lee were in accord on the need to fight defensively. "In defensive warfare he was perfect," Longstreet wrote. "But when the hunt was up, his combativeness was overruling."

Longstreet arrived at Gettysburg late on July 1, too late to participate in the fighting on the battle's first day. Lee had wanted to prevent Union forces from fortifying the heights of Cemetery Ridge, but an overly cau-

At Gettysburg, Longstreet sought to force a Union offensive by maneuvering between their position and Washington. Lee, however, ordered an attack on the Round Tops. *Library of Congress*

Despite delays, logistical problems, and stronger opposition than expected, Longstreet advanced toward the Round Tops. The Union line held, and the tide began to turn for the Confederacy. *Library of Congress*

tious response by Second Corps Commander Richard Ewell, and his division commander, Jubal A. Early, failed to dislodge them.

By the time Longstreet came up, the ridge was heavily fortified. To him that meant opportunity. In his narrative history of the Civil War, Shelby Foote has Longstreet explaining that "all we have to do is throw our army around by their left, and we shall interpose between the Federal army and Washington. We can get a strong position and wait, and if they fail to attack us we shall have everything in condition to move back tomorrow night in the direction of Washington.... They will be sure to attack us."

To Longstreet's mind this was the whole point of the campaign, to force the Union army onto the offensive and destroy it as he had almost done at Fredericksburg. But Lee feared to make a turning movement without J. E. B. Stuart's cavalry as his eyes, and Stuart had yet to show up at Gettysburg. No one knew where he was and, as it turned out, this was a critical loss.

Lee also had no intention of giving up the initiative. "The enemy is there," he said, pointing towards Cemetery Ridge, "and I am going to attack him there."

In later years, the entire future of the war was seen to hinge upon that conversation. Lee could not be dissuaded from taking the offensive, and Longstreet was convinced that such a move would mean disaster. The question then became whether Longstreet deliberately delayed the ordered attack on July 2 for so long that he squandered any chance of its success.

In an early morning meeting, Lee had turned down Longstreet's request for a flanking movement of the Union left. Without Stuart, Lee was going ahead by feel, basing his moves on the reports of inexperienced scouts. A reconnaissance satisfied him that the Little Round Tops, two rocky prominences on the extreme Union left, were not yet heavily manned and could be taken without any further flanking.

He also denied Longstreet's appeal for a delay until General George Pickett's division could reach the field. At 11 A.M., Lee gave the order to proceed, and Longstreet's men began to move. According to later writings, it was Longstreet's understanding that Lee knew the movement would take several hours before an attack could be made. Piston points out that a similar march by Jackson at Chancellorsville had taken eight hours. So Lee must have anticipated a delay of approximately this length.

While conceding that Longstreet was "unenthusiastic about the attack," historians Herman Hattaway and Archer Jones state that he "got his men up to the battle area in the quickest time possible, but circumstances forced him to delay the actual assault."

These "circumstances" involved several complications. The entire attack plan was based on concealment from the Union forces atop Cemetery Ridge. But because of the erratic reconnaissance, it was discovered that the original plan of march would take Longstreet directly into the federal line of vision. The route had to be changed, and in some cases redoubled to use the cover of some nearby woods. A march that had been estimated at three miles at Lee's headquarters had become closer to 12 miles for many in Longstreet's corps.

The first elements of the attacking column were not in position until 3 P.M. To their distress they observed that the Round Tops had become heavily defended. General John Bell Hood quickly sent word back to Longstreet of this development and twice asked permission to extend his flanking movement farther and then attack from the undefended side.

At the Battle of Chickamauga, Longstreet proved himself with an attack that nearly broke the Union line. ***Library of Congress***

But Lee had rejected just such a proposal a few hours earlier. Based on this conversation, Longstreet told Hood, "We must obey the orders of General Lee." Although he realized that he was now ordering a frontal attack, counter to every bit of understanding he had gathered about this war, Longstreet felt he could do no more. He rode out himself at the head of General William Barksdale's Mississippi Brigade.

Barksdale would die a few moments later in the battle for Little Round Top. In the minds of both participants and historians, this was the most desperate and critical struggle of the war. Hood's Texans, fighting their way through underbrush and across rocks, almost gained the summit but could not attack in enough numbers to hold on. Hood himself was severely wounded in the fight.

In the words of Bruce Catton, "It was a test of what men can nerve themselves to attempt and what they can compel themselves to endure, and at shattering cost it proved that the possibilities in both directions are limitless."

At the end of the second day, Longstreet's men held the terrain directly in front of the Round Tops. Many Confederate officers and even the taciturn Longstreet (who had been reported captured, much to his amusement) accepted it as a limited victory. But the Union line had held. While no one recognized it yet, the Confederacy's great chance was already gone.

On the morning of July 3, Lee announced that the Southern artillery would bombard the federal center and Longstreet's corps, with Pickett's division brought up, would attack Cemetery Ridge.

Longstreet, as second in command, again felt that his duty compelled him to express opposition to this plan. "General," he told Lee, "I have been a soldier all my life. I have been with soldiers engaged in fights by couples, by squads, companies, regiments, divisions and armies and should know as well as anyone what soldiers can do. It is my opinion that no 15,000 men ever arrayed for battle can take that position."

In later years, Longstreet's critics would claim that it was his "delays" of the previous day that made this attack necessary and that the dangers inherent in Lee's plan were compounded by his subordinate's "tardiness and lack of confidence."

"Never was I so depressed as I was on that day," Longstreet would write later. After a personal inspection of the terrain over which the charge would have to go, Lee refused to alter his plan. Longstreet repeated to Alexander his conviction that it could not possibly succeed. "I would not make it now, but that General Lee has ordered it and is expecting it," he said.

British observer Arthur J. L. Fremantle, who would write a book shortly afterwards in which he confidently predicted a Confederate victory in the war, noted that once the order was given, "No person could have been more calm or self possessed than General Longstreet. I could now thoroughly appreciate the term 'bulldog,' which I had heard applied to him by the soldiers."

Pickett's Charge resulted in the virtual annihilation of that general's division, and while it is regarded as one of the great feats of valor in all of American warfare, it sealed the Confederate defeat at Gettysburg. After its dreadful conclusion, Lee stated, "All this has been my fault—it is I who have lost this fight."

Historian Allan Nevins described Gettysburg as "a blunder based on ... miscalculations." There was severe criticism of Lee in the South at the time, and there was even some question if he could retain command of the army. Gettysburg was not fully appreciated for the turning point it was until after the war, though, and Longstreet himself urged continued support for Lee.

Two months later, his plan for moving his corps to the western campaign was finally approved. Longstreet arrived in Georgia just in time to throw his forces into the Battle of Chickamauga and very nearly cut the opposing Union line in half.

He was fighting under a new commander, on strange terrain, against an unknown opponent.

Longstreet's forces halted a Union counterattack at The Wilderness on May 6, 1864. When he came up to take charge, bullets from his own troops struck him in the throat. ***Library of Congress***

"Longstreet was a man who liked to take his own time getting everything ready before he fought," wrote Catton, "and he had precious little time here; but he adapted himself this once." His blow sent the forces of his old West Point friend, General Rosecrans, reeling. Only the resolute stand of General George Thomas, who would henceforth be known as the Rock of Chickamauga, prevented a complete Union disaster.

Longstreet, too, came out of the battle with a new nickname. He was now the Bull of the Woods, and his prestige was never higher.

But in November 1863, with another battle for Chattanooga looming, Bragg decided to send Longstreet off to capture Knoxville. This move has been described, perhaps charitably, as "misguided," since it gave Bragg no advantage in the more important campaign in front of him. But the two generals were then barely on speaking terms, and Bragg brooded that Longstreet was deliberately trying to make him look bad, although there is no evidence such intent existed anywhere outside of Bragg's imagination. Very few people were able to get along with Bragg.

Moreover, when given a second independent command, Longstreet once more was ineffectual. Burnside and his Union troops managed to reach Knoxville ahead of him and held the city through a month of poorly coordinated Confederate attacks. Longstreet's subordinates were quarreling, trusted aides refused to cooperate, morale sank, supplies were exhausted, and he seriously considered resigning.

He revived his grand strategic plan to join the general he most admired, Joseph E. Johnston, in the west. He advocated an invasion of Kentucky in concert with him and Beauregard, seeing it as a way of demoralizing the North before the 1864 elections. Jefferson Davis rejected the idea as impractical, however, and instead returned Longstreet's corps to the Army of Northern Virginia and Lee.

The two men seemed genuinely glad to be reunited. U. S. Grant had been placed in command of the Army of the Potomac in March 1864, and the feeling in Richmond was that he would be no match for Lee. Although the material condition of the Confederacy was faltering, there was hope that Lee would once more gain the battlefield initiative and convince the Union that it could not hope to win this war.

Longstreet wasn't so sure. "We must make up our minds to get into the line of battle and stay there," he told an officer on Lee's staff. "For that man [Grant] will fight us every day and every hour until the end of the war. In order to whip him we must outmaneuver him and husband our strength as best we can."

But again that was not the campaign Lee envisioned. He intended to hit Grant first at The Wilderness, where he and Jackson had achieved their greatest success one year before. On May 5, 1864, he struck. This time, however, the federal line did not break, and Grant's counterattack, instead, sent the forces of Ambrose P. Hill reeling back.

Just as at Chickamauga, however, Longstreet came up at the critical time. On May 6, Hood's Texas Brigade stopped the Union advance and began to drive it back. But in the confusion of the battle, fought in a thick and gloomy forest, as Longstreet rode up to take charge, he was wounded by shots fired by his own men.

The bullet passed through his throat, and for the rest of his life he had difficulty speaking loudly. Lee could only wring his hands in despair as he saw Longstreet carried to the rear. His recuperation would take five months, depriving Lee of his most trusted aide at this critical time of the war.

Grant had taken high casualties at The Wilderness but unlike his predecessors, and true to Longstreet's prediction, he just kept on coming at Lee. This was a different kind of opponent, and in 11 more months his advantage in manpower and material would bring the war to its conclusion.

By the time Longstreet was able to return to action, in October 1864, with his arm still partly paralyzed, Lee already was bottled up in Richmond. There was little to do but try to put off the end as long as possible. His men cheered wildly when Longstreet returned, and his relations with Lee remained close. That was regarded by Longstreet as a personal triumph. His aide, Goree, wrote home that "It is gratifying for General L to know that he is no favorite with the President and Bragg yet he had what is much better, the unbounded confidence of Gen. Lee. . . ."

Longstreet's corps retained its discipline to the end,

when he advised Lee that he could count on the courtesy and generosity of Grant at the formal surrender at Appomattox. Afterwards, Lee embraced him warmly, turned to Goree and said: "Captain, I am going to put my old War Horse under your charge. I want you to take good care of him."

In April 1865, few Southern heroes ranked higher than Longstreet. He was quickly paroled by federal authorities and made his way to New Orleans where he became a cotton factor and started an insurance business. The city was a popular retirement home for Confederate generals, and for a time Longstreet lived in comfort and easy affability with them.

Just as he had in the war, however, he continued to think of the larger political picture. To Longstreet it was imperative for the South to regain control of its own destiny. He felt it could never do that as long as it remained wholly Democrat and out of political power. It made much more sense, he felt, to work within the Republican Party in order to gain hold of the levers of policy.

To most Southerners, this was like going over to the Devil. In the late 1860s, the Republicans were seen as feasting at the table of the helpless South, looting its wealth, and installing newly freed slaves in positions of authority to deliberately humiliate its people.

Longstreet announced his position in a letter to the *New Orleans Times*, in June 1867, even though his trusted uncle, Augustus, had warned him that its publication "will be your ruin." Longstreet, accordingly, was ostracized by his former associates.

Though vilified in the South as the man who lost the Battle of Gettysburg, Longstreet maintained favor with the Republicans. He received numerous appointments, including U.S. ambassador to Turkey. ***National Archives and Records Division***

After the war, Longstreet determined to work from within the Republican party to aid the South. President Ulysses S. Grant appointed him to a post with the New Orleans customs office. ***Library of Congress***

Grant was elected president in 1868 and appointed Longstreet, now a fellow Republican, to a post in the customs office at New Orleans. The two men were old friends and regarded each other as relatives. Nonetheless, the job was perceived as a sellout in the South, and Longstreet was regarded with increased contempt.

Matters soon became much worse. With the initial shock of defeat absorbed, Southerners were trying to make sense of the war. How could it possibly have been lost, except through incompetence and betrayal? The story of the war became transformed into the Lost Cause, a saga of courage and righteousness undone from within.

With the perspective of a few years, it was now seen that Gettysburg had been the turning point. An explanation was needed to explain why that battle, and subsequently the war, was lost.

There was no point blaming Stuart. He was dead. After Lee passed away in 1870, his memory became unassailable. Although he had come in for his share of the blame at the time of the battle, this was all forgotten because his memory was now sacrosanct. His statement after Gettysburg, "This was all my fault," was now seen as a manly effort to deflect blame from subordinates rather than as an admission of culpability.

Another of Lee's top aides, Early, had returned from exile in Canada in 1869 and began to write his version of the war's major events. He was also a Virginian and eager to embellish the growing legend sur-

Seven years after the death of his first wife, the seventy-six-year-old Longstreet married the much younger Helen Dortch. ***Library of Congress***

rounding Lee. He was especially eager on that count, perhaps, because his reluctance to attack the outnumbered Northern forces on Cemetery Ridge on the battle's first day can also be regarded as a major reason for the eventual defeat.

In his writings and during a speech delivered on Lee's birthday in 1872, Early directly blamed Longstreet for the loss at Gettysburg. He was soon joined by a rising chorus of other Virginians. They read into Longstreet's actions on the second day of the battle a betrayal of Lee's masterful plan.

He had become, in his biographer Piston's phrase, "the Judas, the Antichrist of the Lost Cause." As he tried to defend himself in magazine articles, he only outraged his critics even more. He now dared to criticize the sainted Lee, and that truly was unforgivable.

Driven from Louisiana, he returned to his boyhood home in Gainesville, Georgia, and was appointed postmaster there in 1879. Successive Republican administrations continued to make sure he was taken care of, appointing him as the U.S. ambassador to Turkey and then U.S. marshall for Georgia in 1881.

He bought a farm outside Gainesville and then purchased the Piedmont Hotel in the middle of town. The building still stands near downtown and is in the process of being restored, while documents relating to his years in Gainesville are exhibited in the town's Georgia Mountains Museum.

His wife died in 1890, just a few months after their home burned to the ground, destroying most documents relating to Longstreet's life. Nonetheless, he kept working on the book that was intended to be the definitive justification of his career, *From Manassas to Appomattox.*

It was published in 1896. Its tone was brusque and often argumentative, much as Longstreet's personal conversation, and it only seemed to harden the verdict against him. When historians found several errors and major distortions in the work, owing to his inability to consult his lost papers, Longstreet's reputation suffered even more.

The following year he married Helen Dortch in a ceremony in the Governor's Mansion in Atlanta. Longstreet was now 76 years old, and his wife's age was reported variously as being anywhere between 22 and 34. The younger figure seems more probable since she volunteered to work in a defense plant almost 50 years later, during World War II, when several national publications did feature stories about her.

Longstreet remained a popular attraction at Northern Civil War reunions, where he attracted large, enthusiastic crowds. "Everywhere except in the South," he wrote, "soldiers are accepted as comrades upon equal terms without regards to their political affiliations."

Early passed away in 1894 and soon the opposition to Longstreet became less strident. He was greeted warmly at several Confederate reunions, and it seemed that time was healing things. But that was a fallacy. The men who knew him best, those who had served under him, were leaving the scene, and the reputation that had become attached to him after the war now grew even stronger. When he was named U.S. commissioner of railroads, in 1898, several Southern senators voted against the appointment because he had criticized Lee in his autobiography.

He died of cancer, complicated by pneumonia, in 1904. His last words, addressed to his wife, were, "Helen, we shall be happier in this post."

His wife received a warm letter from President Theodore Roosevelt, who praised Longstreet for his efforts towards national reconciliation between former enemies. Many Southern newspapers wrote warm editorials about him, and his funeral in Gainesville was attended by many dignitaries.

Fewer than five percent of the posts of the United Confederate Veterans passed resolutions honoring him, however, and not until 1998 was a statue of Longstreet finally placed among the Confederate lines at Gettysburg.

The Cavalrymen

JAMES EWELL BROWN STUART

"Deep in the hearts of all true cavalrymen, North and South, will ever burn a sentiment of admiration mingled with regret for this knightly soldier and generous man."

U.S. General T. F. Rodenbough in Photographic History of the Civil War

No officer on his staff could ever recall seeing Robert E. Lee so upset. The eyes of his army were missing. Major General Jeb Stuart and his cavalry had been out of touch for a week, and on the eve of the Battle of Gettysburg, Lee was driving blind.

He had no idea where the Federals were, or in what force, or even who was in command of their army. He greeted any officer who approached him with the same anxious question: "Can you tell me where General Stuart is?"

There was no answer. At this critical moment, the man whom Lee had come to rely on absolutely, who "never brought me a piece of false information," had failed to bring him any information at all.

The one flaw in the character of a brilliant and innovative soldier, as if ordained by fate, had risen up at the worst possible time. Stuart's boyish love of glory, acclaim, and praise had led him on a meaningless raid through Pennsylvania, miles away from where Lee wanted him. In the minds of many historians of this critical battle, his absence opened the door to the Southern defeat.

His death, just 10 months later, at the age of 31, would lift much of the criticism he received at the time and leave General James Longstreet as the sole surviving scapegoat for the loss. But if Stuart had been on the field, the battle plan over which Longstreet and Lee had disagreed could have been put into effect.

The Confederates would have positioned themselves between the Union army and Washington, D.C., and forced the Federals to attack them. But without Stuart's screening cavalry, Lee would not risk the necessary turning movement of his army and, instead, it was he who was forced to take the offensive at Gettysburg, with tragic results.

Jeb Stuart, nonetheless, has come down through history as an incomparable cavalryman. He was also the roguish cavalier, a man who could extract the full measure of gallantry from the bloody business of war. While General William T. Sherman famously said, "War is hell," to Stuart and his men it was more like an ongoing hunting party or a pageant out of a romantic novel.

The general kept a banjo player on his staff and would ride into battle singing. "If you want to have a good fight, j'in the cavalry," was the preferred tune, recorded by Mitch Miller and his Chorus 100 years later and turned into a Hit Parade chart topper.

The description of Stuart by his favorite staff officer, Fitzhugh Lee, nephew of the commanding general, has come down as a classic: "His strong figure, his big brown beard, his piercing, laughing blue eyes, the drooping hat and black feather, the 'fighting jacket' as he termed it, the tall cavalry boots, formed one of the most jubilant and striking figures of the war."

Stuart's jacket shone "with dazzling buttons," wrote John Esten Cooke, in *Wearing of the Gray.* "It was cov-

A dashing and brilliant cavalry leader, J. E. B. Stuart's love of glory led him astray at Gettysburg, depriving Lee of much-needed reconnaissance information. ***Museum of the Confederacy, Richmond, Virginia***

ered with gold braid. His hat was looped up with a golden star and decorated with a black ostrich plume; his fine buff gauntlets reached to his elbow; around his waist was tied a splendid yellow sash and his spurs were of pure gold."

But the uniform reveals an insight into the heart of the man who wore it. In the end, the impetuosity that spurred him to attempt great deeds was the quality that kept him from true greatness.

The future cavalry leader grew up on a plantation in the foothills of Virginia's Blue Ridge country, the perfect setting to foster a love of the open. The land that made up his father's property, Laurel Hill, has been acquired and set aside as a park by the Stuart Memorial Trust. In visiting the place, just a few hundred yards above the North Carolina border, one sees a landscape almost unchanged from the days when Stuart was born there in 1833.

His father, Archibald Stuart, had represented his district for one term in Congress and also was a delegate to two state constitutional conventions. Young Jeb seemed to inherit a pugnacious nature from him and a love of literature and music from his Welsh mother, Elizabeth Letcher Pannill, the granddaughter of a Revolutionary War hero.

His personality had thus been shaped when he entered West Point at the age of 17. He was repeatedly involved in fights with other cadets, challenges he met "with thankful acceptance," even though he lost more often that not. The elder Stuart approved. "I did not consider you so much to blame," he wrote his son after one such episode. "An insult should be resented under all circumstances."

Nonetheless, he was a better student than most would give him credit for. He graduated 13th in the 46-member class of 1854, indicating the more studious side to his nature.

His nickname was "Beauty," and it was not intended as a compliment. Stuart, in fact, was a rather homely man, with a receding chin, a large nose, and a square, stocky physique. His flowing beard was grown in an effort to mask the less attractive features of his physiognomy.

But he never had any problem attracting the ladies. His courtly treatment of them and gallant bearing made him irresistible. Throughout the war, he was surrounded by feminine admirers, who gave him flowers and other keepsakes. But everyone who knew him swore that he was always faithful to his wife, Flora, and that the attachments were merely chivalric.

He had met her while serving with the First U.S. Cavalry in Kansas as a young second lieutenant. Flora Cooke was the colonel's daughter, and the two married after a brief, intense courtship in 1855.

Kansas in the 1850s was a lively place to be stationed. The border conflict between abolitionist settlers and pro-slavery forces from Missouri made the territory a cauldron of violence, with atrocities committed on both sides. In addition, Indian warfare flared up intermittently in the western part of Kansas.

In July 1857, Stuart was seriously wounded during a battle with the Cheyenne and is credited with leading his unit back through hostile country for 200 miles before accepting medical attention. It was the only wound he ever received, until the bullet that killed him.

Stuart was given consistently outstanding reports

Stuart grew up in the foothills of Virginia's Blue Ridge country. ***Library of Congress***

during his frontier service. His mind was engaged in other areas, too. In 1859, he perfected a device that would attach a cavalry saber to the belt without encumbrance. He was allowed to return east that year in the hopes of patenting the attachment and selling it to the War Department.

Instead, he found himself in the middle of a major precursor to war: John Brown's raid at Harpers Ferry. Stuart was sent by the War Department to deliver a sealed message to Lieutenant Colonel Robert E. Lee, who had been superintendent of West Point during his time as a cadet. When Stuart learned that Lee's instructions were to put down the insurrection at the U.S. armory, he asked to go along as his aide and was accepted.

In an account that Stuart wrote in a letter to his mother, he said that he was assigned to approach the door of the engine house where the raiders, whose identity was still unknown, were barricaded. He was to ask their leader, "Mr. Smith," for surrender, and when the expected refusal was given, Stuart was to wave his hat as a signal for the storming party to advance.

"I approached the door in the presence of perhaps two thousand spectators," he wrote, "and told Mr. Smith that I had a communication for him from Colonel Lee. He opened the door about four inches and placed his body against the crack with a cocked carbine in his hand; hence his remark after his capture that he could have wiped me out like a mosquito.

"When Smith first came to the door I recognized old Osawatomie Brown who had given us so much trouble in Kansas. No one present but myself could have performed that service.... I got his bowie knife from his person and have it yet."

Stuart gave the agreed-upon signal, and in a matter of moments Brown was clubbed to the ground by the U.S. Marine storming party. The raid was over, but by the time Stuart returned to Kansas, he realized from what he had seen and heard back east that the time for a decision was coming.

By January 1861, he had made it. He sent forward an application for a commission in the new Confederate army. His official resignation from the U.S. Army came just 11 days after he was notified of his promotion to captain.

It had not been a decision made lightly. His father-in-law, General Philip St. George Cooke, also Virginia born, chose to stay with the Union. But Stuart's brother-in-law, Colonel John R. Cooke, joined the Confederacy. In a letter to the younger Cooke, Stuart called the family split "a misfortune" and said that, "General Cooke will regret it but once and that will be continually."

Stuart would soon have the chance to hasten the day of regret.

Receiving the rank of captain, Stuart was sent to the Shenandoah Valley. He served under General Joseph E. Johnston and soon won his admiration. "He is a rare man," wrote Johnston in an official report of August 1861, "wonderfully endowed by nature with the qualities necessary for an officer of light cavalry. Calm, firm, active and enterprising. I know of no one more competent than he to estimate the occurrences before him at their true value."

He skillfully screened Johnston's movements on the way to reinforce General P. G. T. Beauregard at First Manassas that summer. In the battle itself, he fought well and was commended by Beauregard for his reconnaissance work and a charge he led on the Confederate left that swept the opposition from the field. By September, he had been promoted to brigadier general.

But over the course of the next nine months, Stuart's assignments were routine. He fared poorly in a short fight at Dranesville, Virginia, with federal cavalry in December, but it was an inconsequential action.

Then in June 1862 came the chance he was waiting for, the opportunity that would make his name on both sides of the war. Lee had taken over from the wounded Johnston to direct the Peninsula Campaign, southeast of Richmond. He needed information about the disposition of General George McClellan's troops on the federal right and condition of the roads in the area.

Stuart's homely looks earned him the nickname "Beauty." *Museum of the Confederacy, Richmond, Virginia*

Lee instructed the young brigadier on June 11, to "return as soon as the object of your expedition is accomplished." But to Stuart's ears that sounded like an open-ended order. After all, who could say when and how the "object" of this assignment could change. He rode out with 1,200 chosen men the next day, with the idea for a far more expansive expedition planted in his mind.

His starting point was Hanover Court House, and after riding 14 miles the initial assignment had been completed. But Stuart made brief contact with a federal cavalry unit, and it convinced him that he would be looked for if he went back the way he started. So he made the audacious choice to ride completely around McClellan's army.

This was what he had been waiting for, and his report on the decision almost throbs with pent-up anticipation.

"There was something of the sublime," he wrote, "in the implicit confidence and unquestioning trust of the rank and file in a leader guiding them straight, apparently, into the very jaws of the enemy, every step appearing to them to diminish the faintest hope of extrication."

He was, at times, closely pursued and had to cross the Chickahominy River perilously by knocking down trees and stretching them from one bank to the other. But on June 15 he returned to the Southern lines after destroying federal stores and capturing 165 prisoners and 260 horses and mules, while losing just one man.

The "Ride Around McClellan" turned Stuart into an instant hero. When he went into Richmond to report to Virginia's governor, he was cheered in the streets and compelled to make a short speech. He said that he had "ridden out to see some old friends in the United States Army but they very uncivilly turned their backs upon me."

Among those friends was his father-in-law, who was incapable of organizing a pursuit of Stuart, lost his command, and was shunted off to Louisiana as a recruiter.

Some commentators criticize the ride because it alerted McClellan that his situation had been observed

In the 1850s, Stuart served with the First U.S. Cavalry in Kansas. In addition to violent conflicts between pro-slavery and abolitionist forces, he dealt with Indian warfare. *Library of Congress*

At Harpers Ferry, Stuart bore the request for surrender to John Brown and his men. Upon their refusal, he gave the signal that initiated the advance of the storming party. *Library of Congress*

and he had best change his base. But Lee never made that judgment and, instead, seemed delighted by Stuart's actions. The information he received was more than he had hoped for.

In his book, *Wearing of the Grey*, John Esten Cooke, who rode with Stuart, recounts how he and the general discussed the tight situation at the Chickahominy crossing. Cooke said that if the Federals had come upon them, "you would have been compelled to surrender."

Stuart disagreed and said there would have been another alternative. "To die game," he said.

Before the end of this campaign, Lee's first major success, Stuart's headstrong nature would lead to disappointment. As McClellan's troops withdrew to their ships and prepared to return North, Stuart seized Evelington Heights, left unguarded through an oversight.

The place looked directly down upon the federal loading docks, and the excited Stuart could not bring himself to send for reinforcements and wait for their arrival. So he opened fire with his lone howitzer. That alerted the Union forces to his presence, however, and heavy return artillery soon drove him from the heights.

Historian Douglas Southall Freeman and others fault the action, making the point that if Stuart had simply turned in his report, Southern forces could have quickly occupied the heights and inflicted severe damage on the federal retreat. Nonetheless, Stuart already had made his reputation, and in a few more weeks the legend would grow.

Lee soon began the move north that would end at

Stuart's father-in-law, General Philip St. George Cooke, chose to remain with the Union. *National Archives and Records Division*

In June 1862, Stuart set out to reconnoiter McClellan's army. He ended up leading his cavalry in a complete circuit of the Union forces. *Library of Congress*

Antietam, and on August 17, 1862, Stuart arrived at the town of Verdiersville, Virginia. He was wearing a new plumed hat. According to some accounts, the hat was the payoff of a bet he had made with two old friends in the Union army.

They had met under a flag of truce after the Battle of Cedar Mountain, a week earlier. Stonewall Jackson managed to rally his troops to victory there, but Stuart bet his friends that in the Northern press it would be described as a Confederate defeat.

A few days later, a courier under another flag of truce delivered the hat to Stuart, along with a copy of a New York newspaper proclaiming a federal victory. Stuart was delighted, and as he bedded down for the night he kept the hat right beside him.

But a critical road into Verdiersville was left unguarded, and a Union cavalry unit slipped through on the attack. Stuart was awakened by pistol shots and had to scramble into the saddle. In the melee and frantic ride to escape, he lost his hat.

Stuart brooded about this, but five days later he got his chance for revenge. Lee approved a raid behind the Union lines to Catlett Station, where the Orange and Alexandria Railroad bridged a small creek. The expedition bogged down in heavy thunderstorms, and the search for other federal encampments was stymied.

Then a captured slave volunteered to lead Stuart's men through the rainy night to a major prize: the headquarters of Union commanding general, John Pope. The surprise raid led to the capture of several of Pope's officers and horses, as well as the general's dispatch book, hat, and dress uniform.

Stuart had to admit that he could not destroy the bridge, which was his primary objective, because it was too wet to burn. But the other booty more than made up for the raid's lack of military value, and Lee gained valuable insight into Union plans before the Battle of Second Manassas. Pope's hat and uniform were exhibited at the capitol in Richmond, lifting Southern morale and making Stuart a hero again.

He was also a hero to his men. "He was the most approachable of major generals and jested with the private soldiers of his command as jovially as though he had been one of themselves," wrote his first biographer, Cooke.

One of his officers, Colonel John S. Mosby, described riding with Stuart as "a carnival of fun." "Nobody thought of danger or sleep ... all had perfect confidence in their leader."

Others recalled his singing, his cheerfulness even after a night in the saddle, the way he twisted his beard until a problem was solved and then the relaxed laughter that followed. Stuart was truly adored. Even the dour Jackson was won over by his irrepressible colleague.

"Jackson was more free and familiar with Stuart than with any other officer in the army," wrote Henry Kyd Douglas in his book, *I Rode with Stonewall.* "And Stuart loved Jackson more than he did any living man."

When Stuart presented Jackson with a resplendent new uniform coat, Stonewall admired it, folded it up, and put it away. "The coat is much too handsome for me," he told Major Heros van Borcke, "but I shall take the best care of it and shall prize it highly as a souvenir." Van Borcke then convinced Jackson to wear the coat at dinner as a special favor to Stuart and wrote that "soldiers came running by the hundreds to the spot, desirous of seeing their beloved Stonewall in his new attire."

On another occasion, Stuart arrived late in Jackson's camp and crawled into bed fully clothed with the general. During the course of the night, Stuart pulled most of the blankets onto himself and was an especially restless sleeping companion.

"General Stuart," said Stonewall the next morning,

Stuart led a raid behind Union lines to Catlett Station, where he attacked a Federal encampment that included General John Pope's headquarters. ***Library of Congress***

"I'm always glad to see you here. But you must not get into my bed with your boots and spurs on and ride me around like a cavalry horse all night."

In September 1862, while at Urbana, Maryland, Stuart organized a dance for his staff and local families, sympathizers of North and South alike. In the midst of the music, the alarm went out that federal raiders were attacking the lines. Men left their partners and dashed to their horses, promising to return when the scuffle was over. By 1:30 A.M., Stuart and his staff were back, and the dance went on. Even the arrival of wounded soldiers did not interrupt the merriment for long.

At about the same time, he was presented with a gift of a pair of spurs by the "Women of Baltimore." For a time, Stuart took to signing his personal letters with the initials K.G.S.: Knight of the Golden Spurs.

Nonetheless, Stuart was a strict teetotaler and a sincere member of the Episcopal Church. There was no dancing allowed in his presence on Sundays. Those closest to him said that he never played cards and "never dreamed of uttering an oath under any provocation, nor would he permit it at his headquarters."

On October 9, he rode off to bedevil McClellan once more. After a farewell dance that lasted until 1 A.M., he and 1,800 of his best men set off towards Pennsylvania from northern Virginia. They had orders from Lee to destroy the railroad bridge at Chambersburg. Again, however, the orders were open-ended, and Stuart interpreted them liberally.

The bridge was iron and could not be damaged, but Stuart's forces came away with badly needed federal stores, including weapons and clothing. Thirty civic leaders were held hostage for the release of Confederate prisoners. About $250,000 in damage was done to the rail line.

But the Federals were alerted to his presence and determined to cut him off before he could reach safety. "Not a man should be permitted to return to Virginia," came the urgent orders out of Washington.

Instead, Stuart baffled his pursuers again, just as he had in June, by completing the circuit eastward rather than returning the way he had come. Once more he had ridden completely around McClellan, crossing the Potomac with no fatalities.

Abraham Lincoln was not amused when he heard the news. "When I was a boy we used to play a game," the president remarked on a steamer excursion upon the same river. "Three times round and out. Stuart has been around him twice. If he goes around him once more, gentlemen, McClellan will be out."

Stuart's showmanship also earned him some enemies in his own army. General Lafayette McLaws, who distrusted his close relationship with Jackson, noted with contempt that Stuart carried a banjo player with him on his campaigns. "This claptrap is noticed and lauded as a peculiarity of a genius," he said, "when, in fact, it is nothing else but the act of a buffoon. . . ."

Others were not as outspoken in their animosity but

Colonel John Mosby, another legendary cavalryman, served under Stuart's command. *National Archives and Records Division*

regarded Stuart as a leader who was not to be taken seriously. The British observer, Arthur J. L. Fremantle, described him as "roaming over the country at his own discretion…turning up at the right moment and hitherto he has not got himself into any serious trouble."

But Colonel A. Scheibert, detached from the Prussian army, noted approvingly that, "Before Stuart undertook any movement, he spared nothing in the way of preparation which might make it succeed.… He omitted no precaution and spared no pains or effort to secure the best possible results."

Lee went out of his way in an official report to "express my sense of [Stuart's] boldness, judgment and prudence." He even demonstrated an ability to command artillery effectively during the Battle of Fredericksburg, in December 1862. Yet even that could not overcome a conviction that Stuart's style outweighed his substance.

In the spring of 1863, Lee began to move north again, and Stuart was placed in charge of securing Jackson's route towards Chancellorsville. Stonewall would die of wounds suffered during his sweeping victory there, and his subordinate, Ambrose P. Hill, was incapacitated, both legs struck by shell fragments.

Hill called on Stuart to take command, and on the night of May 2 the cavalry leader assumed his dear friend Jackson's post. Unaware of how seriously Stonewall was wounded, he sent messengers to find out how he was to proceed. Jackson, fighting to remain conscious, could only murmur, "I don't know. I can't tell. Say to General Stuart he must do what he thinks best."

But Lee added that, "Those people must be pressed today," and Stuart took him at his word. When the Stonewall Brigade ran into furious opposition the next morning, Stuart rallied them personally, urging them to avenge Jackson and leading a chorus of his favorite song: "If you want to have a good fight, j'in the cavalry."

The Southern line held, securing the victory. When a description of this scene was brought to Jackson, he wept. "It was just like them to do so," he said. "Just like them. They are a noble body of men."

Stuart's performance was superb, and there continues to be debate over whether he should have been named Jackson's successor. The possibility was certainly discussed by Lee, but there is no indication that he gave it serious consideration. Stuart's report of his actions at Chancellorsville had been, as usual, self-laudatory and that had not been well received. His frenetic behavior, including breaking into song to exhort his men, was remarked upon, too.

There is also the chance that he was simply too valuable to Lee as the head of his cavalry to assume any other command. Still, other officers thought it was an injustice. "He had won the right to it," wrote General E. P. Alexander. "I believe he had all of Jackson's genius and dash and originality. Stuart, however, possessed the rare quality of being always equal to himself at his very best."

At any rate, the army was expanded from two corps to three, and the promotions went to Hill and Richard Ewell. Stuart remained at the head of the heretofore invincible Confederate cavalry, but within weeks he would receive a rude jolt at a place called Brandy Station.

This was the opening engagement of the campaign that culminated at Gettysburg. It revealed that the Union cavalry was suddenly a force to be reckoned with. Reorganized and placed under the command of Major General Alfred Pleasonton, this formerly bumbling outfit had gathered together some of the finest horsemen in the army and placed them under youthful leadership.

Stuart was an excellent leader, but part of his reputation was also based on the fact that his opposition was so inept. At his base near Culpeper, Virginia, he passed the time holding reviews featuring mock cavalry charges, complete with cannon going off. Young ladies were invited to attend and fainted with excitement. Lee was also asked to observe and was highly amused, finding Stuart "in all his glory."

But on June 9, it all became real. Pleasonton led 10,000 horsemen on a raid across the Rappahannock River, completely surprising Stuart. The battle at Brandy Station was the largest cavalry engagement ever fought in North America, with more than 17,000 riders engaged in

At Chambersburg, Stuart captured much needed Federal stores. To avoid his pursuers, he again rode completely around McClellan's army. ***Library of Congress***

the fight. Stuart nearly found himself encircled at one point and was forced to fight his way out in unaccustomed desperation.

The Federals withdrew and suffered slightly more casualties than the Confederates. But Pleasonton was pleased at what the battle had shown him about the fighting capabilities of his new mounted force. And Stuart was highly embarrassed.

For the first time, he was roundly criticized in the Southern press. "If he is to be the eyes and ears of the army," wrote the *Richmond Enquirer*, "we should advise him to see more and be seen less." Even other officers were upset with him. In a letter home, General Dorsey Pender called the fight "a sad affair" and added: "I suppose it is all right that Stuart should get all the blame, for when anything handsome is done he gets all the credit."

Stuart heard the snickers, and several historians feel that is the explanation for what followed. On June 23, he received orders from Lee to move north into Maryland. "Take position on General Ewell's right, place yourself in communication with him, guard his flank, keep him informed of the enemy's movements and collect all the supplies you can for the use of the army."

As usual, he was given a good deal of leeway. Stuart, mindful of how his greatest exploits had begun in a similar manner, was all too ready to strike off once more in another daring raid to wipe out the memory of Brandy Station.

But he was delayed in crossing the Potomac when he unexpectedly ran into a heavy concentration of General Joseph Hooker's troops. He had to skirt them and couldn't make the ford until June 28. By that time he had lost contact with Ewell.

General Alfred Pleasonton surprised Stuart at Brandy Station. The ensuing cavalry engagement was the largest ever in North America. ***Library of Congress***

Instead of turning back to find him, however, Stuart went on to Rockville, Maryland, on the very outskirts of Washington. He was able to follow up there on part of Lee's instructions, gathering supplies meant for the Union army. But the captured goods slowed his advance

Following his retreat from Brandy Station, Stuart went on a raid for supplies. Delays kept him from Gettysburg, and he arrived late on the battle's second day. ***Museum of the Confederacy, Richmond, Virginia***

even more, and his men by now were dead tired, having spent several nights in the saddle.

He knew that the main body of Lee's army was to his west, but he couldn't tell where. He began moving in that direction, raided the town of Hanover, Pennsylvania, and shelled the U.S. Cavalry barracks at Carlisle. But not until July 1, eight days after the raid began, did his scouts return with the report of a major battle underway at Gettysburg.

Stuart was now 30 miles from the fight, and at 1 A.M. on July 2 he finally began heading to it. He wasn't able to reach Lee, however, until late afternoon of the battle's second day.

Those who witnessed their meeting said that it was almost too painful to bear. The father-son relationship the two men had formed had nearly been severed.

"General Stuart, where have you been," said Lee, lifting an arm—some observers said in reproach, others in exasperation. "I have not heard from you in days, and you the eyes and ears of my army."

Stuart was mortified and tried to put the best possible face on it.

"I have brought you 125 wagons and their teams, General," he said.

"Yes, General," replied Lee icily. "But they are an impediment to me now."

Then with Stuart standing before him, utterly shattered, Lee relented. "Let me ask your help now," he said. "We will not discuss this longer. Help me fight these people."

Stuart did participate in the third day of the battle, but even his defenders concede that his work was "ineffectual." Instead of redeeming his reputation, Stuart had placed a shadow on it for all time.

After the defeat, there were recriminations. In Richmond, calls came for Lee's dismissal, or even a court-

General Philip Sheridan took the offensive to force Stuart into a fight. Their engagement at Yellow Tavern on May 11, 1864 was Stuart's last. ***National Archives and Records Division***

After being shot during a fierce cavalry battle, the 31-year-old Stuart died on May 12, 1864. ***Library of Congress***

martial. But as more details of the battle became known, the focus of criticism shifted to Stuart, who was accused of using his cavalry "to gratify his personal pride."

But while Lee had told Stuart to keep in contact with Ewell's corps, he had never given similar instructions to Ewell. As a result, Ewell made no attempt to try to find Stuart, assuming the cavalry leader was where he should have been. Moreover, Lee did have cavalry at his disposal, several brigades under the command of Stuart's subordinates. From all appearances, however, he did not trust them to do the sort of reconnaissance that Stuart performed for him.

But the Confederate cavalry was now exhausted. The weeks of hard riding and combat had caught up to them, and they needed time to heal. Still, Stuart expertly screened Lee's withdrawal after Gettysburg. Later that fall, he also dealt Union cavalry under General George A. Custer a sharp defeat at Buckland Mills, Virginia, a rout that became known as the Buckland Races.

But the glory days were coming to a close. By the spring of 1864, U. S. Grant was ready to start his massive coordinated assault on the South's pressure points—Lee's army in Virginia and Joseph E. Johnston in Georgia. Stuart's job was to screen Lee's movements at the Battle of The Wilderness, on May 5 and 6, and then to impede the Union advance to Spotsylvania Court House.

Shelby Foote calls Stuart's work at Spotsylvania among the greatest he performed in the entire war "although the action promised little of the glory he had chased in former times."

On May 9, however, the trumpets sounded again. General Philip Sheridan had convinced Grant to turn him loose on a raid behind the Southern lines. "We are going to fight Stuart's cavalry," he announced to his division commanders. "I shall expect nothing but success."

Sheridan had the numbers. His line of 12,000 mounted troopers ran 13 miles in length. "Keep on moving, boys," he shouted to his officers. "We're going through. There isn't cavalry enough in all the Southern Confederacy to stop us."

Stuart recognized that the purpose of the raid was to force him into a battle and shatter his outnumbered force. He wouldn't let that happen if he could help it. But he also didn't know exactly where Sheridan was headed.

Sheridan was on the road to Richmond, and there wasn't much in the way of troops between him and the Confederate capital. But he also might curl around and attack Lee from the rear at Spotsylvania. His massive raiding force had left Grant stripped of cavalry, in a precarious position in the event of any movement by Lee. But Stuart deliberately left part of his force behind to give Lee an advantage. All he could do was try to trail Sheridan as best he could with his far lesser numbers. When the chance came, he intended to hit him from the side.

The routes of the two forces would intersect north of Richmond, on May 11, at a deserted stagecoach inn called Yellow Tavern. Stuart got there first and dismounted, aligning his men in the shape of a V and waiting for Sheridan to attack.

The fight raged for two hours until Michigan troops under Custer, getting his revenge for Buckland, found the weak spot in the Confederate center. Stuart hurried up to rally his men, taking a position against a fence in the far forward position. Having come through the war unscathed, he had started to think of himself as invulnerable, and when an aide suggested he go back to a safer spot, his reply was "I don't reckon there's any danger."

As the Union forces prepared another assault, Stuart shouted "Give it to them." An instant later his head sagged. A trooper named John Huff, deliberately aiming at the magnificently dressed officer 30 feet away from him, brought Stuart down with a bullet to the abdomen.

As his men heard the news, they clustered to his side in disbelief. "Go back," he shouted to them, sitting up on the litter that had been brought to carry him off the field. "Go back and do your duty as I have done mine, and our country will be safe. Go back! Go back!"

As the men left to resume the fight, Stuart turned to an officer and asked, "How do I look in the face." Told that he would be all right, he replied, "Well, I don't know how this will turn out, but if it is God's will that I shall die, I am ready."

He knew that he could not survive, but he lingered on for several hours after being carried to his sister-in-law's house in Richmond. Jefferson Davis came to see him and was told by his physician that the internal bleeding was unstoppable. Nonetheless, he seemed "so calm and physically so strong," Davis said later.

He sang a chorus of "Rock of Ages" with a clergyman and died on the evening of May 12, a few hours before his wife and children could reach his bedside.

Lee could barely bring himself to speak when he received the news. "A most valuable and able officer," he began. He then had to put his hand over his face to conceal his emotion and retired to his tent. "I can scarcely think of him without weeping," he said later.

Stuart was 31 years old, and it was recognized on both sides of the conflict that a sad milestone had been reached.

His death, said Sheridan, "inflicted a blow from which entire recovery was impossible." On more than one occasion in the months to come, Lee would shake his head and sigh. "If I had my poor Stuart with me," he said, "I should know all about what those people are doing."

But it was more than that, too. It seemed somehow that everything symbolizing the panache, the spirit, the sheer brightness of the Confederate endeavor had flickered out when Jeb Stuart was lowered into his grave.

NATHAN BEDFORD FORREST

"Forrest is the very devil and I think he got some of our troops under cower. I will order Washington to make up a force and go out and follow Forrest to the death, if it costs 10,000 lives and breaks the Treasury. There will never be peace in Tennessee till Forrest is dead."

General William T. Sherman, 1864

He may have been the greatest natural military genius in American history. He understood nothing of textbook war or West Point doctrine. Instead, Nathan B. Forrest had an instinctive feel for what to do on the battlefield and how to disrupt and destroy an enemy's plans.

He entered the war as a private and left it as a lieutenant general. No other soldier on either side rose that high from so low a start. Of course, he did get a bit of a boost from the fact that he was rich. Forrest had made a fortune in slave trading, which caused him to be suspect in the eyes of the more fastidious elements of Southern society. They did not shy away from enriching themselves at slave labor but looked down upon the men who supplied its human sinew.

But money alone did not grease Forrest's path. He killed about 30 men in hand-to-hand combat, including one of his own officers, and had almost that many horses shot out from under him. In one fight after another, he taught the Union generals to fear him for his unpredictable behavior and his unrestrained ferocity when he sensed an advantage.

He understood the use of fear and did not hesitate to employ it. "Keeping the scare up" was part of his planning. He would frequently demand immediate surrender "or you may expect no quarter" and would attack a tired opponent relentlessly.

He was a six-footer at a time when most men were of lesser stature and was not above inflicting a physical beating to instill discipline. He even threatened to punch his commanding general, Braxton Bragg, in the jaw—although that was a desire shared by many in the Southern army. His soldiers would say later that they were more afraid of Forrest than they were of the Yankees.

In the final summary, however, it may be that his readiness to use these tactics was the reason for the two dark questions that still hover above his name: the massacre of black Union soldiers at Fort Pillow and the founding of the Ku Klux Klan. His defenders insist upon his innocence on both counts. But the historical record is more ambiguous, and a century after his death he is still tainted in some quarters by suspicions of violent racism.

He probably never uttered the most famous quotation attributed to him: "I get there fustest with the mostest." That was an invention by those trying to replicate his manner of speech. He was unlettered, and his writings did indicate a certain imprecision in grammar. But in conversation he was clear, his meaning direct.

"War means fightin'," he would say at Shiloh, "and fightin' means killin.'" No historical analyst with a Ph.D. ever put it any better.

Still, when a female admirer asked him why his beard was black while the hair on his head had turned white, he responded: "That's because I use my brains more than my mouth." His gift for analysis and concentration on the task at hand characterized his leadership abilities just as much as his aggressiveness did.

Forrest was born in 1821 in a backwoods Tennessee log cabin, southeast of Nashville, in what was then Bedford County. The geography apparently supplied his middle name.

A fierce fighter and a cavalry commander with a flair for tactical innovation, Nathan Bedford Forrest instilled fear in his opponents. ***U.S. Army Military History Institute***

The Forrests had followed the frontier west, from Virginia to North Carolina and into Tennessee, starting in the 1730s. Unlike other great Confederate cavalry leaders, John Hunt Morgan and Jeb Stuart, there was nothing of the chivalric in his upbringing. The family lived a hardscrabble existence, fending off poverty with the strength in their backs.

Nathan's twin sister, Fanny, died in childhood of typhoid, as did his other two sisters and two of his eight brothers. His father, William, worked as a blacksmith, but as his health failed, the family lost whatever slim hold they may have had on ease.

The Forrests moved to an even more isolated farm, in northern Mississippi, in 1834. William's death three years later, when Nathan was 16 years old, left the family to its own resources. Fortunately, his mother, Mariam Beck, was a strapping woman of just under six feet in height, with a will that matched her body.

Under her guidance, Nathan and his brothers managed to run the small family farm successfully. After a brief visit to Texas as a volunteer when it appeared that war with Mexico was imminent (which it wasn't), Nathan returned home and took up trading in livestock.

By the time he was 21, he had gone into business with his father's brother, Jonathan, in the town of Hernando, Mississippi, just south of Memphis. His uncle was killed three years later in an altercation with a family named Matlock, a brawl in which Nathan shot their two adversaries. That left the young man as sole proprietor of the struggling business.

In the same year, he also wed Mary Ann Montgomery. She came from a far more illustrious family than Forrest, claiming kinship to General Richard Montgomery, who had fallen at Quebec during the Revolutionary War. Her uncle and guardian, a Presbyterian minister, was less than pleased when Nathan showed up to ask for her hand.

"I couldn't consent," he was told. "You cuss and gamble, and Mary Ann is a Christian girl."

"I know it," said Forrest with disarming candor, "and that's just why I want her."

Forrest was never quite able to rid himself of these bad habits, but his respect for women was universally noted.

By the late 1840s, he had expanded his business to include slaves. In that time and place, it was a natural extension of dealing in livestock. Memphis was growing into the commercial center of the Mississippi Delta, where cotton plantations were thriving. There was an almost unlimited demand for slaves imported from the older states of the Southeast where produc-

Though Forrest eventually made his fortune as a slave trader, he was born into difficult circumstances. He shared none of his fellow Confederates' chivalric ideals. ***Library of Congress***

tion was shifting to less labor-intensive crops. But the cotton boom turned Memphis into the leading slave market in the South, and Forrest grew rich from it.

In 1852, he moved to the city and steadily built up his business with a number of partners. By the end of decade, he was a man of some standing and was elected an alderman. His income was close to $100,000 a year, a fabulous sum, and he invested much of it in plantation property in Mississippi and Arkansas.

Nonetheless, to some of the aristocratic young men whom he later led into battle, his unsavory trade marked him permanently as a man of dubious standing. "I must express my distaste at being commanded by a man with no pretension to gentility," wrote one such Mississippi gentleman. "Forrest may be, and no doubt is, the best cavalry officer in the West, but I object to a tyrannical, hot-headed vulgarian commanding me."

Even his great wealth, however, couldn't protect his six-year-old daughter, Fanny, named for his own deceased twin. The girl died of dysentery in 1854, a wrenching blow to the young family.

Forrest was 40 years old when the Civil War began, a comfortable, well-connected man in middle age with no prior military experience. Yet six days after Tennessee voted for secession, in June 1861, Forrest and his 15-year-old son, William, enlisted together as privates in a company of "Mounted Rifles."

He didn't stay a private for long. According to his biographer, Jack Hurst, his appointment as a lieutenant colonel came through about a month after he joined the army, courtesy of Tennessee's Governor Isham G. Harris, a longtime associate. He was authorized to recruit a company of mounted rangers at his own expense to operate independently of any regular army command.

By November he had put together a 650-man battalion, made up of like-minded fighters drawn mostly from Kentucky and Alabama. They fought well in their first campaign, around the Bowling Green, Kentucky, area, and Forrest himself made an indelible impression.

"Standing in the stirrups," according to Shelby Foote's description, "swinging his sword and roaring 'Charge! Charge!' in a voice that rang like brass, the colonel personally accounted for three enemy officers, killing two and wounding one; he shot the first, sabered the second and dislocated the shoulder of a third by knocking him off his horse."

Unencumbered by prior conceptions, Forrest was starting to put together the concept of using the cavalry as mounted infantry. British military historian Field Marshal Viscount Garnet J. Wolsely wrote that Forrest was the first in modern warfare to recognize the "use of the dragoon, the rifleman on horseback who from being mounted has all the mobility of the horse soldier."

Refusing to accept surrender at Fort Donelson, Forrest fought his way past the advancing Union force. ***Library of Congress***

His ideas were the direct precursor of the panzer corps and armored infantry of World War II.

But he was still formulating all of that when he was sent to Fort Donelson, in February 1862, to help defend the critical outpost from the advance of U. S. Grant. He recognized early that the fort was in the hands of incompetents who meant to surrender their troops and make good their own escape. Forrest would have no part of that.

"I did not come here for the purpose of surrendering my command," he informed the hapless General Simon Bolivar Buckner, who had been given command of the fort when his two superiors passed on it. Buckner gave him permission to try to fight his way out as best he could.

Forrest not only got his men out but managed to evacuate many infantrymen who rode double with his own troopers. Totally disgusted by the ineptitude he saw at Donelson, he proceeded to Nashville only to find the city in a panic. The army was ready to abandon valuable stores to the oncoming Union forces. Forrest stayed on for four days and organized an orderly retreat. When some local citizens objected to the removal of the stores, Forrest had fire hoses turned on them. His actions saved irreplaceable machinery, weapons, and food for the military.

He rejoined the main body of the army at Corinth, Mississippi, and within two months found himself in the midst of the inferno at Shiloh. Once more he was dismayed at the hesitance of commanding officers to take decisive steps to win the battle, not merely to avoid defeat.

Trying to cross the Tennessee River, Forrest found a Federal force blocking his path while a second approached from the rear. "Charge both ways," he commanded. ***National Archives and Records Division***

Scouting on his own after the battle's first night, he saw that Grant was being reinforced by General Don Carlos Buell, the very thing the Southern offensive was designed to stop. The only way to get out of the battlefield with a victory was to attack Grant immediately, while there was still confusion on the Union side, or to withdraw.

Instead, he was told that the orders had been given to dig in until morning. Forrest was furious. "If the enemy comes on us in the morning, we'll be whipped like hell," he raged.

He was exactly right, and in covering the predicted retreat under fire, Forrest was seriously wounded. Waiting for the moment when the pursuing Union troops lost their straight alignment, he ordered a charge into their midst. The problem was he got too far ahead of his own men and found himself in the middle of the enemy all by himself.

A shotgun blast to his side nearly took him from the saddle, but he recovered, hoisted a Union soldier onto his horse, and using him as a shield, fought his way back to his own lines. The men on both sides were awestruck at what they had witnessed.

The bullet lodged beside his spine and was removed in an operation performed without anesthetic. Forrest went back home to Memphis to recuperate and think about what he had seen in battle. But by late June, he already was raising more recruits ("Come on, boys, if you want a heap of fun and to kill some Yankees") and was promoted to brigadier general.

He also understood, along with Morgan, that the only way to stop the Union advance into Mississippi was to go after Grant's supply lines to his rear: railroads and depots in Kentucky and Tennessee. On July 9, the two cavalry leaders left from Chattanooga on the first of their raids.

Forrest captured Murfreesboro four days later. Two Union garrisons continued to hold out, but Forrest dismissed suggestions that he withdraw before reinforcements arrived. "I didn't come here to make half a job of it," he said. "I'm going to have them all."

He then employed two tactics that he would use repeatedly. He sent a note demanding immediate surrender "to prevent the further effusion of blood" and also repeatedly paraded the same group of men within sight of the holdouts, to convince their officers that they were confronted by overpowering numbers. Both commanders quickly surrendered.

Forrest had destroyed the railhead, taken 1,200 prisoners, and stopped the advance on Chattanooga, preparing the way for Bragg's counteroffensive into Kentucky later in the summer.

In December 1862, he struck again, destroying the railroads around Jackson, Tennessee, and capturing Colonel Robert G. Ingersoll, who would go on to a career as one of the most influential orators and pamphleteers of the late nineteenth century.

On his return, however, his passage across the Tennessee River was blocked by federal troops and gunboats at Parker's Cross Roads. He was then surprised by another force coming up on his rear. His response added to the legend that was growing around him. When asked by a panicked staff officer what to do, Forrest supposedly answered, "Charge both ways."

The unexpected response broke the Union lines, and Forrest was able to return most of his command to Chattanooga. It would subsequently adopt the name of the Old Brigade and become one of the proudest units in the Confederate army.

By April 1863, Grant had caught on to the Southern tactics. But Forrest had become a constant annoyance to him. When he learned that Forrest was commanding, said a staff officer of the Union general, "he at once became apprehensive, because Forrest was amenable to no known rules of procedure, was a law unto himself for all military acts and was constantly doing the unexpected at all times and places."

So Grant decided to give Forrest a taste of his own medicine. He sent the 1,500-man cavalry brigade of Colonel Abel D. Streight on a raid against Confederate rail lines in north Alabama and west Georgia. They left from Eastport, Mississippi, on the Tennessee River, on April 21, and were mounted on mules because Streight felt those animals would be more effective in hilly terrain.

The raid came as a complete surprise, but within nine days Forrest had caught up to Streight with a 600-man force. For the next three days the two sides fought an extended running battle.

Streight laid a masterful ambush at Day's Gap, Alabama, wounding Forrest's brother in the fight. Although heavily outnumbered, Forrest still pursued Streight continuously, giving his opponent no time to rest in the hostile country through which he was operating. "Shoot at everything blue and keep up the scare," he ordered.

Streight planned to reach Gadsden first and then get away from Forrest by destroying the bridge at Black Creek. But a 16-year-old girl, Emma Sanson, showed Forrest a shallow ford across the creek, and the chase went on. Forrest stopped long enough to write a note to the young lady, sending his "highest regards ... for her gallant conduct" and requesting a lock of her hair. A monument to Emma still stands in downtown Gadsden.

By May 3, Streight could run no further and decided to make a stand at Cedar Bluff, just short of the Georgia line. Forrest trotted out his usual tactics, demanding surrender to prevent bloodshed and sending his only two guns over the same road seven times while the astonished Streight looked on. He had better than a two to one advantage on Forrest, but psychologically he was no match for him. He quickly surrendered.

While Streight did not accomplish his goal, Grant did have the satisfaction of knowing that he had taken Forrest away from Mississippi as he was preparing the campaign against Vicksburg.

Forrest's less attractive side was also making itself evident. He had quarreled with another cavalry leader, General Joseph Wheeler, in February over an unsuccessful attack on Fort Donelson. "I will be in my coffin before I will fight again under your command," he told him and stalked off.

An even uglier incident occurred in June when Forrest got into a vicious fight with a subordinate, Lieutenant A. W. Gould. He had severely criticized the man following the ambush at Day's Gap and ordered him transferred from his command.

Forrest pursued the cavalry of Colonel Abel D. Streight for three days before finally forcing his surrender. ***Library of Congress***

According to Forrest, Gould accused him of questioning his courage and pulled a gun on him, discharging a single shot into the general's side. Forrest had been picking his teeth with a penknife before Gould's arrival. While holding his assailant's gun hand in the air, he opened the blade of the knife with his teeth and jabbed it into Gould's side.

Gould, blood pouring from the wound, staggered from the room with Forrest, thinking he had been injured mortally, in pursuit. Gould collapsed in the street and was taken to a nearby tailor shop. Doctors were trying to stop the bleeding there when Forrest burst through the door carrying two pistols and took a shot at him, the bullet ricocheting and wounding a soldier in the leg.

Gould jumped up and started to run again, but passed out in a field. He died two days later. An examination revealed that Gould's shot had missed all of Forrest's vital organs, and within two weeks he was back in the saddle.

In later life Forrest expressed remorse over the incident, saying that he "never wanted to kill anybody except an enemy, and then only when fighting for his country."

In July, he joined Bragg's command. It was in the

During the Battle of Chattanooga, Forrest was disgusted when General Braxton Bragg refused to press his advantage and retake the town. ***Library of Congress***

process of falling back to Chattanooga after being outmaneuvered by Union forces under General William S. Rosecrans. As the army retreated through Cowan, Tennessee, an angry woman berated one of the officers. "You great big cowardly rascal," she screamed. "I wish old Forrest was here. He'd make you fight."

As it turned out, her comments had been directed at Forrest, who was greatly amused by them. But his attitude changed as he watched Bragg bungle the fighting around the critical rail center.

After stopping the Federals at Chickamauga, just south of the city, Forrest expected the commander to follow up the advantage and "keep up the scare," driving the enemy back through Chattanooga. "I think we ought to press forward as rapidly as possible," he informed Bragg urgently after a scouting trip to the city's outskirts.

He was told that Bragg did not want to move because of a lack of supplies. "We can get all the supplies our army needs in Chattanooga," the exasperated Forrest told his staff. "What does he fight battles for?"

Bragg settled down, instead, for a siege, much to the disgust of his leading generals. Then on September 28, Forrest was ordered to turn over the troops under his command to Wheeler, who was planning a raid behind federal lines. He sent an outraged letter of protest to Bragg and then left on a brief visit with his wife. While on leave, he was told the transfer would be permanent.

These were seasoned troops Forrest had raised and trained himself, and now they were under the command of Wheeler, a man he hated. Forrest returned to Bragg's headquarters in a fury.

"I have stood by your meanness as long as I intend to," he snarled at his commander. "You have played the part of a damned scoundrel and are a coward, and if you were any part of a man I would slap your jaws and force you to resent it. You may as well not issue any more orders to me for I will not obey them ... and I say to you that if you ever again try to interfere with me or cross my path it will be at the peril of your life."

Astonishingly, Forrest was neither disciplined nor court-martialed for this insubordination. He had predicted as much, saying that Bragg would be "the last man to mention it." Bragg did not regard Forrest as part of the regular army and also recognized his value. He merely approved his transfer to Mississippi and then forgot about it.

Forrest managed to retain 300 men from the Old Brigade and recruited about 3,000 more from behind Union lines in Tennessee. But the quality of these new troops was questionable. Many of them had previously avoided conscription, and some were deserters.

Sherman, behind the opposing lines, was unimpressed. "Every conscript they catch will cost a good man to watch," he snickered. "Forrest may cavort about that country as much as he pleases."

But in February 1864, he took these untested troops and battered a Union force, advancing south from Memphis, at Okolona, Mississippi. As the fighting began and a Confederate soldier started to run away in panic, Forrest grabbed the man, threw him to the ground and started beating him with a tree branch. He then yanked him to his feet and sent him back the way he had come. "God damn you, go back to the front and fight!" he shouted at the terrified soldier. "You might as well be killed there as here for if you ever run away again, you'll not get off so easy."

He pressed the federal column under General William Sooy Smith for miles, repeating the tactics he had employed the previous year against Streight, sending it back to Memphis in disorder and defeat. His brother, Jeffrey, was killed in the fighting but Forrest had again turned his force into a formidable fighting machine.

This set the stage for one of Forrest's greatest raids and the most controversial battle of his career. Leaving Mississippi in late March, he surprised the city of Paducah, Kentucky, and its garrison on March 25, cleaning out the federal depot supplying Sherman's army and holding the town for 10 hours.

When local newspapers gloated afterwards that he had failed to capture 140 horses hidden during the raid, Forrest sent a force back to the city to get them, too. He then turned his attention to Fort Pillow, Tennessee, a federal outpost on the Mississippi River, 50 miles north of Memphis, which supplied gunboats operating on the river.

Many of the defenders were freed slaves who had joined the Northern army. There were also Tennesseans who had remained loyal to the Union. Forrest did not regard either with favor. Forrest arrived on April 12, positioned his troops against the weak federal fortifications, and made his standard demand for immediate surrender or "I cannot be responsible for the fate of your command."

The Union commander, Major William F. Bradford, asked for an hour to consider, but Forrest's scouts reported a gunboat advancing towards the fort. Suspecting a stall, Forrest ordered an immediate attack, and Pillow's defenses were quickly overrun.

Many Union soldiers began to run for the water, having been told the gunboat would rescue them. But it was still too far away to help. As some of them turned back in surrender they were, from most reports, shot down by Confederate troops yelling "No quarter!" Sixty-four percent of the black soldiers in the fort were killed.

Forrest had not led the assault, and observers indicated that when he saw the shootings taking place, he put a stop to them as soon as he could. His troops thought they were carrying out his orders, however, and the incident inflamed public opinion throughout the North. It became known as the Fort Pillow Massacre.

General James Chalmers, who commanded Confederate infantry at the battle, told Union officials later that his soldiers "had such a hatred towards the armed Negro that they could not be restrained from killing [them] after they had captured them." Moreover, Forrest stated three days after the battle, "It is hoped that [this] will demonstrate to the Northern people that Negro soldiers cannot cope with Southerners."

A congressional committee was sent to Tennessee to take testimony from wounded survivors who had been returned to the Union lines. President Lincoln also urged an investigation into "the alleged butchery of our troops." The order was passed along to Sherman with the recommendation that if the reports were accurate "retaliation must be resorted to promptly."

The more lurid accounts, including reports that black prisoners were buried alive and barracks set afire with their occupants inside, were discounted. There was little doubt, however, that African-Americans were targeted by Forrest's troops and gunned down. While he did not order such action, his efforts to stop it appeared to be late and inadequate. The evidence fell short of impelling Sherman to order retaliation, but Fort Pillow remains a severe blemish on Forrest's reputation.

Sherman soon had more pressing concerns about Forrest. By June, he was in position to threaten his rail supply lines, as the Union forces were massing to take Atlanta. Just as four months before, a federal force was

In Paducah, Kentucky, site of Fort Anderson, Forrest's raid cleaned out the Federal depot supplying Sherman's army. ***Library of Congress***

The Fort Pillow Massacre marred Forrest's reputation. This postwar political broadside dubs him "The Butcher Forrest." *Library of Congress*

sent out from Memphis to engage and smash him in northern Mississippi. But again Forrest seized the initiative, and in a classic double envelopment destroyed the Union infantry at Brices Cross Roads.

He kept moving his artillery forward, towards the Union lines. This ran against accepted principles of warfare but had the effect of shredding the enemy's center. "Artillery is made to be captured," he explained to the Confederate officer who directed the fire, "and I wanted to see them take yours."

Brices Cross Roads is regarded by military historians as Forrest at his tactical peak, one of the war's most decisive victories. Union losses were placed at 2,612 men while Forrest's were 495. He was now being called the Wizard of the Saddle.

But Sherman was determined to rid himself of this menace. In July, an even larger Union force reentered Mississippi, and this time it employed scorched earth policies to punish the area's inhabitants. The Federals reached the town of Tupelo and fortified it. Although Forrest later described the defenses as "impregnable," he ordered poorly coordinated assaults on them and suffered a major defeat. The Confederates held the field but suffered twice as many losses as the Union forces.

When asked by General Stephen D. Lee if he had any ideas about what had happened, Forrest grew testy. "I've always got ideas, and I'll tell you one thing, General Lee," he responded. "If I knew as much about West Point tactics as you, the Yankees would whip hell out of me every day."

In the last stages of the fighting, Forrest was wounded in the foot, and a rumor spread through the army that he had been killed. To put the story to rest, he located a farmer's buggy and directed the battle while riding in it.

Just to show that he still had fight in him, he raided his hometown, Memphis, in August. That sent a scare through the place but failed in Forrest's goal of capturing the Union generals who were based there.

He also managed to raise an annoyance along the Tennessee River in November, surprising four Union gunboats with his cavalry at a supply depot near Johnsonville, Tennessee, and destroying them with artillery fire.

But time was running out on the Confederacy. When General James Wilson began a massive cavalry raid into central Alabama with 13,500 men in April 1865, Forrest could do little to stop him. Even his last battle, however, was marked by his personal stamp.

At Ebenezer Church, near Selma, he was wounded by a saber blow while fighting on horseback with a Union captain. Forrest drew a revolver with his other hand and shot the man dead.

"If that boy had known enough to give me the point of his saber instead of the edge," he said later, "I should not have been here to tell about it."

But final surrender was now inevitable, and Forrest pondered his course. "If one road led to hell and the other to Mexico, I would be indifferent which to take" he remarked on the evening before he was to stack arms. In the end, however, he addressed his men and urged reconciliation.

"You have been good soldiers," he told them, "you can be good citizens. Obey the laws, preserve your honor, and the government to which you have surrendered can afford to be and will be magnanimous."

Not very many months would pass before Forrest would have second thoughts about this magnanimity. "I came into the army worth a million and a half dollars," he would say in later years, "and came out a beggar."

Rebuilding a fortune was not easy in the postwar South. Moreover, he was a 44-year-old man, worn out from years of almost constant campaigning. He returned to his plantation in Coahoma County, Mississippi, did some planting, and operated a sawmill. But he could not make money quickly enough to pay off his debts, and he had to mortgage his land. Those who cheered him, he pointed out, were now trying to crush him.

Early in 1866, he was accused of killing a black freedman on his plantation with an axe. But Forrest told the authorities that he was trying to stop the man from beating his wife and that the sharecropper had attacked him first with a knife. No charges were ever brought.

The Fort Pillow Massacre still darkened Forrest's name in the North. This killing, in addition to his background as a slave trader, convinced many people there, including the press, that he was an unrepentant racist.

Forrest moved back to Memphis and entered the insurance business. He also started raising funds for a new railroad to be built between Memphis and Selma, Alabama. But other activities would soon begin taking up his time.

In the winter of 1865, a group of young Confederate veterans in Pulaski, Tennessee, organized a social club to amuse themselves. They called it Kuklos, after the Greek word for "circle." It was, at first, a way to pass the winter months by making up fantastic names for each other and giving parties in a deserted house. After a while, the name was rendered as Ku Klux and then it was an easy matter, as a token of their close ties, to simply add Klan.

But soon the innocent club acquired a darker meaning. Tennessee was the first secessionist state to rejoin the Union. But it was bitterly divided. The eastern part of the state had opposed the Confederacy, and many of its citizens had fought for the Union. Now these men were in control of the state government, and they were disinclined to go gently with those who had seceded.

Many Confederate veterans were excluded from voting, and the Tennessee legislature fell under control of radical Republicans and the blacks whose votes they directed. Most Southerners recoiled because they could not reconcile themselves to the thought of blacks exercising any power over their lives.

The Ku Kluxers found that they had devised an effective instrument for retaliating. Night riders, shots fired, utter secrecy. Word of the organization spread, and soon there were Klans throughout Tennessee and northern Alabama.

In the spring of 1867, it was decided to hold a clandestine meeting of Klan leaders in Nashville to adopt a prescript, or statement of principles, and to coordinate activities. It isn't likely that Forrest attended this meeting, but he soon heard of the Klan through some of his former officers and was intrigued.

The Klan apparently had approached Robert E. Lee to serve as its head, but he declined. A general of Forrest's stature would do almost as well. He took the Klan oath and was quickly elected its chief. But a more suitable title was needed. It was recalled that his old nickname was Wizard of the Saddle, so he became the Klan's first Imperial Wizard.

Forrest handed Federal troops at Brices Cross Roads one of their most decisive defeats of the war, inflicting more than five times the casualties he endured. *Smithsonian Institution, National Portrait Gallery*

The Klan's methods—sudden unexpected appearances and scare tactics—were just the sort of thing Forrest had fostered during the war. He also found his insurance and railroad jobs convenient covers for traveling through the South and spreading Klan doctrine.

By 1868, the Tennessee legislature was threatening to call out the militia and impose martial law to halt Klan raids. Forrest, while never admitting that the Klan existed or that he was its head, made a response.

"If the Radical legislature arms the Negroes and tells them to shoot down all Confederate soldiers," he said, "on the grounds that they are members of this Kuklux Klan, as they call it, and outlaws, then, in my opinion there will be civil war in Tennessee. I don't want to see any more bloodshed.... If they bring this war on us, there is one thing that I will tell you—that I

Forrest accepted the Ku Klux Klan's invitation to become its first Imperial Wizard, but he disassociated himself from the group two years later when its activities grew more violent. *Library of Congress*

Though the postwar years saw Forrest's financial and physical well-being decline and his name blackened in the North, citizens of his hometown Memphis regarded him as a hero. *Library of Congress*

shall not shoot any Negroes so long as I can see a white Radical to shoot, for it is the Radicals who will be to blame for bringing on this war."

But the radical tide had about run its course. By 1870, a more conservative group took control of the legislature and restored the rights of former Confederates. Forrest had disassociated himself from the Klan the preceding year. It was now running out of control, using violence indiscriminately to pillage and rob. "Bad men" had taken it over, he said, and he wanted no part of it.

He was summoned to Washington in 1871 to testify at Congressional hearings on Klan activities. Forrest ducked and weaved, denying all knowledge, but admitted he knew some of the people involved. He sidestepped some questions and pleaded failure of memory on others.

Afterwards, he admitted to "gentlemanly lies." He wanted nothing more to do with the Klan, but felt honor bound to protect former associates. He felt some untruths had been justified.

His finances and his health began failing rapidly in the next few years. His railroad went bust, and he contracted diabetes. By 1875, he was a shadow of himself, wasting away to a 100-pound wraith.

"I am completely broke up," he told friends. "I am broke in fortune, broke in health, broke in spirit."

A few months before his death, he attended a black political barbecue in Memphis. Forrest had undergone a religious conversion and in the time remaining to him seemed to be earnestly trying to right some old wrongs. His speech was a remarkable gesture of reconciliation.

"I came to meet you as friends and welcome you to the white people," he said. "I want you to come nearer to us...We have but one flag, one country. Let us stand together. We may differ in color but not in sentiment...Go to work, be industrious, live honestly and act truly and when you are oppressed, I'll come to your relief."

Four months later, in October 1875, he was on his deathbed. Jefferson Davis came by to pay his last respects and was a pallbearer at his funeral.

"The generals commanding in the Southwest never appreciated his greatness," he said on the ride to the cemetery. "Their judgment was that he was [only] a bold and enterprising raider and rider. I was misled by them and never knew how to measure him.... I saw it all after it was too late."

JOHN HUNT MORGAN

"In my mortal apprehension I never once thought of trusting in God for safety, but wholly relied upon the wisdom and skill of John Morgan."

Confederate soldier Bromfield L. Ridley, March 1863

His career was a distillation of Southern chivalry, the way the war was supposed to have been in romantic novels and Technicolor epics. A son of one of Kentucky's first families, he threw away his livelihood to fight for a cause he believed in. His daring cavalry raids confused and disordered a numerically superior enemy. His courtship and marriage to Mattie Ready in the midst of the war was the stuff of nostalgic fantasy.

To cap it off, John Hunt Morgan, in one rash and wild ride through the states of Indiana and Ohio, led his men farther north than any other Confederate force. But he had gone too far, and his reputation was tarnished when his great raid failed.

By the time of his death, in the late summer of 1864, he had become a marginal figure, reduced to sporadic raids in a sideshow of the war. Moreover, his men were accused of criminal acts when it became apparent that his home state would not rally to the Southern cause.

Still, there is something about Morgan and the galloping hoofbeats of his Raiders that captures the imagination. His admirers called him "The Thunder Bolt of the Confederacy." Children repeated a rhyme: "Morgan, Morgan the Raider and Morgan's terrible men/ With bowie knives and pistols are galloping up the glen." There was a time, in the last six months of 1862, when it seemed that his swift, destructive raids could go on disrupting the federal invasion of Tennessee indefinitely.

The old photographs show a handsome, dark-bearded man in his late 30s, slouch hat set back at a rakish angle, legs crossed so that his high riding boots show to best advantage. He had no formal military training. But his grasp of the role cavalry could play in the war and how it would nullify federal strategy in the western campaign was brilliant.

In just a few raids involving fewer than 3,000 troopers, wrote historian Bruce Catton, Morgan revealed "the living signs that something was wrong with the Federal conduct of the war in the west.... Federal power had let the war get into a condition of unstable equilibrium in which mere incidents could jar it into a new shape."

His cavalry had the ability to create those incidents, destroying supply and communication lines. The Northern armies were trying to control a vast territory that was beyond their grasp. It would be years before the federal command understood that the war could not be won with territorial gains but only by breaking the other side's will to fight. Morgan's raids first drove that lesson home.

He was born in 1825 in Huntsville, Alabama. His mother, Henrietta, had moved there with her new husband, Calvin Cogswell Morgan. The raider's grandfather, John Wesley Hunt, was reputed to be the wealthiest man in Kentucky, the first millionaire in the state. But his father did not have the golden touch, and when the Alabama business failed, the young family had to return to Lexington and the shelter of the Hunt fortune.

Hopemont, the brick mansion Hunt built in 1814, still stands in the fashionable Gratz Park area of town. Then as now it was filled with solemn family portraits and heirlooms. The past spoke to the young Morgan from its walls, reminding him that he sprung from a heritage deeply rooted in this soil. His passion for Kentucky, and his later conviction that it could not fail

John Hunt Morgan's daring raids upset Federal plans to invade Tennessee. In addition, Morgan led his cavalry farther north than any other Confederate force. ***Museum of the Confederacy, Richmond, Virginia***

to cast off wrongful leadership and flock to the Confederate banner, was born in the imposing rooms of this house.

Although Morgan and his five brothers grew up on a farm outside of town, he was a frequent visitor to his grandparents' mansion. The assertive Hunt took responsibility for raising him. He enrolled at Transylvania University, in Lexington, but was too restless for studies. His marks were indifferent, there was a duel, and soon his formal education was over.

But the Mexican War began when he was 21, and this was more to the young man's taste. He enlisted as a private in the First Regiment of Kentucky Volunteers, along with his brother, Calvin, and his father's brother, Alexander Morgan, who turned down a commission to fight beside his two nephews.

The three men found themselves in the thick of the Battle of Buena Vista in February 1847. This was the fight at which Morgan's future commander, Braxton Bragg, won lasting fame. The victory also propelled General Zachary Taylor to the presidency in the following year's election.

The Kentucky troops, outnumbered and driven back by a spirited Mexican assault that overran neighboring units, were forced to dismount and make a stand. Morgan's biographer, James A. Ramage, said the men fought with "promptness and bravery, standing as firm as the rocks of the mountain."

The Mexicans could not sustain the attack and, after two days of desperate battle, retreated. Alexander, however, was cut down by Mexican lancers and died on the field. Nonetheless, it had been Morgan's first taste of battle, and he wanted more. With his service up in June, he returned to Kentucky and raised a company of cavalry. He was elected captain, but before they could get back to Mexico, the war ended. Using his own fortune, Morgan paid back every man in his company for time lost from work

As the oldest Hunt grandson, he was placed in charge of family enterprises. Most important of them was a ropewalk, which manufactured hemp bags and clothing for the Southern market. This was the region where Morgan's commercial ties were centered, and it captured his heart as well.

He married his partner's sister, Rebecca Bruce, and settled into the life of a young businessman. But he found no satisfaction in his home. His wife soon became an invalid, rarely leaving her front door. His business life settled into the routine. Moreover, there were stirrings in the nation and no Kentuckian, especially, could fail to note them.

The state was America's political fulcrum. If it came to secession, it was increasingly apparent that the states of the Deep South would leave the Union. The critical decisions would be made on the border between North and South. Kentucky, which commanded water passage on both the Mississippi and Ohio rivers, was essential to both sides.

"I think to lose Kentucky is nearly the same as to lose the whole game," said Abraham Lincoln, Kentucky-born himself, in the first days of the war. "We would as well consent to separation at once, including the surrender of [Washington]."

When the fight for Kentucky began, Morgan made sure he would be ready. In 1857, at the age of 32, he raised the Lexington Rifles, a militia unit with distinct pro-Southern sympathies. Their drills became a familiar part of the city's scene.

When war was declared, Kentucky proclaimed its

official neutrality. Morgan, however, did not. He defiantly flew a secessionist flag over his factory, and it was well known to federal authorities which side his militia favored. He began smuggling arms to the South. Confiscation of his property was just a matter of course.

But in July 1861, he suddenly became free to make his choice. Rebecca Bruce Morgan, after years of lingering illness, almost mercifully passed away. With a palpable sense of relief, John Hunt Morgan left Lexington to join the Southern army, certain that he would return to liberate his home state within the year.

He slipped off with 25 members of his Rifles and within days enlisted in the Confederate army at Bowling Green. He was soon joined by four of his five brothers and was made a captain of Kentucky volunteers, assigned to conduct scouting missions around the federal army of General Don Carlos Buell.

Buell's base was Louisville, and he controlled the vital Louisville and Nashville Railroad. In a quick strike behind Buell's lines that fall, Morgan took 33 prisoners, destroyed supply trains, set off a series of disruptive alarms, and returned home without losing a man. Moreover, he had accomplished all this with 13 troopers.

Morgan took to this kind of warfare. He was among the first to understand its possibilities, and he wanted to expand and extend its use. But in the early months of 1862, the Confederate line collapsed. Forts Henry and Donelson fell to U. S. Grant, and the Southern armies had to evacuate Nashville and retreat to Corinth, Mississippi.

Morgan's previous raids, however, had brought him to the attention of General Pierre G. T. Beauregard. A few days before the Battle of Shiloh, in April 1862, he was promoted to colonel. Morgan's unit participated in that bloody fight, and at its conclusion he was more convinced than ever that the role of the cavalry had to change.

Its utility would be limited on the battlefield because it was apparent that this would be an infantry war. Because of the state of weapons technology, the entrenched defense had an enormous advantage. The cavalry charge was useless against such concentrated firepower. But opportunities for using cavalry to disrupt an enemy with overextended supply lines were enormous.

Morgan lobbied Beauregard's successor, General Braxton Bragg, constantly, pleading to be turned loose on more extensive raids upon Buell's rear. Finally, Bragg gave Morgan his head.

In May 1862, Morgan started off from Mississippi on a series of quick hits through Tennessee and Kentucky. His tactics were simple: move rapidly, concentrate forces to inflict maximum damage on the objective, split the command to frustrate pursuit, avoid engagements in any numbers, and disappear. He took 400 prisoners at Columbia, Tennessee, and wrecked the railroad at Cave City, Kentucky. The Southern command took note.

By the end of May, it was apparent that the critical rail center of Chattanooga was Buell's target, and Grant's army was poised to roll across Mississippi. In response, Morgan was given the manpower to carry on the sort of guerilla campaign he envisioned.

Hopemont was built in 1814 by John Wesley Hunt, Morgan's grandfather and Kentucky's first millionaire. ***Library of Congress***

During the Mexican War, Morgan joined the First Regiment of Kentucky Volunteers and saw action at the Battle of Buena Vista. ***Library of Congress***

Even before he left Knoxville on July 4 on his first great raid, the legends were attached to him. His bearing, aristocratic lineage and dashing exploits had made him a Southern hero. With the war going badly in the west and no victories on the battlefield to build on, it seemed to the public that Morgan alone would stem the tide.

When Buell, under constant prodding from Washington, began moving on Chattanooga, Morgan and 900 of his "terrible men" fell upon his supply lines. In a raid that covered more than 1,000 miles, his troopers captured 17 Kentucky towns, took 1,200 prisoners from the regular U.S. Army, dispersed 1,500 home guardsmen, wiped out several supply depots and railroad equipment valued at $8 million, and cut Buell off from his Louisville base.

Morgan rode back to Tennessee after 24 days with losses of fewer than 100 men. Buell was stopped in his tracks, and Northern strategists were in shock. Their carefully measured plans had been stymied by fewer than 1,000 men. Union forces in Tennessee could not be sustained if they lost control of their support base in Kentucky. It was a bitter blow to Union morale.

In August, Morgan destroyed the rail tunnel north of Gallatin, Tennessee, and when a Union force was sent out to pursue him, he suddenly wheeled around, attacked it, and captured General R. W. Johnson. But there was more to come.

Early in the war, Morgan harried the forces of General Don Carlos Buell with only a handful of raiders. ***National Archives and Records Division***

After the Mexican War, Morgan settled down to the life of a businessman, managing some of the Hunt family enterprises. ***University of Kentucky***

Morgan was fired with the idea of leading Kentucky out of the Union. In most places he visited on his raids, he was greeted as a conquering hero. He didn't have to commandeer supplies; they were given to him. He felt that a full-scale invasion could roll back the Union army all the way to the Ohio River, place a Confederate government in the state capital at Frankfort and, best of all, win Lexington, stronghold of the Morgans and the Hunts, for the South.

Morgan found a ready listener in Bragg. He became convinced that his army, in combination with General Edmund Kirby Smith, could get behind Buell and force a Union retreat into Kentucky.

By September 5, Bragg had entered Kentucky, and Buell accordingly abandoned his advance on Chattanooga and advised Washington that he would march back to Louisville. "March where you please," came the directive from General-in-Chief Henry Halleck, "provided you find the enemy and fight him."

But that was easier said than done. Once again, the elusive Morgan had been turned loose and was systematically driving Buell crazy. He had learned how to tap into the telegraph wires and was routinely intercepting federal communications. His men would disconnect the wire, hook it up to a portable battery, and amuse themselves by sending contradictory orders to Union commanders or countermanding orders to pursue Morgan. Once they sent a message to Washington complaining about the poor quality of the mules they had captured intended for Buell.

While he had a puckish side, Morgan began to take himself very seriously as a liberator. "Kentuckians," he wrote in a poster that was distributed throughout the state, "I have come to liberate you from the hands of your oppressors." He called for 50,000 recruits, only the bravest need apply. Then he concluded with a poetic exhortation: "Strike—for your altars and your fires./ Strike for the green graves of your sires,/ God, and your native land."

When Lexington fell to Smith's army, Confederate flags flew from almost every window. "Baskets of food and buckets of cold water [were given out] at street corners for the refreshment of tired Confederates, everyone exulting," writes Bruce Catton, in *Terrible Swift Sword.* "The town almost exploded with joy when John Hunt Morgan and his cavalry came through on the gallop; all the church bells rang and people who had no flags waved their handkerchiefs and laughed or wept or cheered as the spirit moved them."

But by September 17, the Confederate advance began to slow. Bragg was reluctant to force a battle, even with numerical superiority over Buell and control of the federal supply lines. Instead, he hesitated, installed a short-lived government at Frankfort, and, when Buell finally attacked him, came off with no better than a draw at the Battle of Perryville. Bragg was then forced to retreat into Tennessee.

In a 24-day raid, Morgan managed with just 900 men to derail Buell's plan to take Chattanooga, depriving him of supplies and cutting him off from his base of operations. ***Library of Congress***

There would be no liberation, but Morgan's men rode nonetheless. In another defiant sweep on the retreat from Kentucky in October, he once more took a terrible toll on Union supplies and morale, destroying rail bridges and isolated military outposts.

However, there had been no general uprising to join the Southern side, no massive flocking of volunteers to the Confederate colors. The new government at Frankfort was swiftly booted out and replaced with Union loyalists. As Morgan returned with Bragg to his base in Murfreesboro, Tennessee, nothing had really changed.

Still, Morgan's reputation was never more glittering. Jefferson Davis visited Murfreesboro in December and was treated to a round of parties and celebrations. He was convinced morale was undiminished in Tennessee and was told that much of the credit went to Morgan. General Joseph E. Johnston used words like "brilliant and indispensable" to describe him and suggested the Confederate president give him an immediate promotion to brigadier general. Davis obligingly placed the stars on Morgan's shoulders himself.

Among those attending the ceremony was Mattie Ready, the 21-year old-belle of Murfreesboro. She was the daughter of former U.S. Congressman Charles Ready, now a Tennessee representative to the Confederate Congress. During a brief federal occupation of the town, the story goes, a Union officer asked her name. "It's Mattie Ready," she replied. "But by the grace of God one day I hope to call myself the wife of John Morgan."

Morgan heard the story and upon arriving in Murfreesboro paid a call on the lady. Although there were 16 years difference in their ages, the couple found that they were a match. They were engaged, and on December 14, the day after Morgan received his promotion, they were wed.

It was a storybook affair, with Bragg and his top commanders standing in attendance and the ceremony performed by General Leonidas Polk, wearing his vestments as a bishop of the Episcopal Church. A brief honeymoon ended one week later with the newlyweds sitting their horses side by side on a knoll near Alexandria, Tennessee, to review Morgan's troops.

"Company after company moved forward into line, with sabers jingling, horses prancing, firearms glistening, bugles blowing and flags waving," wrote local historian Thomas Gray Webb. "Then came the order to halt and the whole command faced its general and his smiling bride. It formed a scene ... which no soldier could look upon without feeling his blood course proudly and his pulse beat bravely."

In Murfreesboro, Morgan wed Mattie Ready, the daughter of former U.S. Congressman Charles Ready. *University of Kentucky Library*

After this charmed interlude, the groom was off again. This third raid of 1862 (which carried over into the new year) took two brigades, amounting to about 4,000 men, on another devastating swing into Kentucky. He captured 1,887 enemy prisoners, destroyed 20 miles of rail lines and four bridges, and did an estimated $2 million damage to Union stores at a toll of two men killed and 24 wounded.

But this raid did not earn Morgan the unqualified plaudits of his earlier exploits. It was true that the blow at Union activity was impressive. But a new man was in charge of the North's Army of the Cumberland. Morgan's first two raids had spooked Buell into a state of paralysis. He sent frantic dispatches to Washington, reporting that "my communications ... are swarming with an immense cavalry force of the enemy. My army cannot be sustained in its present position, much less advanced, until they were made secure."

By late fall, the Union high command had heard enough, and the reluctant Buell was replaced by William S. Rosecrans. This general saw Morgan's absence as an advantage, stripping 4,000 fighting cavalrymen from Bragg's force. Although he knew of the damage being done to his supply lines, Rosecrans decided to move out of Nashville anyhow and carry the fight to Bragg. On December 30, the armies met at Stones River.

Although the bitter four-day battle cost more than 24,000 casualties on both sides, it ended inconclusively. Bragg, however, was forced to withdraw from Murfreesboro and make his new headquarters at Tullahoma, to the southeast. There were some in Richmond who wondered whether the critical factor in the battle had not been the absence of Morgan and his men.

In March, Morgan was badly mauled by a smaller

General William Rosecrans ignored Morgan's threat to his supply line, taking the fight to Bragg at Stones River. *National Archives and Records Division*

On his raid into the North in July 1863, Morgan invaded Salem, Indiana. His men looted stores and destroyed rail depots and bridges. ***Cincinnati Museum Center***

Union force at Vaught's Hill, near Milton, Tennessee, and two weeks later suffered another setback a few miles away at Liberty. Now the whispering began in earnest among those in Bragg's command and in Richmond who felt the Kentuckian had grown a bit too cocky for his own good.

He was officially given a vote of thanks by the Confederate Congress in May for his "varied, heroic and invaluable service." Still, a sense of tarnish had set in, and it was intolerable to one of Morgan's pride. So he began to hatch the plan for what would be his greatest achievement, a raid that would bring the war home to the North and restore his unchallenged position as the greatest cavalry leader in the west.

It was expected that Rosecrans would begin to advance on the great rail center of Chattanooga as soon as the roads were passable in summer. Morgan convinced Bragg that another of his raids would divert forces under General Ambrose Burnside from linking up with Rosecrans for the push on Chattanooga.

Bragg gave his consent, although he didn't know what Morgan really had in mind. Because this time Morgan had no intention of stopping in Kentucky. This time he would push on beyond the Ohio River into Indiana and then either swing west into Illinois or east through Ohio to link up with Robert E. Lee's invasion of Pennsylvania. Absolutely no one in the Confederate command had authorized or even knew about this scheme. That was of no concern to Morgan.

Four of his brothers rode with him on the July 2 departure and his brother-in-law, Colonel Basil Duke, commanded a brigade. Morgan had turned the war into a personal crusade, almost a clan vendetta. That sense was heightened when his brother, Tom, was killed in a clash with Michigan troops just days into this raid, outside Lebanon, Kentucky.

Morgan continued on grimly, through Bardstown, and feinted an attack on Louisville. But he had already planned his next move. Advance raiders had captured two small steamboats, and on July 6 he ferried his 2,500 men across the Ohio River, at Brandenburg, Kentucky, and into Indiana.

What happened over the next three weeks is the stuff of legend. To some Southern sympathizers it was the greatest adventure of the war. But to others it was a pointless exercise that had no discernible military goal and "ended Morgan's usefulness to the Army of Tennessee."

Lee already had retreated at Gettysburg by the time Morgan entered Indiana, but that made no difference. He brushed aside a small force of Home Guards that tried to stop him near Corydon, Indiana, and continued north unencumbered. Celebrations of Lee's defeat turned to panic in Indianapolis as officials became con-

Morgan's raid into Washington, Ohio, prompted panic by its citizens. *University of Kentucky Library*

vinced the state capital was the target of Morgan's assault.

But word that Morgan was on the loose had spread all across the Midwest. In Illinois, they told the story of a bridegroom whose marriage was celebrated with an old fashioned, bell-ringing, pan-banging shivaree. Unfamiliar with the local custom, the young man leaped from his bed and took off down the road in a panic, convinced the racket meant that Morgan's Raiders were upon him.

Morgan never did get to Illinois, but his men sacked the quiet Quaker town of Salem, Indiana, an incident celebrated in Jessamyn West's famous novel, *Friendly Persuasion.* With the entire countryside alerted and Burnside's cavalry in pursuit, Morgan swung east. On July 13, he clattered across the northern suburbs of Cincinnati, sending that city into frantic alarms.

But now the raid was turning from an adventure into an ordeal. He had lost almost 500 men, mostly from weariness and loss of horses. They were in the saddle hour after hour, grabbing tiny slivers of sleep wherever they could. Morgan realized that he had to get back across the Ohio to salvage his command. But by now the Northern pursuit was closing in.

Morgan headed for Buffington Island, Ohio, a place where the river ordinarily was shallow enough to ford. But the Ohio was running high, which not only made the crossing perilous but enabled Union gunboats to come up the river to block him. When Morgan reached the crossing on July 18, he also slowed down to allow stragglers to catch up to the main force. But that allowed Burnside's cavalry, under Brigadier General Edward H. Hobson, to catch up with him, too.

Instead of an escape, Buffington Island had turned into a trap. Morgan was outmanned six to one on land, and the guns of the USS *Moose* controlled the river. He lost 120 men in a running battle across the river plain, and 700 more, including Duke and two of Morgan's brothers, were captured. Only Morgan and 363 others managed to get away by galloping through a ravine.

There was no question now as to the raid's purpose. The only issue was escape. But Hobson's pursuit was relentless, and although Morgan managed to stay ahead of him for another seven days, he was finally cornered and forced to surrender at Salineville, Ohio, on July 26.

The great raid was over. Morgan and his men had covered 700 miles in 25 days, averaging 20 hours a day in the saddle. He had destroyed bridges and tracks, frightened the daylights out of a large portion of the Ohio Valley, and remained behind enemy lines longer than all of J. E. B. Stuart's raids combined. Observers said that Morgan could have crossed the river himself at Blennerhassett Island, near Parkersburg, West Virginia, but chose to return to his men when gunboats closed that escape route for the rest of them.

A highly irritated Burnside ruled him ineligible for parole. Instead, he was sentenced to a maximum security prison for criminals in Columbus, Ohio, and, as the crowning indignity, his beard and long hair were cut off. That last punishment was regarded in the South as a barbaric humiliation, and later the governor of Ohio apologized "for an outrageous and disgraceful act."

Morgan's defenders claim that the raid did accomplish something. It tied up Burnside long enough for Bragg to make an orderly retreat and form a defensive line around Chattanooga, holding up the Union advance for months. It was "incomparably the most brilliant raid of the entire war," wrote Duke in his personal memoir, *A History of Morgan's Cavalry.*

Other historians are not so kind. "The real object of the raid has remained a mystery," writes Mark Mayo Boatner III. "This reckless adventure deprived him of his well-earned reputation." In Richmond, public statements hailed Morgan as a hero, but privately the Confederate command was furious with him for disregarding orders to stay south of the Ohio.

The raid also turned public opinion in Ohio against the Copperheads, Democrats who were sympathetic to the South. That segment of the party had been a strong presence in the state, but after Morgan's raid Ohio turned securely Republican.

Morgan's wife of six months was frantic over his safety and suffered a miscarriage. She tried to mobilize public opinion to protest his treatment as a common criminal. But in just four months, Mattie Ready Morgan received the stunning news that her husband had escaped.

Tunneling from their cells, Morgan and six of his officers hit an air vent, followed it out to an exterior wall, and climbed across to freedom. The men managed to get civilian clothes and boarded a train to Cincinnati. According to legend, Morgan found himself seated next to a Union officer who informed him, as the train passed the prison, that it was where the infamous Confederate raider was being held. Two of the men were later recaptured near Louisville, but Morgan managed to elude his pursuers with the assistance of several sympathizers in Kentucky, and he rejoined his wife at Danville, Virginia, in time for Christmas dinner.

He was welcomed to Richmond on January 2, 1864, with the official statement that "the despicable foe in their futile efforts to degrade you before the world ... have only elevated you in the estimation of all Confederate citizens, and the whole civilized world."

Captured during his great raid, Morgan escaped prison. He returned to service, but was given no command of significant responsibility. ***Library of Congress***

The words were brave. But, in fact, Morgan had squandered his command in the fields of Ohio and along with it the confidence of his superiors.

He was placed in charge of another cavalry force in April, but it was in southwestern Virginia, far from the center of action. There were complaints from other officers that Morgan's men were poorly disciplined. It was also whispered that the great raider had lost his nerve and promised his Mattie that he would take no more chances.

Morgan must have heard the talk, and it ate at him. But there was a way to silence it. He returned to Kentucky once more. There was no longer any strategic advantage to be gained there; it was early June, and the focus of the western campaign was far away in Georgia.

After the war, Morgan's remains were returned to Lexington, where his equestrian statue stands. ***Library of Congress***

This was, instead, an attempt to recapture the aura of his great days.

The raid was a disaster. Morgan took the supply depot at Cynthiana, northeast of Lexington, but decided to make a stand there against a larger pursuing Union force. He was badly beaten, losing all but 400 men out of a force of 1,400.

Moreover, there were reports that when his men captured Mt. Sterling, they held up the local bank for $18,000. Although Morgan swore he knew nothing about the robbery, his failure to recover the money and punish the men responsible was criticized severely in Richmond. He was threatened with a court-martial, and his reputation suffered another blemish.

By late summer, he was in eastern Tennessee, involved in a sideshow: a campaign for the railroad that connected Knoxville with Virginia. Union forces were concentrated at Bull's Gap, the pass through which the rail route crossed the mountains, and Morgan spent the rainy night of September 3 in the nearby town of Greeneville.

This was the part of the Confederacy most loyal to the Union. Many of its residents were, in fact, off fighting with the Northern army, and Andrew Johnson, who was running for vice president on the Republican ticket with Lincoln in the upcoming national election, came from Greeneville. It was not a safe place for any Confederate.

Morgan was also unfortunate in his choice of lodging. The home in which he stayed was owned by C. D. Williams, and also living there was Sarah Thompson. By some accounts, she was an employee of the Williams family and by others a relative. Her husband, a former recruiter for the Union cause, had been shot down by Southern irregulars eight months earlier. Sarah was waiting for a chance to avenge his death.

She slipped out of the house after dark and managed to talk her way past the Confederate pickets in the rainy mist. She then ran to a friend's farm, borrowed a horse, and rode the 16 miles to the Union lines. Her story convinced Major General Alvan Gillem, and he ordered a dawn raid on the sleeping town of Greeneville.

Morgan was caught completely by surprise. By the time his pickets could raise the alarm, the Williams house was surrounded. He barely had time to slip a pair of trousers over his pajamas and run from the rear of the house. While trying to climb a fence, he was shot dead by Private Andrew Campbell, of Tennessee. Campbell said later he thought Morgan was reaching for a weapon. The house in which he spent his final night is undergoing restoration, and there are plans to open it as a museum.

Morgan's body was returned to Richmond and buried in a capital city that already was under siege by the surrounding Union armies, a siege that would not be lifted until the war ended in seven more months. Mattie Ready Morgan outlived her husband by 23 years, eventually remarrying before her death in 1887.

On April 17, 1868, Morgan returned to Lexington for the final time. His remains were carried through the streets of his hometown and laid to rest beside those of his brother Tom, who had been killed in Lebanon, Kentucky, at the start of the great raid almost five years before.

Hundreds of the "terrible men" who once rode with him followed the funeral procession to Lexington Cemetery in solemn rows and former Confederate officers formed the honor guard. Residents agreed the only ceremony Lexington had seen that compared to it was the autumn morning in 1862 when Morgan made his first homecoming, riding at the head of the army and claiming the city forever for the Confederate cause.

The equestrian statue of Morgan, on the east lawn of the Fayette County Courthouse, remains a Lexington landmark. An object of notoriety when first unveiled, it depicts Morgan astride a stallion, when it was well known in Lexington that his favorite horse was a mare, Black Bess.

The Western Commanders

ALBERT SIDNEY JOHNSTON

"If Sidney Johnston is not a general, we had better give up the war, for we have no generals."

Jefferson Davis, February 1862

He was born for heroism, but it always seemed to elude him. Just as the prize appeared within his grasp, events would sweep it away. Finally, on the battleground at Shiloh, at the age of 59, Albert Sidney Johnston realized his goal and, with the full exhilaration of that moment upon him, lost his life.

When he resigned his commission in the U.S. Army to join the Southern cause, he was acclaimed as the greatest soldier in America, the one man who could surely see the Confederacy to victory. By the bitter spring of 1862, however, he was vilified by many of those same voices as an incompetent and a traitor, appointed the South's top field commander only because of his long friendship with Davis.

That debate has raged ever since. Military historians point to Johnston's failure in securing forts Henry and Donelson, the critical outposts blocking the federal advance into Tennessee. "It is hard to find the basis for this almost unchallenged opinion that he was the supremely qualified soldier, that his death was an irremediable catastrophe," writes Stanley F. Horn, in his history of the Army of Tennessee.

Others insist, however, he performed masterfully while outnumbered and forced to defend hopelessly overextended lines. He nearly cut short U. S. Grant's career by surprising him at Shiloh and may have possessed the overall grasp of strategy, the intuitive sense of when to turn from the defensive to a quick and overwhelming attack, that his successors lacked. His death, say his advocates, ended any chance of Confederate success in the western campaign.

Sidney Johnston was born in Washington, Kentucky, in 1803. His father was a physician in this thriving town, which was then the second largest community in the state. Situated at the crest of a hard four-mile climb from the Ohio River, it grew to prominence as the first overnight stop for Kentucky-bound travelers from the East. His birthplace still stands in the historic district of the town.

It was in Washington that Harriet Beecher Stowe, while visiting a school friend, witnessed a slave auction, a memory that would eventually stir her to write *Uncle Tom's Cabin.* But Johnston grew up as a part of Kentucky's slaveholding culture and, in fact, blamed subsequent failure with a cotton plantation on his inability to raise the money to buy slaves.

Johnston's father intended for the young man to enter medicine and enrolled him at the age of 15 in Lexington's Transylvania University. It was there that Johnston met a younger student, Jefferson Davis. Their friendship would endure for the rest of Johnston's life and often take the form of hero-worship by the future president of the Confederacy.

Johnston was a big man, over six feet tall at a time when that was unusual, and close to 200 pounds. He was handsome and cordial, a manly presence with a surprising sense of humor. Davis later called him "the greatest soldier, the ablest man, civil or military, Confederate or Federal, then living." That may have been something of an overstatement, but Johnston seemed to have that effect on people. He inspired respect and confidence through his presence.

He won an appointment to West Point and graduated eighth in the class of 1826. Davis followed his friend there, and their friendship deepened. After graduation, however, Johnston made an unfortunate decision. Invited to join the staff of the Army's most brilliant young commander, Winfield Scott, he felt there would be greater opportunity in the infantry.

Considered the greatest soldier in America at the outbreak of the Civil War, Albert Sidney Johnston's fortunes declined as he commanded the Confederacy's western forces. ***Chicago Historical Society***

Instead, he was shunted off to the Jefferson Barracks, at St. Louis. And there he stayed, aside from some brief, inconsequential activity in the Black Hawk War of 1832. After eight discouraging years as a lieutenant, with no prospect for advancement and a young family to support, he resigned his commission and bought a farm in Missouri. By 1836 his wife and one daughter had died, and the farm was slowly being crushed by debt.

That was the year of the struggle for Texas independence. So Johnston decided to leave his remaining two children with their maternal grandmother in Louisville and put his military experience to use in the service of the new republic's army.

Texas welcomed him enthusiastically, and for the rest of his life Johnston considered it his home. Within months of his arrival, he had advanced from private to senior brigadier general. Unfortunately, the previous holder of this rank, Felix Huston, took Johnston's promotion as a personal insult and called out the new general to a duel.

While recognizing the challenge as absurd, Johnston knew that to refuse it would destroy his authority. So the two men, armed with single-shot pistols, fired at each other four times and missed. On the fifth shot, Johnston went down with a hip wound. With honor duly satisfied, the new brigadier was able to assume command after a month of recuperation.

Once again, however, there was little to command. A threatened invasion by Mexico never took place, and Johnston found himself serving as Texas's secretary of war at a time of extended peace. He turned away from the military life once more and after remarrying, to a cousin of his first wife, tried his luck with farming again, this time in Texas.

He was no more successful there than he had been in Missouri. By 1846, his cotton plantation was grinding him inexorably into poverty. He was 43 years old, his youthful promise unfulfilled either in war or the soil. Johnston seemed about to enter the declining years of a life marked by poor choices and mediocrity.

Then the United States and Mexico went to war. Turned down in his application for a regular army commission, Johnston raised a company of Texas volunteers and was elected colonel. Most of his unit decided, however, to return home as soon as their six-month term of enlistment was up, leaving the frustrated Johnston again without a command. But General Zachary Taylor had been impressed by his bearing and named him a staff officer.

In the battle for Monterrey, in September 1846, he distinguished himself for gallantry and leadership in the attack on the Diablo Redoubt. "Here, there and everywhere the magnificent voice of Johnston ... was to be heard above the din," wrote Mexican War historian Alfred Hoyt Bill. "He encouraged and directed the men with sound common sense." Also participating in this fight were future generals Braxton Bragg, Joseph Hooker, Grant, and Davis, whose path once again had touched that of his old friend.

That engagement ended Johnston's combat experience in the war, and he returned to Texas and an unsuccessful struggle to save his failing plantation. But his luck had turned. Taylor, elected president in 1848, heard of his former officer's plight and assigned him the job of army paymaster for western Texas with the rank of major. Taylor called him "the finest soldier I ever commanded," and the word was out to find Johnston a more suitable position. The new post, at least,

An etching based on a miniature portrait of Johnston shows the general at age 35, around the time of his service in Texas. ***Battles and Leaders of the Civil War***

gave him the chance to stabilize his finances until a better opportunity came.

That occurred when Davis, now elevated to secretary of war, named him commander of the newly formed Second Cavalry with the rank of colonel. This elite unit included an old West Point friend, Robert E. Lee. Also serving under him were future Confederate general William J. Hardee, who would be with Johnston in Kentucky in 1861, and the future Union general, George Thomas.

Johnston was then promoted to the command of the Department of Texas, further enhancing a growing reputation for competence. General Scott, who had invited him to join his staff three decades before and was now the highest ranking officer in the military, called him "a Godsend to the Army and to the country."

In 1857, Johnston was handed the most delicate assignment of his career. Concern was growing over the Mormon territory of Utah. There were reports that Brigham Young was leading the church into open defiance of American law and had instituted theocratic rule.

This came as a welcome diversion in Washington, where political leaders around President James Buchanan were eager to rouse public opinion over something other than the intractable issue of slavery. It was decided to send a military expedition against the Mormons and restore federal authority.

But Young was not inclined to give in. He called in all the far-flung settlements of the church and prepared to make a stand in the Great Salt Lake Valley. Advance parties were sent east along the Oregon Trail to destroy available forage for the advancing federal army, which was forced to spend an ineffectual winter near Fort Bridger, Idaho. Public opinion turned sharply against the expedition, and the press began calling it "Buchanan's Blunder."

It was then that Johnston was thrust into the middle of this mess, promoted to brigadier and placed in command of the stalled force. It was a prickly situation. Johnston had 2,000 men, but it would have taken ten times that number to pacify and occupy Utah. Instead, he patiently reached a compromise. Through interme-

After impressing General Zachary Taylor with his command of Texas volunteers, Johnston distinguished himself at the Battle of Monterrey. ***Library of Congress***

Johnston's fortunes improved following the Mexican War as influential associates secured for him high-ranking positions in the army. *Texas State Library and Archives Commission*

diaries, the Mormons apologized for destroying government provisions. Johnston decided that was good enough and accepted it. Young then gave consent for the troops to enter Utah. They marched quietly through Salt Lake City and settled uneventfully in a base south of the capital.

That seemed to satisfy everyone. The Mormons relaxed, the troops stayed on with nothing much to do for three years, and Johnston's diplomatic skills won him a promotion to commander of the military department of California. He was able to bring his family west to the beautiful U.S. Army post in the middle of San Francisco Bay, Alcatraz. According to the grapevine, he was now in line to succeed Scott in Washington when the old general decided to retire.

But events outran such plans. When Johnston was told that Texas had voted for secession, he resigned his commission in April 1861 and announced that he would join the Confederacy. He felt honor-bound, however, to remain at his post until officially relieved. When he was told later that federal authorities had feared he would turn the post over to the Confederacy, Johnston was scandalized.

Even his return to the South was the stuff of epic. Along with 30 other officers who chose the Confederate cause, he rode on horseback from Los Angeles across the Southwest, dodging U.S. Army patrols and Apache raiders, until making it back to Texas in late July. From the moment he arrived in New Orleans by steamship and embarked on the train trip to Richmond, he was greeted as a hero. Cheering crowds turned out to salute him at every stop along the way.

When he arrived at the presidential residence, Davis leaped from a sickbed to hail him, saying that he recognized his tread upon the staircase. "I hoped and expected that I had others who would be generals," said Davis. "But I knew I had one, and that was Sidney Johnston."

Celebration over the Southern victory at Manassas was still in progress when Johnston received his appointment as a full general, with command over the whole of western operations. Davis postdated the appointment so that his old friend would outrank every other field commander in the Confederacy. No one minded. The rest of the South had caught Davis's enthusiasm, and as Johnston returned west to take up his post in Nashville, it was believed that the best possible man had assumed command in the war's most critical region.

Johnston, however, had no idea what he was walking into. He was being asked to defend a front that stretched for 500 miles, from the Cumberland Gap in eastern Kentucky all the way across the Mississippi River and into Arkansas. Four federal armies opposed him along this line, and to counter all this Johnston had fewer than 50,000 men. He was made to understand very quickly that there was small chance of reinforcement.

When he appealed to the governors of neighboring states for men, he was immediately rebuffed. "Our own coast is threatened," wired the governor of Alabama. "It is utterly impossible for me to comply with your request," was the response from Georgia.

"Our people do not comprehend the magnitude of the danger that threatens," he complained to his old friend, Davis. But when the Confederate president received Johnston's request for help, he grew agitated. "My God," he exclaimed. "Why did General Johnston send for arms and reinforcements?... Where am I to get arms or men?"

Weak central authority and the doctrine of states' rights, which in Southern minds was the whole point of the war, made Johnston's request impossible to fill. Ultimately, Mississippi and Tennessee, realizing the

Johnston's diplomacy defused a tense situation with Brigham Young and his Mormon community, allowing a peaceful procession of troops through Salt Lake City. ***Library of Congress***

threat to their territory if the line broke, did send him additional regiments. But they could not arrive fast enough to ward off a Union blow, and he was on his own as far as Richmond was concerned.

The three federal armies in Kentucky totaled about 75,000 men. There were three natural invasion routes by which they could move against Johnston—the Mississippi, Tennessee, and Cumberland rivers. In addition, the Louisville and Nashville Railroad was aimed right at the heart of his defenses. He had to worry about movement along each of those routes.

Johnston did have some advantages, though. His command was unified. He was greatly respected by the Union forces. Most of all, the opposition had no idea what his intentions were. For all they knew, he was about to launch an invasion of Kentucky and try to take that slaveholding border state out of the Union.

Johnston understood that and knew how to capitalize on it. He issued deliberately misleading statements to Southern newspapers, exaggerating the size of his forces and promising an imminent move north, aimed at Louisville and Cincinnati.

He certainly convinced General William T. Sherman, who faced the center of Johnston's line. He wired Washington insistently that he was about to be hit by

Following his success in Utah, Johnston took command of the military department in California. ***Battles and Leaders of the Civil War***

the full force of a Southern attack. After several such alarms, Sherman was placed on medical leave with what was described later as a nervous collapse. General George McClellan observed succinctly, "Sherman's gone in the head."

But Johnston's psychological warfare could only work for so long, and it would not make up for the shortage of manpower. Eventually, the Northern armies would probe and find that out.

When that happened, it was imperative that the two forts, Henry and Donelson, located 12 miles apart and guarding the river passage to Tennessee's interior, be rigorously defended. If they did not stand fast, the line would be shattered. Johnston ordered the high ground at both places fortified. When the inevitable blow came, there he felt he could withstand it.

Unfortunately, the overall plan had a flaw in it, and that was the incompetence of his subordinates. In January 1862, Johnston's plan began to come apart on the eastern flank, at Cumberland Gap. Although the inexperienced General Felix Zollicoffer, a newspaper editor in civilian life, had been ordered to keep his army on the south side of the Cumberland, he crossed over and prepared to engage a numerically superior Union army with the river at his back.

He was routed at Beech Grove, and when the near-sighted commander, clad in a white raincoat, lost his way in the rain and began shouting orders to federal troops, he was shot dead.

Upon hearing of this fiasco, Johnston issued a call from his Nashville headquarters to prepare for the coming onslaught at his center. "The country must now be roused to make the greatest effort it will be called upon to make during the war," he said. "No matter what the sacrifice may be, it must be made, and without loss of time.... All the resources of the Confederacy are now needed for the defense of Tennessee."

It was typical of his direct and inspirational style. But he might as well have been shouting at the wind. The Union army was equipped with ironclad gunboats, and they were advancing down the Tennessee River on a totally unprepared Fort Henry.

While Johnston had ordered the high ground fortified, General Lloyd Tilghman, although an engineer by training, couldn't quite seem to grasp the urgency of the situation. "It is most extraordinary," Johnston said when informed of the lagging work. "I ordered General Polk [Tilghman's superior] four months ago to at once construct those works. And now, with the enemy upon us, nothing of importance has been done. It is most extraordinary."

He then wired Tilghman to work all night if need be to complete the defensive works. Too late. U. S. Grant and his ironclads arrived at the fort on February

When Johnston resigned to join the Confederacy, he rode across the Southwest, from California to Texas. *Library of Congress*

Despite Johnston's efforts to reinforce key points in his line, Union gunboats advanced on and captured Fort Henry. Fort Donelson surrendered shortly thereafter. ***Library of Congress***

6. Tilghman knew his defenses were wholly inadequate to withstand the coming assault. He sent most of his garrison overland to Fort Donelson, on the Cumberland River, offered what resistance he could, and surrendered the following day.

The situation was even worse at Donelson. When Fort Henry fell, Johnston understood that his position at Nashville was now untenable. Instead of evacuating Fort Donelson, however, and saving his forces there, he chose to try to hold up the Union advance. Once more he selected an inept commander, General John B. Floyd, for this critical assignment.

Floyd and his second in command, General Gideon J. Pillow, first decided they could not hold on to the fort, which was probably the correct assumption. Their best move, they felt, was to attack the federal lines before the gunboats could come up and retreat southeast through the breach they created. If they had stuck to that plan, the garrison could have been saved. Instead, after making a successful assault, they sent everyone back inside Donelson and tried to hold the fort.

When the gunboats arrived and began lobbing shells into the fort, the two generals realized they had made a big mistake. They decided to get out while they could. The two of them set off for Nashville by boat and left the garrison to negotiate a surrender.

Watching all this was cavalry Colonel Nathan Bedford Forrest. As the bombardment began, he turned to a chaplain standing nearby and said, "Parson, for God's sake pray. Nothing but God Almighty can save this fort."

Forrest had no intention of spending the rest of the war in a prison camp. Assembling his men, he told them, "Boys, these people are talking about surrendering, and I am going out of this place before they do or bust hell wide open." Forrest did make it out and was invaluable in bringing order to the subsequent Confederate evacuation of Nashville. But 12,000 men were taken prisoner in the first major Union victory of the war, a huge disaster for the South.

In the space of a few days, Johnston had lost Kentucky, middle Tennessee, and the city of Nashville, site of the South's largest iron and powder works. It was the first major urban area to fall to the North. Desperate to save the remainder of his army, Johnston managed to retreat to the rail line in Decatur, Alabama, and awaited developments.

What developed immediately was a call for his head. Southerners had taken his deliberately overoptimistic reports of the winter at face value. They could not understand how Johnston could possibly have been beaten so easily with that sort of numerical advantage, never realizing the numbers he had given out were a sham.

Historians have criticized him for handling his

Johnston faced the forces of Gen. Ulysses S. Grant during his western campaign. ***National Archives and Records Division***

bumbling subordinates with such diffidence. If he meant to defend Donelson, many of them have said, he should have taken command himself instead of leaving it to a pair of incompetents.

Johnston understood that ultimate responsibility rested with him. "The test of merit in my profession with the people is success," he wrote to a friend at this low ebb. "It is a hard rule but I think it is right." He explained to Davis: "I observed silence, as it seemed to me the best way to serve the cause of the country."

A delegation from Tennessee called upon Davis to demand Johnston's removal because he was "no general." The president waved them away. "If Sidney Johnston is no general," he told them, "we had better give up the war, because we have no generals."

Fortunately for Johnston, the condition of Tennessee's roads in late winter made it impossible for the armies of Grant and Don Carlos Buell to pursue him. Grant, instead, proceeded by water along the Tennessee River. He encamped near the town of Pittsburg Landing, just north of the Mississippi border, waiting for better weather to finish off Johnston.

But Johnston recognized that Grant's delay was his chance. If he could not blunt or halt the Northern advance where it stood, Grant would roll over Mississippi in a matter of weeks.

Another Confederate force under General Pierre G. T. Beauregard had assembled at Corinth, Mississippi, 20 miles south of Grant's position. Because he commanded interior lines of rail communication, Johnston was able to gather 40,000 men at Corinth in a matter of days. That was almost equal to the number Grant had. But the advantage would quickly dissipate. Buell was moving south to join Grant, and when the two federal armies were unified, they would outnumber Johnston by 35,000 men.

These few weeks at the end of March were Johnston's defining moment as a soldier. He had to make a battered army believe in itself again, convince his men that they had the capacity to fight, and draw up a plan to strike Grant before he knew the blow was coming.

Across the Confederate command, the critical fight taking shape was well understood. Davis sent eager messages of encouragement, and so did Johnston's old friend, Lee. "No one has sympathized with you in the troubles with which you are surrounded more sincerely than myself," wrote his colleague. "You have [the enemy] divided, keep him so if you can."

But there was so little time. Buell would probably arrive in the first week of April, and if the attack did not come by then, the opportunity would be gone. Moreover, an anticipated supporting force of 15,000 troops from Arkansas found itself involved there in the Battle of Pea Ridge and could not get to Corinth in time.

On April 2, Johnston ordered a movement on Grant within two days. Beauregard was given the responsibility. The Creole general used as his model, of all things, Napoleon's battle plan at Waterloo, which called for attacks coordinated in three distinct waves. Beauregard, apparently, chose to disregard the final outcome of that engagement.

Napoleon's troops also were seasoned veterans, accustomed to the face of war. Johnston's men, although enthusiastic, were not. Few of them had ever been under fire. Even getting them into the right order of march from the base camp at Corinth turned out to be an ordeal. Units turned up missing, blocked from joining the proper corps by other units similarly lost.

Beauregard was distraught, rain came pouring down, and the offensive was bogged in the mud before it could even begin. When a few recruits fired their rifles to see if they would still work in the rain, their horrified superiors ran to quiet them before they gave away their approach to the Union pickets.

Johnston remained unperturbed by the absence of

At Shiloh, Grant had to rally his forces after initial Union retreat. During this same battle, Johnston died from blood loss after a Minie ball struck him in the leg. ***Library of Congress***

the Arkansas forces or by the weather or the confusion. When Beauregard implored him to hold off and return to Corinth because the army was not ready to attack, Johnston shook his head. "I would fight them if they were a million," he said. "They can present no greater front … than we can, and the more men they crowd in there the worse we can make it for them."

On April 6, two days later than planned, his forces were finally in position to strike.

Until this April morning, one week short of a year after the guns had begun firing at Fort Sumter, no one really understood the calamitous nature of this war. There had only been three major battles, so far. At the biggest of them, First Manassas, the total dead on both sides was given as 805, with a casualty rate at less than 10 percent of total forces engaged. But here at Shiloh, there would be 3,477 dead and almost one of every four of the 102,000 soldiers involved would be killed, wounded, or missing. It dashed any hope that the war would be anything short of a long and bloody ordeal.

Johnston had a message to the troops read by each regiment's colonel. It concluded: "The eyes and hopes of eight millions of people rest upon you. You are expected to show yourself worthy of your race and lineage; worthy of the women of the South, whose noble devotion in this war has never been exceeded in any time. With such incentives to brave deeds, and with the trust that God is with us, your generals will lead you confidently to the combat, assured of success."

Right until the moment that the guns opened up, however, Beauregard was still arguing for a return to Corinth. The noise stopped him as he spoke.

"The battle has opened, gentlemen," said Johnston. "It is too late to change our dispositions. Tonight we will water our horses in the Tennessee River."

With that he signaled his horse, Fire-Eater, to move towards the sound of the guns. His life now could be numbered in hours.

Despite all the dire predictions, the first Confederate assault swept forward with surprising ease. Grant, astonishingly, had not entrenched. His entire attention was focused on combining his force with Buell's and continuing his offensive. He never imagined that he would be attacked.

There had been a few scattered indications, but the only Union general who observed them was Sherman. Returned from sick leave, he was very cautious about reporting a suspected attack for fear he would be permanently labeled as mentally unstable. Johnston had fooled him once, and Sherman would not let it happen again. Even when the actual attack began, Sherman refused to believe the reports. "You must be badly scared over there," was his reply.

The horrified Grant rode quickly to the front to try

At turns celebrated and vilified, Johnston in death reestablished his hero's status. Thousands turned out to witness his body's return to Texas for burial. ***Library of Congress***

to stem the wholesale retreat. With Beauregard controlling the rear area from Shiloh Church, the log structure that would give its name to the battlefield, Johnston, rode to his forward lines. The troops stood and cheered as he passed by.

Historian Bruce Catton described Shiloh as "a grab bag full of separate combats." No distinct front lines formed on the first day of battle as men tried to form up with whomever they saw and fire back on those firing at them. Beauregard's own New Orleans unit, dressed in blue, came under attack from other Confederates.

Not only was there confusion in the fighting, but many of the Southern troops, some of whom hadn't eaten a full meal since leaving Corinth, stopped to plunder the abandoned Union tents. Johnston was horrified at this breakdown in discipline and railed at the men, ordering them forward.

"None of that, sir," he called out to a young lieutenant in rebuke. "We are not here for plunder." Then, realizing the men were looting out of hunger, he leaned down from the saddle and picked up a tin cup from the Union mess. "Let this be my share of the spoils today," he said, and directed the soldiers to the front. He held the cup in his hand for the rest of the day.

The battle plan called for turning Grant's left and cutting him off from the river. But several federal units combined to make a stand at a narrow lane overgrown with brush, known afterwards as the Sunken Road. Resistance here was so fierce that the Confederates referred to the position as "the Hornets' Nest."

Every attempt to charge the nest frontally was cut to bits by the Union forces. The holdup here meant that the left wing of the Confederate assault was dangerously overextended and in danger of being cut off by a Union counterattack. Johnston, greatly concerned, rode to a peach orchard where artillery had been concentrated to blast away at the hornets.

"Men, they are stubborn," he called, as he tried to organize another charge. He extended his tin cup and touched the tip of a soldier's bayonet. "We must use the bayonet. These must do the work. I will lead you."

With that, Johnston galloped towards the front. His troops, cheering wildly, raced behind him, clearing away all opposition in their path. It was the culminating moment of the general's career, an exhibition of gallantry that lived forever in the memories of those who witnessed it.

Johnston returned to the original position, his eyes shining with a warrior's glee. The air had been alive with bullets, and his uniform was shredded in several places. The sole of one boot had been cut in half. "They didn't trip me up this time," he said to one of his aides, Governor Isham G. Harris of Tennessee.

Suddenly, Johnston reeled in the saddle and slumped to one side. Harris quickly grabbed his shoulders to prevent him from falling and called, "General, are you hurt?" "Yes," was Johnston's reply, "and I fear seriously."

Harris guided the general's horse to a ravine and pulled Johnston from the saddle, frantically searching for the wound. Finally, he saw that his right boot was filled with blood. A bullet had struck the femoral artery in his leg, and Johnston was bleeding to death.

A tourniquet might have been able to staunch the flow of blood until medical help arrived, and there was one in the general's pocket. But Johnston had insisted that his own staff physician be used to treat a group of wounded Union prisoners. Neither Harris nor any of the other aides at hand had any medical training. Instead of applying a tourniquet, they tried giving the general brandy.

Apparently in no pain, Johnston looked at them blankly, the liquid running out of his mouth. "Johnston," cried Harris desperately, "do you know me? Do you know me?"

There was no answer. The general was dead. It was about 2:30 P.M., seven and a half hours after the first shots of the battle were fired. The tree under which he died remains encircled by an iron fence as a memorial at the Shiloh National Military Park.

A later autopsy revealed that he had been struck by a Minie ball fired by an Enfield rifle. Given the angle of entry, it was quite possible that the shot had been fired by one of the Southern soldiers behind him during the charge on the Union lines. Historians have pointed out that Enfields were not generally used by federal troops in the Western theater at this point of the war.

Within days, the man who had been vilified in the South only weeks before was being hailed as a fallen hero whose loss was irreparable. Davis was inconsolable when he learned of the death of his old friend. "The fortunes of a country hung by a single thread on the life that was yielded on the field of Shiloh," he said. Many Confederate leaders were similarly convinced that if Johnston had lived, his army would have carried on the momentum and won the battle—perhaps, even, the war. That, however, is a rather thin supposition.

By the evening of the first day, a unit of Mississippi cavalry, as Johnston had promised, did water their horses at the Tennessee River. But these few were the only Confederate soldiers to advance that far. By that time, the force of the Southern assault was spent.

Grant had managed to form a defensive line, and although Beauregard pressed the attack on the next day, keeping the news of Johnston's death from the troops, the two federal armies had at last combined and achieved numerical superiority. Even if Johnston had lived, it is unlikely that the outcome at Shiloh would have been any different.

Historian Albert Castel says that Johnston was undone throughout his brief tenure by incompetent subordinates, and there is little reason to believe that situation would have improved as the war progressed. "Probably the most he could have done," writes Castel, "was prolong effective Confederate resistance in the West by avoiding the blunders and consequent disasters of his successors. This may not seem like much, but it might have been enough ... to cause the North to lose the will to continue fighting."

Johnston was entombed in New Orleans. When the war was over, the remains were taken to his adopted home state, Texas. Federal authorities declared that no public display would be allowed at his funeral procession. But thousands of Texans followed his coffin silently through the streets of Galveston, Houston, and finally Austin, where he was laid to rest in a hero's grave on the lawn of the State Capitol.

JOHN BELL HOOD

"Hood is a bold fighter. I am doubtful as to other qualities necessary."

Robert E. Lee to Jefferson Davis, July 12, 1864

Everyone who met him liked him almost at once. He was a tall man, six foot two, big-chested and broad-shouldered, like a soldier out of a romantic novel. His beard was almost blond, and his dark blue eyes, as women noticed instantly, were deeply sad.

His voice was clear, and he moved with a sort of graceful strength. John Bell Hood was, in short, the image of a brilliant leader, a man who inspired respect and admiration.

And the man could fight. In a few short months, Hood's Brigade became the most formidable unit in the Army of Northern Virginia, a fearless band led by a man who wanted to be where the battle was the thickest.

He was adored by his men. But he possessed two major flaws. He was incapable of exercising independent command, and he was too ready to blame subordinates when his plans did not turn out.

While his career under Lee and James Longstreet is filled with one glorious episode after another, as the commander of the Army of Tennessee he was an utter failure. He finally resigned his command after leading his troops into two of the worst defeats suffered by the Confederates in the war.

One arm was shattered at Gettysburg, and no sooner did he return to battle than a leg was lost at Chickamauga. He had to be strapped into his saddle like a latter-day El Cid, but that only seemed to enhance the aura about him.

He was, indeed, reported slain at Chickamauga, and if that had actually occurred, he would be remembered as among the most successful of Southern generals. But it was Hood's fate to be promoted beyond his capacity, and the fact that he had deliberately undercut the man he succeeded made his final failure all the more poignant.

His eagerness to do battle with superior forces was described by Douglas Southall Freeman as "an irrepressible rashness." But that is exactly what Davis admired in him. He was tired of generals who gave up ground without a fight, never realizing that it was the wisest way to conduct a portion of the war.

"I have so often urged that we should force the enemy to give us battle," Hood wrote to General Braxton Bragg just before being given command of the western army, "as to almost be regarded as reckless by the officers high in rank in this army, since their views have been so directly opposite."

As it turned out, those officers were right, and Hood's gallant notions were devastating.

Although he rose to fame as the leader of a Texas brigade, men who sang "The Yellow Rose of Texas" as they entered battle, Hood lived in that state only briefly. He was a Kentuckian by birth but came to identify with Texas during his military service on the frontier. When his own state failed to secede, it seemed natural to him to join the Confederate Army as a Texan.

He was the son of a doctor, as was his fellow Kentuckian Albert Sidney Johnston. Hood, in fact, served under Johnston, who also came to regard himself as a Texan, in the Second Cavalry.

Dr. John W. Hood had planned a medical career for his son. The Hoods came to Kentucky in 1784 from Virginia, and the doctor's father, Luke Hood, was an enthusiastic Indian fighter. He accompanied General Anthony Wayne on his Ohio expedition of 1794 and fought at Fallen Timbers.

Luke's children grew up in Bluegrass comfort, however, and John W. studied medicine at the University of Pennsylvania. He never actually earned a medical degree, but that wasn't especially regarded as necessary in those times.

Hood was practicing in the town of Owingsville when John Bell was born in 1831. Within a few years, the doctor was a prosperous landowner and traveled east each year to lecture on his theory of using "abdominal supports" (apparently, some sort of truss) to correct all health problems. He gathered a group of young students around him in Kentucky. They were drawn by his ideas, although it was nothing quite as grand as a "medical school," which is how his son described it in his memoirs.

Dr. Hood offered his son a European education if he studied medicine. But the bellicose spirit of his grandfather, having skipped a generation, now descended upon John Bell. He talked his father into allowing him to attend West Point instead, although the doctor was none too happy about this career path.

John P. Dyer, in the biography *The Gallant Hood*, quotes the elder Hood as saying: "If you can't behave, don't come home. Go to the nearest gatepost and butt your brains out."

While Hood's performance at the Military Academy never reached that level of desperation, it was far from outstanding. He ranked 44th in his 55-man class of 1853. At one point, he had accumulated 196 demerits, four short of expulsion, and only an encouraging talk with his classmate, the future Union Lieutenant General John Schofield, persuaded him to stay.

Upon graduation, he was immediately posted to California, where he served with Captain U. S. Grant but was overcome by the boredom of the remote setting. It was with relief that he was transferred to the Second Cavalry, under the command of Lieutenant Colonel Albert Sidney Johnston and Colonel Robert E. Lee.

This was an elite regiment, about to be transferred from the Jefferson Barracks, in St. Louis, to Texas. Hood's father had taken sick and would die in 1857, and during this time he developed a rather filial attachment to Lee, who had been superintendent at West Point during his cadet days.

Noticing the way the young officer's good looks attracted some of the less reputable women in the area, Lee gave him some fatherly advice. "Never marry," he said, "unless you can do so in a family which will enable your children to feel proud of both sides of the house."

It was spoken like a true Virginia aristocrat and Hood, apparently, took it to heart. He would not marry for another 11 years, and when he did it was into a suitable New Orleans family.

Hood did have an outlet for his youthful recklessness, though. In the summer of 1857, while on patrol in Comanche country, he ran headlong into an ambush. He took an arrow through his left hand, pulling the shaft out himself, but managed to fight off the attackers at a cost of two dead. It was his first combat experience, and he was commended for it. But a pattern of attacking against great odds had been set.

A tenacious fighter, John Bell Hood commanded one of the most formidable brigades in Lee's Army of Northern Virginia. He did not fare so well in the West. ***Library of Congress***

A number of assignments in Texas followed. But when he went home in 1860 to help clear up his father's estate, he was told to report to West Point as chief of cavalry. It was a prestigious appointment for a 29-year-old officer, but Hood asked that it be rescinded.

He found no appeal in a staff job and felt that the assignment would leave him at a disadvantage in the event of war, an event which he clearly saw coming. By the time he returned to Texas, in the spring of 1861, the

A Kentuckian by birth, Hood identified himself as a Texan after his service in that state in the Second Cavalry. ***Library of Congress***

national break had been made, and Hood knew which side he was on.

He resigned from the U.S. Army, went to the temporary Confederate capital at Montgomery to receive a commission as first lieutenant, and was sent on to Richmond.

The young officer was assigned to General John Magruder, and because Hood identified himself as a Texan, he was placed in charge of the rough-hewn Fourth Texas Infantry. Hood proved to be an inspirational leader who turned a rather ragtag bunch of frontiersmen into a highly motivated unit.

"I lost no opportunity whenever the officers or men came to my quarters," he would write, "or whenever I chanced to be in conversation with them, to arouse their pride, to impress upon them that no regiment in the army should ever be allowed to go forth upon the battlefield and return with more trophies of war than the 4th Texas."

Magruder was so impressed with the results that he promoted Hood to captain. This offended captains with more seniority, so Magruder solved that problem by making Hood a major. By March of 1862, he was regarded as one of the most promising young officers in the army and was promoted to brigadier general.

All that was satisfying, but the true test was battle, and Hood's Brigade had not yet met it. That chance would come in May, at Eltham's Landing, Virginia. This was a small engagement in which Hood was ordered to hold up a federal force, part of George McClellan's advance against Richmond, until General Joseph E. Johnston could retreat to new lines.

Hood was riding 50 feet in front of his men when he encountered a federal skirmish line. He had ordered his men not to load until they were told, because he didn't want to risk confused firing in this heavily wooded area. One of his men, fortunately, had disregarded the order and brought down a skirmisher who had Hood in his sights.

The fight was only a scrape, but it established Hood's reputation for gallantry. It was at Gaines Mill, however, on June 27, that this reputation would soar.

Lee's counteroffensive in the Seven Days Battles had come to a halt against stout Union defenses. Repeated attacks on them were thrown back in a full day of fighting. Finally, at 7 P.M. in the long midsummer twilight, Lee asked Hood if he could break the line.

"I don't know whether I can or not," was the reply. "But I can try." Hood then returned to his men and told them to drop their knapsacks and blankets and get ready to follow him to the Union lines.

Wounded men from General Ambrose P. Hill's division, which had tried for hours to take the position, actually grabbed at their legs and tried to stop Hood's Brigade from making what they regarded as a charge into certain death. But Hood and the Georgians of Colonel Evander Law broke through the defenses that had stopped them.

When Stonewall Jackson surveyed the battlefield later, he would say: "These men are soldiers indeed!"

The official report on the battle noted that almost all of the dead in Hood's Brigade were on the side of the swamp where the attack had begun, with very few at the federal line. As Freeman notes: "Evidently, the Federals had abandoned all resistance on that part of the line as soon as those fierce soldiers were upon them."

Hood's charge was regarded as the single most brilliant achievement during the Seven Days, and his soldiers were viewed as the best combat troops in the army. He was now 32 years old and obviously being measured for bigger things.

An indication of how big came when his temper got him into trouble with Longstreet in August, immediately after Second Manassas. Several new federal ambulances were captured in the fight by Hood's scouts. A few days later, the commander of another brigade asserted his authority over these vehicles and ordered Hood to turn them over to him.

Hood refused, saying that "I would cheerfully have obeyed directions to deliver them to General Lee's Quartermaster for the use of the army," but another brigadier was not entitled to them. The complaint was brought to Longstreet, who ordered Hood arrested for insubordination and sent back from his troops to await trial.

Lee quickly reversed the decision, allowing Hood to remain with his men although not exercising command. He knew that he would be needed soon. Lee said, in fact, that with a word of apology from Hood he would rescind the entire matter. Hood refused, saying that he was not to blame.

Lee decided he would take no action until after the upcoming battle. Following Hood's performance at Antietam, however, the ambulance case was a dead issue.

During the opening of this engagement, Hood's Brigade was held in reserve behind Jackson to give his men a chance to cook the first hot breakfast rations they had been issued in weeks. But Jackson's position, in a cornfield on the Confederate left, came under enormous pressure from the artillery of General Joseph Hooker.

Just as it seemed that Hooker's infantry would sweep over Jackson, the Texans under Hood came rushing into the fight. They arrived in a bad mood, too, because they had been forced to throw aside their hot meal when the call came in.

Antietam was one of the worst engagements of the war in terms of casualties as a percentage of troops engaged. Losses on both sides totaled more than 26,000 out of 127,000 men involved. What made it even more appalling was how rapidly the losses of high officers mounted. By the time Hood's Brigade came in, all but two of the regimental commanders in one Confederate division had gone down, and elsewhere colonels had to assume division command.

With Hood holding the breach in the line, Jackson sent couriers to him, asking whether he needed help. Hood's reply was repeated for weeks throughout the army: "Tell General Jackson unless I get reinforcements I must be forced back … but I am going on while I can."

And so he did, advancing into a fire even more deadly than at Gaines Mill. So thickly were the bodies piled here that Hood would write later: "Never before was I so consciously troubled with fear that my horse would further injure some wounded fellow soldier, lying helpless on the ground."

With Jackson unable to send any help to him, the order came from Lee to release two more divisions to help Hood. When one of the officers arrived at the scene of this carnage, he asked Hood: "Where is your division?" Hood answered, "Dead on the field."

Hood's attack had prevented a Confederate disaster and even the hard-to-please Jackson was enormously impressed. "It gives me pleasure to say," he wrote in urging Hood's promotion to major general, "that his duties were discharged with such ability and zeal as to command my admiration. I regard him as one of the most promising officers of the army."

Lee let the ambulance affair dwindle away, and on October 11 Hood received his promotion. He was assigned to Longstreet's corps. Although his Brigade had suffered enormously at Antietam, it would remain a first-rate fighting unit throughout the war. While led by different commanders, it would always bear the name of Hood.

His reputation as a fighter was secure, but there soon would be questions over his effectiveness as an administrator. An inspection in November had turned up numerous deficiencies in arms and supplies and showed "inexcusable neglect on the part of its officers."

Arms were in bad order, according to the official report. The camp was dirty and 60 men were barefoot, while only one-third were "decently clad." The report presaged difficulties ahead. It did Hood no immediate damage, but one who filed it away in his mind for future reference was Lee. It had raised some doubts.

Early in 1863, Hood was sent with Longstreet to the futile campaign in southern Virginia to keep supply routes open from North Carolina. He was bored and frustrated with the assignment, far from both the adoring ladies of Richmond and the excitement of Lee's preparations for the Battle of Chancellorsville.

Upon enlisting in the Confederate army, Hood was assigned to General John Magruder, pictured here standing on left, who quickly promoted him. *National Archives and Records Division*

At Gaines Mill, Hood broke the Federal line that had thrown back numerous previous charges. ***Library of Congress***

In the first category, he was surely one of the war's most effective campaigners. Diarist Mary Boykin Chesnut described Hood's "sad Quixotic face, the face of an old Crusader, who believed in his cause, his cross and his crown."

"To those who combined military skills with social graces," wrote Freeman, "all doors were opened. Hood ... was of the company that every hostess, however exacting, rejoiced to have in her drawing room. He not only had the reputation of being a desperate fighter, but he also had a magnificent physique, cordial manners and the suavity of a cavalier."

Throughout his life Hood had no difficulty attracting women, and from every indication he enjoyed the game.

But he was just as thoroughly attracted to battle. "Here we are in front of the enemy again," he wrote Lee from his post at Suffolk, Virginia. "I presume we will leave here so soon as we gather all the bacon in the country. When we leave here it is my desire to return to you. If any troops come to the Rappahannock, please don't forget me."

He would be recalled by Lee soon enough and get all the fighting he could want. On May 31, he rejoined the Army of Northern Virginia as it prepared for its great advance into Pennsylvania. Even then, however, Hood had to indulge himself in a bit of one-upmanship.

Jeb Stuart had organized a gala show, a review of his entire cavalry, at Culpeper, Virginia, on June 8. All the top generals were invited to attend. Hood was asked to "come and see the review and bring any of your people."

This was intended to mean a few of his staff officers. Hood, instead, showed up with his entire division. "You invited me and my people," he said to Stuart's subordinate, General Fitzhugh Lee. "And you see I have brought them."

There was an intense rivalry between infantry and cavalry, and Hood was warned by Fitzhugh to restrain any of his men from shouting the standard challenge: "Where's your mule?" That usually led to a fist-swinging brawl, an unseemly event with the commanding general in attendance.

In his book, *Wearing of the Gray*, John Esten Cooke quotes one of Hood's troopers as muttering, "Wouldn't we clean 'em out if old Hood would only let us loose on 'em." But it went no further than mutters.

Besides, things would turn serious quickly. Within days came the opening of the Gettysburg campaign. On the second day of the battle, it was Hood who was called on for the critical assault on the Round Tops, on the far Union left.

But a badly flawed reconnaissance had failed to spot the federal buildup there. Lee's plans unintentionally called for a direct assault against a large body of well-entrenched troops. Lee and Longstreet had already debated the battle plan, and Longstreet reluctantly—there are those who would use the word belatedly—accepted the commander's decision.

As Hood approached his position, however, he could see the large force that lay opposite him on the heights. He urgently sent a courier to Longstreet reporting that his scouts had found that the southern edge of the Round Tops was almost undefended. If he could delay the attack and flank their position instead, Hood was sure he could take it easily.

But Longstreet already had squabbled with Lee and been overruled. He was in no mood to try again. "General Lee's orders are to attack up the Emmitsburg Road," he told the messenger, and said that should be relayed to Hood.

Within moments a second and then a third messenger came from Hood, asking in increasingly forceful terms whether the plans could be redrawn. The answers he received were identical. The attack had to be where Lee had ordered it.

Hood finally accepted what had to be. Within 20 minutes of the start of the assault, he went down with a wound that would leave his left arm permanently crippled. Although it at first appeared to be minor, the pain was unbearable and left him dazed. Hood realized he would have to leave the field and relinquish command.

The assault continued under Law, and after a hand-to-hand struggle, portions of the division managed to establish a forward defensive line. But it was almost completely exposed on three sides. Longstreet had held back the supporting force, anticipating that he would throw it into the fight at a time when the Union defenders had been weakened by the battering of Hood's assault.

But the piecemeal plan could not dislodge the troops on Little Round Tops, and its failure led to the next day's debacle with General George Pickett.

Hood was removed to a hospital in Charlottesville, Virginia, where the arm was saved from amputation. He would, however, never regain full use of it.

Little more than two months after Hood suffered his wound, Longstreet's corps was ordered by Lee to join General Braxton Bragg in Georgia, outside of Chattanooga. Hood had been courting the lovely Sally Preston in Richmond, and before he left, his arm still in a sling, he proposed to her. She gave him no answer, although Hood was under the impression that she would accept.

According to Mary Boykin Chesnut, every officer romantically linked with Sally had been killed or seriously wounded immediately thereafter. Now it was Hood who was smitten, and he was heading for Chickamauga.

His train arrived on September 18. Upon hearing the sound of firing from seven miles away, he mounted his horse while it was still in the boxcar and then leaped out to find the battle. By evening he was involved in the fight and quickly took an important crossing of Chickamauga Creek, at Reed's Bridge.

Longstreet wouldn't arrive until late the next day and Bragg placed Hood in command of his own three brigades, as well as two divisions from the Army of Tennessee. He was dismayed at the low morale he found among the officers of this army and resolved to get their attitude straightened out as quickly as possible. It was Hood's experience that the best way of doing that was to go on the attack.

He got his wish on September 20. Longstreet's assault that day broke through the federal lines. But as Hood rode forward to rally his men, with the offensive reaching its critical point, he toppled from his horse. He had been hit in the upper thigh by a rifle bullet. The bone was shattered, and the leg had to be cut off on the field.

"Go ahead," he murmured before falling into unconsciousness, "and keep ahead of everything." Three days later, Sally Preston read in the Richmond papers that her lover was dead and being eulogized as "a noble leader of gallant soldiers." But on the following day, Longstreet wired Richmond that Hood was recovering at the home of one of his officers and being recommended for promotion to lieutenant general.

By October, he was restlessly asking when he could return to the field. Members of his old Brigade passed

Hood's brigade held a breach in the Confederate line at Antietam, preventing a Confederate disaster, but the death toll on both sides was high. *Library of Congress*

Diarist Mary Boykin Chesnut described Hood's countenance as a "sad Quixotic face, the face of an old Crusader." *Dictionary of American Portraits*

Hood followed his orders to assault the heavily defended Round Tops at Gettysburg. Early in the fight, he received a wound that permanently crippled his arm. *Library of Congress*

the hat, and although he would never lead them again, they raised $5,000 to buy their beloved general an artificial limb.

But when Sally saw her soldier again in November, he was not the same man. At the age of 32 he now moved painfully on crutches, trouser leg hanging empty, with a face that seemed to have aged years in just a matter of weeks.

When he heard rumors that she was to be engaged to other Richmond bachelors, Hood bitterly responded: "I think I will set a mantrap near your door and break some of those young fellows' legs."

But his promotion had come through, and he was about to leave again, joining Joseph E. Johnston's army in Georgia. Against her family's protests, Sally accepted Hood's proposal and was engaged.

"Do you believe I like him now," she asked Mrs. Chesnut defiantly. Mrs. Chesnut wrote in her diary that she doubted it.

He joined Johnston at his headquarters in Dalton, Georgia in February 1864. Until now he had served under generals who used the defensive as part of an overall approach that ultimately relied upon going on the attack. But with Johnston he was dealing with the consummate defensive tactician, and Hood soon found that he had absolutely no sympathy for this philosophy.

But he was in perfect accord with Davis, who felt that Johnston's tactics in all his campaigns had been defeatist. He blamed him for losing Vicksburg and, being a Mississippian, never forgave him for it. Now he felt that Johnston was following the same script in Georgia.

Although Hood was just five months past the loss of his leg, Johnston was happy to have such a fighter for the struggle ahead. His delight would have been tempered if he knew that Hood was filing secret reports to Davis and Bragg and seeking to undercut him.

These communications reinforced Davis's conviction that Johnston could attack the army of William T. Sherman if he really wanted to. He just didn't have it in him.

Strangely enough, when Johnston did feel that he was in position to make an attack on Sherman, near Cassville, Georgia, on May 19, Hood demurred, arguing that federal concentrations against him were too strong. None of Johnston's reports indicated such strength, nor was that the opinion of his other top general, William J. Hardee. But if Hood felt he could not attack, Johnston was not inclined to make him do so, and the army fell back again.

As Johnston reached the outskirts of Atlanta, the demand for his job was overwhelming. Davis's key cabinet advisor, Secretary of War Judah P. Benjamin, wanted Johnston out. Bragg, sent out to report on the competence of the man who was sent in to replace him for incompetence, predictably filed a statement that Johnston had to go. Powerful politicians in Georgia, fearing the damage being done to their state, also called for his dismissal.

In fact, about the only man supporting Johnston

Riding forward to rally his men at Chickamauga, Hood again received a crippling wound, this time losing his leg. ***Library of Congress***

was Lee. When informed by Davis that it was necessary to replace Johnston, Lee responded: "I regret the fact stated. It is a bad time to release the commander of an army situated as that of Tennessee. We may lose Atlanta and the army, too."

His concern was heightened when he learned that Hood was the choice as Johnston's replacement. He remembered the concerns he had about him in the past.

"Hood is a good fighter, very industrious on the battlefield, careless off," he wrote to Davis. "I have had no opportunity of judging his action when the whole responsibility rested upon him. I have a high opinion of his gallantry, earnestness and zeal. General Hardee has more experience in managing an army."

Lee's assessment was deadly accurate, but Davis was of no mind to heed. On July 17, 1864, Hood was made commander of the Army of Tennessee with the expectation that he would go on the offensive immediately. So even if Hood had been more prudent and wanted to wait for a better time to attack, he really had no choice.

In his book, *Never Call Retreat,* historian Bruce Catton summarized what followed. "As a result, the South lost 20,000 good soldiers, Atlanta, the presidential election and most of what remained of the war.... The black mark against Hood is that after he overtried his army and broke it, he complained that his soldiers had let him down."

His first attack on Sherman, three days after succeeding Johnston, was swatted aside. He planned to hit Major General George Thomas while he was in the process of crossing Peachtree Creek, northwest of the city. But Hood's information was bad, and his

Following the removal of General Joseph Johnston, Hood took over as commander of the Army of Tennessee. His three battles to save Atlanta, however, all ended in defeat. ***Library of Congress***

Sherman thwarted Hood's plan to cut his supply line by sending troops to defend his rear while taking the rest of his force on his devastating March to the Sea. *Library of Congress*

movements were too slow. By the time the corps of Hardee and General Alexander Stewart made their attack, Thomas was completely across the stream and well entrenched. The assault was a failure, with 5,000 casualties.

Hood then attempted to move Hardee's men 15 miles, clear around the Union left, which was commanded by the brilliant young Major General James B. McPherson. It was a well-designed plan. While Hood would convince Sherman that he was concentrated against his center, Hardee was to smash into McPherson's rear along the Decatur Road.

Hood attempted to retake Nashville to draw Sherman from Georgia, but he ended up losing his army and finally resigning. *National Archives and Records Division*

But Hood's plan didn't account for the weariness of the soldiers or the midsummer Georgia heat. Hardee's corps was simply too exhausted to make it all the way around McPherson in time. When the attack came, it was on the Union flank, instead.

Even so, it almost succeeded. McPherson was killed during the initial assault. Against all expectations, however, one of the North's political generals, John A. Logan, appointed by Abraham Lincoln to please friends in Illinois, rose to the occasion.

Logan rallied his men and held the line. Instead of turning the Union army, Hardee was pushed back with horrible losses, by some estimates 8,500 men. Yet another attack, on July 28 at Ezra Church, also ended in disaster, with 5,000 losses, and Sherman was still coming on.

Besides sealing the fate of Atlanta, these three battles are credited with deciding the presidential election of 1864. There was evidence throughout the summer that the North was sick of the war. Jubal A. Early was raiding again in Pennsylvania, the siege of Petersburg was taking thousands of lives, and Sherman's campaign in Georgia seemed to be going on forever.

But the Confederate evacuation of Atlanta in September gave Lincoln the battlefield success he needed to rally the electorate. Davis's change in command had only assured reelection for the man who was determined to pursue the war through to total victory.

Hood explained to Richmond that none of this had been his fault. "It seems the troops had been so long confined to trenches and had been taught to believe that intrenchments cannot be taken, so that they attacked without spirit and retired without proper effort."

But he had another plan. He would cut off Sherman's supply line by destroying the railroad in northern Georgia, forcing the Union army to withdraw to the north. Again, there was no arguing with the logic. But as it developed, Davis gave the strategy away, and Sherman refused to cooperate.

In a series of speeches in Georgia and South Carolina, Davis attempted to rally Southern spirits by asserting that Sherman had walked into a trap. He then blurted out exactly how Hood intended to attack him and compared what would happen afterwards to Napoleon's retreat from Moscow.

Grant was paying close attention and urged Sherman to take the proper countermeasures. But Sherman was in no mood to go back the way he had just come. He felt a "retrograde movement" to Tennessee would be harmful to morale. While he had no great regard for Hood as a general, Sherman knew that his army had not been destroyed, and it was still out there, 39,000 strong, waiting for him to come out of Atlanta.

What Sherman did, instead, was to send Thomas's corps north to guard his supply line and rear, and he then set out with most of his army on his devastating March to the Sea across the heart of Georgia.

"Instead of being on the defensive, I would be on the offensive," he wrote Grant, in convincing him of this strategy. "Instead of guessing at what he means to do, he would have to guess at my plans. The difference in war is full 25 percent."

With Hood off to the north, Sherman was able to sack Georgia at his leisure. The blow to Southern morale and supplies was incalculable.

Moreover, the Union force sent up to protect the railroad was able to beat off the cavalry raids ordered by Hood. It handed Stewart a major defeat at Allatoona Pass in October.

Failing to cut the railroad and with Sherman heading off in the opposite direction, Hood decided the best thing for him to do was go to Tennessee. He intended to recapture Nashville, which had fallen during the winter of 1862. That figured to be a blow to Northern morale. Afterwards, he would either head further north to threaten the Ohio River area or turn east and link up with Lee in Virginia. Surely these moves would convince Sherman to give up on Georgia and turn back north to deal with the threat.

Hood trapped the forces of General John Schofield, but they escaped and handed the Confederates a devastating loss at Franklin. *Dictionary of American Portraits*

The plan was never grounded in reality, but Hood managed to convince Lieutenant General P. G. T. Beauregard, who supervised western operations. Beauregard had a weakness for grand Napoleonic schemes, and this one was a dandy. He sent Hood on his way.

But Hood displayed a strange irresolution, almost a reluctance to getting himself in motion. It was November 21 before he finally started north. By that time Sherman already was gone from Atlanta, heading southeast to Savannah, and Thomas was back in Nashville waiting for Hood. The numerical advantage he once enjoyed over Thomas was gone.

Nonetheless, once he got himself going, he moved quickly. He managed to outflank the army of his old West Point friend, Schofield, on its way to Nashville, and was in position to cut it off at Spring Hill, north of Columbia. Hood controlled the Nashville road and had Schofield trapped between the two wings of the Army of Tennessee.

But coordination broke down among the various units. The crucial road was left unguarded overnight, and Schofield discovered the gap. With a desperate march through the darkness, which passed within a few hundred yards of the Confederate pickets, he escaped Hood's trap.

Hood was infuriated when he heard what had happened. "The best move in my career as a soldier," he wrote later, "I was thus destined to behold come to naught."

He called in his top generals, including the always dependable Patrick Cleburne, and upbraided them for failing to close his carefully laid trap.

The failure at Spring Hill has been studied exhaustively by historians, with no conclusive blame assigned. All that can be determined is that it was just another of the repeated lapses in the command structure of the Army of Tennessee.

But it redoubled Hood's determination to get at this Union force on the next day, November 30, at Franklin. In his frustration, he seemingly dispensed with all caution and attacked Schofield head-on. The result was a fiasco.

His army was shattered, taking 7,300 casualties, or three times as many as the Federals. Included in this number were 12 Confederate generals, Cleburne among them. Schofield easily escaped and moved into Nashville to join Thomas.

Hood was now too weak to mount any credible threat on the city, but he refused to retreat. Thomas slowly gathered his strength, resisting repeated messages from Grant to attack Hood immediately before he got it in his head to move towards the Ohio River. Thomas knew that was impossible, and when he delivered the blow, on December 15, he crushed what was left of Hood's army.

The Battle of Nashville cost another 6,500 Confederate casualties and the survivors straggled back to Mississippi as best they could. The Army of Tennessee had ceased to exist as a significant fighting force. Hood took full responsibility for the debacle. Once back in Tupelo, he resigned his command and left the army on January 23, 1865.

He returned to Richmond, facing severe criticism but still unbroken in spirit. He had a gallant new plan: to return to Texas and raise a force to continue the war in the west.

Before he could do it, however, Lee surrendered. Heading south with the fleeing Confederate government, Hood paid a final visit to Sally Preston at her home in South Carolina. This visit convinced him that their romance was finished, too. She would accompany her family to exile in Paris, returning in 1867 to marry the wealthy Rollins Lowndes.

Hood's vain attempt to reach Texas ended on May 30 when he was captured by a federal patrol near Natchez, Mississippi. He was, however, paroled the next day.

On his return to his adopted state, he found himself greeted as a hero. The deeds of Hood's Brigade, although now two years in the past, were still alive there. He made some business connections and soon was set up in New Orleans as a cotton factor.

In 1868, he married Anna Marie Hennen, member of a wealthy family prominent in Louisiana legal circles. They moved into a handsome home in the city's Garden District, and over the next 11 years he fathered 11 children, including three sets of twins. The joke in New Orleans was that this was the new version of Hood's Brigade.

Following the war, Hood settled in New Orleans, married, and fathered 11 children. ***National Archives and Records Division***

But he suffered a string of business reversals in 1878, many of them connected with an outbreak of yellow fever that brought business activity in New Orleans to a halt. He didn't have the funds to take his family to healthier surroundings the following summer. And when the pestilence returned, in August 1879, they were in the city.

His wife died first, on August 24, and he came down with the disease immediately afterwards. After many hours of fever and delirium, Hood followed her in death, along with his oldest daughter, on August 30. He was 48.

He left behind 10 children. A subscription program was started throughout the South to care for them. Eventually, however, it was decided that they had to be placed in separate homes, and the family was broken apart.

Those who knew Hood remarked on the look of great sadness that always seemed to be behind his eyes. In assessing his life, it seems the sadness was well founded, because any success he ever enjoyed was fated to end in tragedy.

PATRICK CLEBURNE

"He is young, ardent, exceedingly gallant but sufficiently prudent ... and has the admiration of his command."

Braxton Bragg to Jefferson Davis, in a letter recommending Cleburne's promotion to major-general, December 1862

He was born and raised in Ireland in a place called Bride Park, near the great seaport of Cork. A man of many talents, he was a pharmacist and a lawyer before finding his true calling as a military commander.

Historians call Patrick Cleburne one of the least appreciated of the Confederacy's great generals. His most recent biography, written by Craig Symonds, was, in fact, titled *Stonewall of the West,* which is not an exaggeration to those who have studied his career.

In spite of fighting under the inept commanders Braxton Bragg and John Bell Hood for most of his career, he turned his division into one of the most reliable and "hardest-hitting" forces in the Army of Tennessee. His actions during the campaigns around Chattanooga and Atlanta are regarded as masterpieces of planning matched with ferocity.

But although he had lived in Arkansas for 11 years before the war, he never truly understood the South. He could not grasp the implacable hold of slavery upon the Confederate mind and cause.

So his proposal to replace the army's depleted manpower in 1864 by freeing and arming Southern blacks was met with appalled silence. It also killed any hope of further advancement for him. Only when it was much too late did Richmond seriously consider what Cleburne had proposed and put it, hesitatingly, into effect.

By that time, Cleburne had fallen at the Battle of Franklin, one of the most sweeping and unnecessary defeats suffered by any Southern army in the entire war.

His father, Joseph Cleburne, was a medical doctor and farmer. From his mother, Mary Ann Ronayne, he was reputedly descended from English nobility. It was whispered in the family that his mother had married beneath her, but since she was already 31 at the time of the wedding, there was little more to be expected.

Patrick was named for the saint upon whose day he was born, in 1828, the third child of the family. His mother died after a difficult fourth childbirth when Patrick was only 19 months old. Joseph Cleburne then married a 19-year-old governess, Isabella Stuart, whom he had hired for his children, and Patrick regarded her as his mother for the rest of his life.

He grew up as a privileged youth, a member of the Protestant gentry in an impoverished Catholic land. When he was eight years old, the family moved to a manor, Grange House, which was regarded as the finest home in the area. He was taught by private tutors, but their instruction was weak in the Classics and in French, areas of knowledge regarded as critical for a university education.

At the death of Joseph Cleburne, in 1843, Patrick was apprenticed to a friend of his father in a nearby town and set out to prepare for the field of medicine as an apothecary. But his weakness in Latin doomed his application to Trinity College.

Ireland was then caught in the middle of the horrific potato famine. The entire country was on the move. Starving farmers and their families were evicted from their homes and wandered into the cities to beg. Others were leaving the country altogether—for England, Australia, North America, or anywhere else they could get to.

At a time when many of his future colleagues were

A native of Ireland, Patrick Cleburne strove under difficult circumstances to turn his troops into some of the toughest and most reliable in the West. ***Museum of the Confederacy, Richmond, Virginia***

learning their trade in the Mexican War, Cleburne, surrounded by this historic catastrophe, also turned to the military. With no other way to support himself, the 17-year-old youth joined the British 41st Infantry Regiment, lying about his age to gain early admission.

He joined up in the expectation that he would be sent to India, which sounded like an attractive alternative to the desolation he saw around him. He also did his best to cover up his past, although whether he did it from humiliation over failing to gain admission to the university or as a way of asserting independence from his family remains a matter of conjecture.

Because of conditions in Ireland, however, he never left the island. His regiment remained there to deal with social unrest. He was promoted to corporal, but after three years his family found where he was and purchased his discharge with a sum from his father's estate.

He had no intention, however, of remaining in Ireland. Just 12 days after his discharge, in November 1849, he was on a boat bound for New Orleans with three of his siblings, joining the great Irish migration to the United States.

He was still a man of some means compared to the abject poverty that surrounded him. But Cleburne hoped to find greater opportunities in a place unmarred by the religious and class hatreds of his homeland.

"The elements of decay and destruction," he wrote his stepmother, "seemed to me to be so deeply seated in the heart of the body social or politic that to stay would only be to witness a lingering dissolution."

Cleburne and his family moved briefly to Cincinnati, where Patrick became a clerk in a drugstore. But in the spring of 1850 he heard of a promising opportunity in the Mississippi River town of Helena, Arkansas. A friend of his employer had recently purchased a pharmacy there and was looking for a manager, perhaps one who had a view to buying into the business.

Patrick accepted and, leaving his two brothers and sister—all of whom would remain in the North—set off by steamboat to his new home. Helena, Arkansas's only port, was thriving in the midst of the great cotton boom in the Mississippi Delta region. Mark Twain was a visitor in those years and left descriptions of the place "occupying one of the prettiest situations on the Mississippi ... a perch on the southernmost group of hills on the river."

Helena was also a young place, just the sort of home Cleburne had hoped to find, with no ghosts of the past to darken it. He quickly earned a partnership in the drugstore and found several educated and congenial companions. The town, in fact, furnished no fewer than seven generals to the Confederate side, an astonishing number for such a small place.

Cleburne was born and raised in Bride Park, Ireland, near the seaport of Cork. ***Library of Congress***

In Helena, Arkansas, Cleburne struck up a friendship with Thomas Hindman, who also served as a general in the Confederacy. ***Library of Congress***

He became one of the top marksmen in the area and also acquired a love of chess. But with time to study and read, Cleburne found he had a strong interest in the law and politics. He was drawn into a friendship with Thomas Hindman (who would become another of the Helena generals), and became active in the Democratic Party.

He chose the Democrats predominantly because they opposed the Know-Nothings, a party that supported policies directed against new immigrants, especially the Irish. But in the tangled political climate of the 1850s, the Know-Nothings were allied with the Abolitionists and would provide part of the core for the new Republican Party. Cleburne's political affiliations placed him firmly on the side of the pro-slavery South.

It also nearly killed him. The vicious political squabbles of the era spilled over into a street fight in which he and Hindman exchanged gunshots with three antagonists. Cleburne killed his man but was severely wounded and for a time was given up for lost. The injury left him with permanent lung damage.

But he was cleared of any criminal charges and became something of a local hero for his show of spunk. His reputation soared even higher in his hometown in 1855. He and Hindman along with a few others remained behind during a yellow fever epidemic to nurse the sick when most of Helena's residents had fled.

So when he was admitted to the bar in 1856, Cleburne was one of the town's leading citizens, and in a few years had become one of its wealthiest, too. He acquired land, took part in railroad speculation, and developed a firm loyalty to Arkansas. More than Ireland had ever been to him it was home.

"These people have been my friends and have stood up for me on all occasions," he wrote one of his brothers. "I am with Arkansas in weal or woe."

Cleburne helped to organize a local militia, the Yell Rifles, in 1860, as men of property with some military background were doing all across the South. Even before Arkansas seceded, Cleburne went to Little Rock with his company to help seize the federal arsenal in January 1861.

The governor demanded its return to avoid trouble, and it would be another four months before the state officially left the Union. But there was little doubt where its sympathies lay.

When secession came, the Yell Rifles joined the Confederate Army. Cleburne was made a captain and then a colonel of the 15th Infantry Regiment. The outfit found itself in the thick of fighting at Shiloh, in 1862, and Cleburne, who had been promoted to brigadier general, was commended for valor.

By the time Bragg and Edmund Kirby Smith began their invasion of Kentucky late that summer, Cleburne had become one of the army's most trusted generals. At Richmond, on August 30, he was in command of a two-

Cleburne became an influential citizen of Helena, holding successful business concerns, dabbling in politics, and taking up a career in law. ***Museum of the Confederacy, Richmond, Virginia***

During the engagement at Perryville, Cleburne's troops pushed farther into the Union lines than any other Confederate unit. ***Battles and Leaders of the Civil War***

hour artillery barrage, followed by a masterfully conceived charge that rolled up the federal center.

The victory opened the way to Lexington, but Cleburne was forced out of the action for a time. While in the midst of a battlefield conversation at Richmond, he was struck by a Minie ball in his left cheek. It knocked out the teeth in his lower jaw and then exited through his still open mouth. He said later that he had "spat it out."

The wound was superficial but left him unable to speak for the remainder of the fight. Nonetheless, he was given part of the credit for its success and returned in time for the small but vicious engagement at Perryville, Kentucky, in October.

Once more, Cleburne's brigade fought well, driving Union troops from the high ground they occupied near the battlefield's center and pushing further into the federal lines than any other unit. That advance left his position exposed on both sides, however, and his horse was shot out from under him during the confusion. He also suffered a slight leg wound when a shell exploded nearby.

While most of the Confederate command regarded Perryville as a victory, Bragg decided afterwards to withdraw from Kentucky. Despite the criticism this decision drew, he had lost 20 percent of his men in the battle and failed to receive the cordial reception and military enlistments he had anticipated from Kentuckians. Withdrawal may have been the prudent thing to do, but Cleburne's actions at the two battles in the state earned him a promotion to major general in December.

Bragg's continued insistence on pulling back ever deeper into the Southern heartland, however, was starting to shake the confidence of several of his generals, including Cleburne. The retreat from Murfreesboro, Tennessee, in January 1863, following the Battle of Stones River, was met with disgust throughout the Army of Tennessee.

"I have consulted with my brigade commanders," Cleburne responded when solicited by Bragg for his written opinion. "They unite with me in personal regard for yourself...but at the same time they see with regret, and it has also met my observation, that you do not possess the confidence of the army in other respects in that degree necessary to secure success."

Other commanders responded in the same vein. But when General Joseph E. Johnston, Bragg's superior, was asked by Richmond if he would assume command, he declined. He said it would be a breach of etiquette to remove an officer and then take over the position himself. So Bragg remained at the head of a badly fractured army.

But Cleburne's greatest successes, the basis of his military reputation, were now at hand. By the middle of August, Bragg was gathering strength in nearby Georgia. He hoped that with the reinforcements finally being sent to him by Richmond he could attain a clear numerical advantage over the opposing federal force.

He also was trying to lure Union General William S. Rosecrans south of Chattanooga by convincing him that it was safe to overextend his lines, then trapping him between the mountainous spurs of Missionary Ridge and Lookout Mountain.

Bragg made his counter attack at Chickamauga Creek on September 19. There were 127,000 men engaged in this epic battle, and Bragg for once did have a slight advantage in manpower, if not the overwhelming number he was hoping for.

The two sides fought to a bloody stalemate on the

first day. With night falling and the federal left thinking it had fought off the worst that Bragg could throw at it, Cleburne suddenly came rushing out of the darkness with 5,000 men.

They had waded across the chilly creek, because getting to a bridge would have slowed them down, and then marched another four miles in soggy discomfort before launching the attack.

The Union forces had not been given time to properly entrench and Brigadier General St. John R. Liddell knew it. Cleburne was reluctant to attack in the dark over unfamiliar terrain with tired troops who had not seen action for nine months. But Liddell urged him on. "General, a minute now will be worth an hour tomorrow," he told Cleburne.

Cleburne had drilled his men long hours on firing rapidly as they advanced, and this tactic seemed to confuse the Union defenders, who thought they were being attacked by a far larger force.

"For half an hour," Cleburne said later, "the firing was the heaviest I have ever heard." An Indiana captain on the receiving end described it as "a display of fireworks that one does not like to see more than once in a lifetime."

But Cleburne's exhausted troops could not pursue the opposition in the dark, and because of a misunderstanding of orders there was a delay of several hours before the attack could be renewed in the morning. That was all the time needed for Union General George Thomas to prepare his defenses for the stand that would keep the federal army from being cut in half and earn him the nickname of the Rock of Chickamauga.

Cleburne's attack eventually crashed against this rock and fell back. But his success on the previous night had badly shredded the Union left, which then required reinforcements from other sections of the federal line. That enabled General James Longstreet to roll up its right wing and send Rosecrans hurrying back to Chattanooga.

But he had escaped the trap, and Bragg's reluctance to follow up his advantage by pressing the attack into the city made the victory at Chickamauga a hollow one. Moreover, Rosecrans had been replaced by a far more formidable opponent. Lincoln, after receiving communications from Rosecrans that, to the president, sounded "confused and stunned like a duck hit on the head," was removed in favor of U. S. Grant.

After General William T. Sherman and 20,000

At Chickamauga, Cleburne surprised Union troops exhausted from a day of fighting with a concentrated attack that nearly cut their line in two. *Library of Congress*

General George Thomas mounted the resolute defense against the Confederate assault at Chickamauga. ***Library of Congress***

additional troops arrived from Mississippi in November, Grant decided to smash his way out of the Chattanooga bottleneck. He sent Sherman against the Confederate right on Missionary Ridge, a 500-foot-high escarpment.

For the best part of a year, Sherman had rolled over every Confederate commander who had been in his way. But this time he ran up against Cleburne, who was defending Tunnel Hill, the portion of the ridge where the railroad tracks cut through the mountain.

Sherman sent six divisions against Cleburne's one in eight hours of intense fighting. But he could not move him back and, in addition, took 1,500 casualties, many of them injured when Cleburne's men rolled rocks down the hillside on their heads.

Sherman was convinced that the only way he could have been held up was if the Confederates had reinforced the line in front of him, weakening other parts of their defenses. "Go signal Grant," he told a major on his staff. "The orders were that I should get as many in front of me as possible, and God knows there are enough."

But he was wrong. There was only Cleburne and five brigades, and they had incurred just one-sixth as many casualties as they inflicted on Sherman.

Cleburne's efforts went in vain, however, because the Confederate center could not hold. On the following day, November 25, the gallant charge of General Philip Sheridan's troops broke the Southern line. It was a bitter, demoralizing defeat because Bragg had all the advantages of terrain and still could not hold on.

The retreat turned into a rout, and only Cleburne's rearguard actions managed to stave off complete disaster.

He first held off Sherman once more at Chickamauga Creek until the army could make its way across the water. "By 9 P.M. everything was across," he reported, "except the dead and a few stragglers lingering here and there under the shadows of the trees for the purpose of being captured; faint-hearted patriots succumbing to the hardships of the war and the imagined hopelessness of the hour."

But the Union pursuit into Georgia was relentless, and Bragg realized he would be overtaken unless the enemy could be delayed at Ringgold Gap, a narrow pass through which ran the rail line to Atlanta. He ordered Cleburne to "hold this position at all hazards and keep back the enemy until the artillery and transportation of the army are secure."

It was a suicide mission, and Cleburne knew it. But he didn't have to abandon hope. In the few hours left to him before the November dawn, he concealed his guns and 4,100 men at the mouth of the gap and waited for the Union troops to come. At 8 A.M., Major General Joseph Hooker obliged him, with 12,000 men.

The first five regiments that entered the gap were thrown back with heavy losses. When Hooker tried to flank Cleburne, he found the Confederate leader had anticipated the move and repulsed him again. Hooker went back at the center for a third assault and once more Cleburne could not be moved.

Finally, Grant came up, assessed the situation, and ordered Hooker to hold off until his heavy guns could be brought up in a few more hours. By that time Bragg would be out of the mountains in Dalton, Georgia, and able to get his army back in order. As soon as Cleburne received word that Bragg was safe, he ordered a withdrawal from Ringgold and rejoined the main body of the army.

He had lost 221 men, inflicted twice that many casualties on Hooker, and allowed the Army of Tennessee to survive. Grant called the affair "unfortunate," and it took away the last shred of confidence he had in Hooker's abilities.

Cleburne's official report fully reflects the pride he felt in his division's accomplishments. "Our immense train was still in view," he wrote, "struggling through the fords of the creek ... and my division, silent but cool and ready was the only barrier between it and the flushed and eager advance of the pursuing Federal army."

For his efforts, Cleburne was given a joint resolution of thanks from the Confederate Congress. It was also said in the army that he had never given up a foot of ground he was assigned to defend. This is when he began to be known as "Stonewall of the West." Six months after the original Stonewall's death, no higher accolade could be given in the South.

But Ringgold Gap was to be the pinnacle of his career. In another two months, Cleburne would drop the bomb that would blast his prospects for further advancement right off the table.

By the winter of 1864, it was generally recognized that the Confederate cause was desperate. The South, in fact, would never successfully take the offensive again. The two-to-one federal advantage in manpower finally was beginning to tell, and Lincoln was determined to get another half million men in arms during the coming year.

The South had virtually every male between the ages of 18 and 45 in uniform, with wounded veterans handling noncombat jobs. Moreover, the rate of desertions was beginning to climb. It was to this situation that Cleburne applied his lawyer's logic.

Not only was the South running short of men, he reasoned, the main reason it could not get support from overseas was because the war was perceived in Europe as a battle to maintain slavery.

Cleburne had stated before the war began that the issue of slavery was irrelevant to him. He saw the conflict as being wholly related to states' rights. "I believe the North is about to wage a brutal and unholy war on a people who have done them no wrong," he wrote in 1861, "in violation of the Constitution and the fundamental principles of government."

Many educated people in the South shared that opinion, but with the Emancipation Proclamation, Lincoln had deftly altered the perception of the war. Cleburne sincerely believed that slavery was doomed whatever happened, but the South's black population could yet be used to advantage.

On January 3, 1864, he requested to read a paper to General Joseph E. Johnston, who had finally taken over command from Bragg, and several other senior officers. In it he outlined his proposal for freeing the slaves and enlisting them in the army.

"This measure will deprive the North," he wrote, "of the moral and material aid which it now derives from the bitter prejudices with which foreigners view the institution, and its war, if continued, will henceforth be so despicable in their eyes that the sources of

With a single division, Cleburne held off the six divisions under General William T. Sherman at Missionary Ridge, inflicting six times the casualties he sustained. ***Library of Congress***

To slow the Union pursuit, Cleburne held off the troops of General Joseph Hooker at Ringgold Gap, repulsing three assaults. *National Archives and Records Division*

recruiting will be dried up. It will leave the enemy's Negro army no motive to fight for, and will exhaust the source from which it has been recruited."

Such an action, Cleburne insisted, "would remove forever every selfish taint from our cause and place independence above every question of property. The very magnitude of the sacrifice ... would appall our enemies and fill our hearts with a pride and singleness of purpose which would clothe us with a new strength in battle."

Cleburne was undeniably sincere, although the possibility that great numbers of freed slaves would want to fight alongside their former masters, who had done their best to refuse their freedom, is dubious, at best.

The officers to whom the proposal was read could barely hide their disgust. Johnston decided against forwarding it to Richmond on the grounds that it was political, and not military, in nature and so lay outside the army's responsibility. Thirteen officers did agree to sign it, however.

General Patton Anderson, who had attended the meeting, called it "monstrous ... revolting to Southern sentiment, Southern pride and Southern honor." General William H. G. Walker called it treason and said the army would mutiny if its details ever came out.

Walker was so furious that he secretly forwarded the proposal to the Confederate government in Richmond. Jefferson Davis read it and declared that its dissemination would be "productive only of discouragement, distraction and dissension." He ordered that Cleburne's paper not only be suppressed but that no discussion of its content be permitted. The proposal was buried in the Confederate archives for 30 years before being uncovered.

Secretary of War James A. Seddon assured Johnston that the paper would not be held against Cleburne, who was still considered the finest division commander in the South. Despite his continuing outstanding performance, however, Cleburne was never promoted again.

Historian D. Y. Thomas and others are convinced that if the proposal had not been written it would have been Cleburne, and not Hood, who succeeded Johnston when he was removed from command of the western army six months later outside Atlanta.

While this storm was raging, Cleburne's best friend and mentor in the army, Major General William J. Hardee, was married in Mobile on January 13. He asked Cleburne to accompany him as his best man. No sooner had the 36-year-old bachelor met the maid of honor, Susan Tarleton, than he was smitten.

He wooed her avidly and within 10 days, just as his furlough expired, asked for her hand. Letters followed, swearing romantic fidelity in courtly phrases. After another brief visit in March, she accepted his proposal. They never saw each other again.

By May, the federal drive towards Atlanta had

While serving as best man for General William J. Hardee, Cleburne fell in love with maid of honor Susan Tarleton. *Dictionary of American Portraits*

Sherman sent troops under General Oliver O. Howard against Cleburne at Pickett's Mill, but Cleburne's smaller force prevailed. ***Library of Congress***

resumed. With Cleburne on the extreme right of the Confederate line, Sherman sent three divisions under General Oliver O. Howard to turn him at Pickett's Mill. In the words of Shelby Foote, it was Howard's "ill fortune ... that the division posted in his path was Cleburne's, by common consent the best in Johnston's army."

Cleburne's well-entrenched, rapid-firing troops stopped the attack in its tracks with horrendous losses. With its survivors trying to take cover in a ravine, Cleburne ordered a counterattack in the dark, and that finished the job. Federal losses were reported at 1,457, while Cleburne's were 448. Once again he had inflicted serious damage on a much larger force.

One Union officer called the engagement "a crime." Cleburne himself was sobered at the sight of the dead in the ravine in front of his position. They had "displayed a courage worthy of an honorable cause," he wrote in his report. "The piles of his dead on this front were pronounced by the officers who have seen the most service to be greater than they had ever seen before."

Despite such defeats, nothing could stop Sherman, who simply shifted his forces to the east, forcing Johnston to overextend his army and slowly continue to retreat.

In late July, Davis replaced the prudently withdrawing Johnston with Hood, who was perceived as a man of action. Cleburne told friends privately that he doubted the wisdom of Hood's plan to go on the offensive and carry the war to the North.

"We are going to carry the war to Africa," he said, referring to the strategy of Rome's general in the Punic Wars of classical times. "But I fear that we will not be as successful as Scipio was."

Cleburne had one more price to exact from the Union army before Atlanta fell. In fighting on the outskirts of the city, on July 22, Cleburne's division found a gap in the Union line and threatened to attack the federal army from the rear.

When news of the breakthrough was brought to Major General James B. McPherson, he galloped off to view the area for himself. McPherson was regarded as the most brilliant young commander in the Union army, surely designated for higher responsibilities. Sherman was convinced that, eventually, McPherson would replace him and possibly Grant.

While riding towards the fight this day, McPherson ran into a body of Cleburne's skirmishers, who had penetrated the Union lines, and was shot dead. It was a stunning loss to the North, and Sherman wept when he received the news.

But while Cleburne's men hung on to their position on Leggett's Hill until the end of the battle, Confederate losses rose to almost 8,500 men. Hood had to withdraw, his counteroffensive a failure.

With Atlanta lost, Hood was more determined than ever to hit Sherman where it would hurt the most. But his attempt in October 1864 to cut off Sherman's supply lines in northern Georgia failed.

Hood then received the approval of western commander P. G. T. Beauregard to drive into Tennessee and then swing east to link up with Robert E. Lee's army in Virginia. This impractical, poorly executed plan came to a bloody culmination at Franklin, Tennessee, on November 30, 1864. A total of 20,000 men in 18 brigades took part in the Confederate attack at Franklin. More than one-third of them became casualties, including 13 generals either fallen or captured.

Cleburne's troops actually managed to penetrate the federal center. He had promised Hood personally that he would. Cleburne was stung by Hood's implication that he had failed to carry out his assignment at Spring Hill on the previous day's fighting, thus allowing the federal force to get away intact.

But he also knew that Hood's attack plan was inept. As he prepared his men, Cleburne spoke briefly to fellow Arkansan, Brigadier General Daniel Govan. "If we are to die," he told him with uncharacteristic grimness, "let us die like men."

After reaching the federal works, Cleburne's division came under fierce attack when federal reinforce-

After having penetrated the Union center at Franklin, Cleburne was shot through the heart. General Robert E. Lee called him "a meteor shooting from a clouded sky." *Arkansas History Commission*

ments were brought up against their exposed position. They held on as long as they could, at one point separated from the Union troops only by a mound of earthworks.

It wasn't until they fell back to their own lines that they discovered Cleburne was missing. As survivors pieced together their stories, they learned that after having two horses shot out from under him, Cleburne had been shot through the heart on the initial charge, 50 yards short of the federal lines.

A legend grew up, repeated by author Irvin S. Cobb, that Cleburne had died in his stocking feet because he had given his boots to an Arkansas soldier who had lost his own. More likely, however, the boots were taken from the corpse by scavengers, who also took his sword and watch.

He was buried near Columbia, Tennessee, before his remains were finally returned permanently to Helena in 1870.

When Susan Tarleton was given the news, she was overcome and wore mourning for a year. She did, eventually, marry another Confederate officer in 1867 but lived only one more year.

Lee called Cleburne "a meteor shooting from a clouded sky." A soldier who had fought under him recalled later that, "Men seemed afraid to be afraid where he was."

But his dear friend Hardee wrote the best epitaph. "Where this division defended, no odds broke its line; where it attacked, no numbers resisted its onslaught, save only once; and there is the grave of Cleburne."

The Difficult Men

JUBAL A. EARLY

"He is much stooped and enfeebled, but as bitter and violent as an adder. Boasts of his being unreconstructed and that he won't accept a pardon for his rebellious offenses. He has fought his battles so many times that he has worked himself into the belief that many of the exaggerated and some ridiculous stories he tells are true."

former Union General George Crook, after speaking with Early in 1890

As the summer of 1864 began, the war seemed just about finished in Northern eyes.

Robert E. Lee and his troublesome Army of Northern Virginia were bottled up behind their siege lines in Petersburg and Richmond. General Sherman was poised to take Atlanta. Surely, after three hard years, a Union victory was near.

Instead, galloping up from the Shenandoah Valley like the return of a nightmare, came Jubal Early. He raided unmolested across the upper Potomac Valley. He burned down Chambersburg, Pennsylvania. For a few days, he threatened Washington itself, coming closer to the city than any other Confederate force during the war.

Rather than Richmond falling, it seemed that it was the Union capital that would be captured. In frustration and disbelief, morale plummeted across the Northern states. Even the reelection of Lincoln, which had seemed assured beyond question a few weeks earlier, was now at risk.

For the tobacco-chewing, short-tempered, profanity-spouting Early, this was rich payback, indeed. Turned loose from the Richmond line to raise whatever havoc he could and draw away some of U. S. Grant's forces from Lee's front, Early was making the most of his chance.

Lee called him affectionately a "bad old man." Although the two were total opposites in temperament, Early had his complete confidence. The war in the Shenandoah had turned mean, a cycle of murder and fire and revenge. Early was the best man to carry on such a war.

He cared nothing for gallantry and didn't especially want to be loved. Stooped by chronic arthritis, he looked much older than his 47 years. Even after the war ended, he fought on for another 29 years with anyone unwise enough to cross him, be it the U.S. government or a former colleague.

In the end, however, he was undone by a ghost. Everything he did in the Shenandoah was compared to Stonewall Jackson's classic campaign of 1862. Early was fighting with a much smaller force, in altered circumstances, against much more formidable opposition. It didn't matter. He couldn't match the memory of Stonewall. He lost the confidence of the public, and Lee, reluctantly, finally had to recall him from command.

His family was Old Virginia, certainly not as socially prominent as the Lees but well connected in their neighborhood. They had established themselves around the town of Rocky Mount, in the foothills of the Blue Ridge, in 1789. His father Joab (the family had a tradition of giving their sons Biblical names starting with the letter J) had served in the state legislature, was a colonel in the county militia, and owned 1,000 acres, planted primarily in tobacco.

His mother's family, the Hairstons, were also wealthy planters. So Early, born in 1816, and his nine siblings grew up with assured position and comfort.

When he decided to attend the U.S. Military Academy, his family connections made the appointment a mere formality, and he arrived at West Point for the start of the 1834 term.

Early's academic performance was credible enough. He finished 18th in his class of 50. That was

Jubal A. Early raised Confederate hopes in 1864 with his raids throughout the Shenandoah Valley, coming closer to Washington, D.C., than any other rebel force. ***Virginia Historical Society***

somewhat behind Braxton Bragg, but well ahead of two other future generals: John Sedgwick, who was killed fighting for the Union, and John Pemberton, a Pennsylvanian who would fight for the South.

"I was not a very exemplary soldier," he would write in later life. "I had very little taste for scrubbing brass and cared very little for the advancement to be obtained by the exercise of that most useful art."

Nonetheless, his standing earned him the right to choose the artillery as his branch of service. He was sent in that capacity to the Seminole War. Before leaving for Florida, however, he was given a leave and spent it at the resort of White Sulphur Springs, now in West Virginia. It was during this time that he was smitten with a wealthy young woman, named Lavinia, from Philadelphia.

There was an understanding to meet in one year at the same place and, in Early's mind at least, something of a deeper commitment, too.

His stay in Florida was brief and uneventful. Neither the climate nor the conduct of this inconclusive Indian war appealed to him. So in 1838, just one year after graduation, he decided to resign his commission and return to civilian life.

Before he reached home, he received two bits of news. His promotion to first lieutenant had come through. Early wrote later that had he known about that sooner, he might have stayed in the military. He also received a newspaper clipping from Lavinia, announcing her marriage to another man.

Early never married, although he did have four children, whom he supported throughout his life, by Julia McNealey, a young woman from Rocky Mount. The experience with the fair Lavinia, apparently, had left its scars.

With his life changing course at the age 22, he decided to go into law. He studied with a local attorney, Norborne Taliaferro, and was admitted to the bar in 1840. It was the profession he practiced, with few interruptions, for the next 21 years.

He earned a reputation as a solid, if unspectacular lawyer. With a good family name behind him, he ran for the county's seat in the state legislature and was elected in 1841, the youngest member of that body.

Early was affiliated with the Whigs, which was generally the party of men of property in the South. But in the Democratic tide of 1842, he was beaten for re-election. As luck would have it, the man who defeated him was his old friend Taliaferro, who had been the appointed prosecuting attorney in Rocky Mount. The two men wound up simply exchanging jobs.

But Early had not entirely gotten the military out of his system. When the Mexican War began, he felt the stirring again and in 1847 was appointed a major in the First Virginia Regiment. Unlike many of his future colleagues, however, he never saw action, remaining on garrison duty near Monterrey for most of the war.

He blamed the arthritis that afflicted him for the rest of his life on a fever he developed there. The illness resulted in his being sent home on leave and, indirectly, was almost the end of him. A steamboat carrying him back to Mexico exploded on the Ohio River. Fourteen people were killed, and Early was badly burned on his feet.

Oddly enough, he reported, the experience seemed to relieve his arthritis "though I would not advise blowing up in a western steamboat as an infallible remedy."

He was mustered out of the army in April 1848 and returned to his law practice. Privately, Rocky Mount may have questioned his domestic arrangement with Julia. But there was no denying his qualities as a lawyer.

"So clear were his deductions from the law," read one newspaper description of him in 1852, "the adaptation, fitness and cogency with which he applied them; his lofty and Virginia bearing to the court" that he easily bested a team of lawyers opposing him.

He was less successful politically, however, losing elections to a state constitutional convention and to another term in the legislature, in 1853. But he did win a seat at the most critical political gathering of his life: the 1861 convention at which Virginia would consider secession.

Early was against it. He was still a Whig and rose before the convention to defend Lincoln's inaugural address. Early urged his fellow delegates to give the president time, noting that he had pledged to carry out the laws in all states. He said it should be "hailed as a guarantee that he would perform his duty and that we should have peace and protection for our property." By that last word, Early meant slaves.

But he was ridiculed by the secessionist majority and almost ended up in a duel with another delegate who challenged his opinions. Even the fall of Fort Sumter did not shake his Unionist convictions. But his views could not prevail over the emotion that swept the convention. On April 17, it voted 88–55 for secession, with Early in the minority. He said that the vote "wrung from me bitter tears of grief."

Four days later, however, he offered his services to the state militia and was commissioned as a colonel. A man who had voted against secession right down to the wire, Early would become the most unreconstructed of rebels.

He was sent to Lynchburg to organize and train three regiments and in just three months found himself in command of the Sixth Brigade at Manassas. Placed in a support position and given vague, imprecise orders, Early somehow arrived on the extreme left flank just in time to reinforce the line. Later reports indicated that his arrival time was cut so closely because he got lost on the way.

Nonetheless, Early's last-minute appearance, just as General P. G. T. Beauregard was considering a withdrawal, gave the Confederates the manpower to begin the charge that swept the Union forces from the field.

His men already referred to him as Old Jube and had learned to fear his biting sarcasm and stern disciplinary demands. He was also known to treat subordinates harshly. His promotion to brigadier general was not universally applauded by those closest to him.

According to one story, at a subsequent gathering of officers he imbibed too much, refused to drink a toast to the fallen generals of Manassas unless a Virginian was named as well, then went out and fell asleep against a tree in the snow. The episode is recounted by Charles C. Osborne, in his book *Jubal.* Osborne could find no independent confirmation of the tale but concluded that "it has the ring of truth. Early was certainly capable of striking the harsh, incongruous note."

Early started at the U.S. Military Academy at West Point in 1834. ***Library of Congress***

After spending a year in Florida fighting in the Seminole War, Early left the service. ***Library of Congress***

Early's brigade was part of the withdrawal to Richmond, ordered by General Joseph E. Johnston at the start of the Peninsula Campaign in May 1862. But with heavy rains hampering his movements, Northern forces caught up to Johnston near Williamsburg. Early, part of the rear guard, was waiting on the campus of the College of William and Mary when he was summoned to go to the support of the hard-pressed General James Longstreet at Fort Magruder.

Early's last-minute appearance at Manassas provided the necessary support to turn the tide of battle. ***Library of Congress***

When Early came up, he saw nine federal guns shelling the fort. They were about 800 yards from his position and at a right angle to it. Pivoting about, Early decided to charge the guns.

But the attack broke down in confusion. There was no coordination with the supporting force led by General Daniel Harvey Hill. Casualties were high. Early himself went down with a Minie ball through his shoulder and had to turn back. It also turned out that the federal guns were in the process of pulling out when Early charged them.

In what was an overall Confederate victory, Early's actions had contributed to 38 percent of the Southern casualties. Longstreet described it in his report as "an impetuous assault," and his assessment was marked by its absence of praise for Early. Many who saw the action described it as a gallant charge, but to no good purpose.

As a result, Early developed a reputation for recklessness. Because he had to return to Rocky Mount to recover from his wounds, he had no immediate chance to change it.

His recuperation took close to three months, and he was treated as a local hero at home. In his book, *The End of an Era*, John Wise describes Early at this time, sitting on a tavern porch and regaling friends with his forthright, critical opinions of the war.

His comments, wrote Wise, "in my opinion… about his superiors, civic and military, and their conduct of affairs, were sufficient to have convicted him a hundred times over before any court martial."

But this argumentative nature was at the core of who Early was.

With his arm still in a sling, Early was assigned to Stonewall Jackson's corps upon his return to the army and was at the forefront of the hard-fought August 1862 engagement at Cedar Mountain. Just as at Williamsburg, the critical part he played in the battle had to do with heavy guns. But this time he was protecting them instead of charging them, and it turned out much better for Early.

He observed that two Southern batteries had been left in a vulnerable position, just a few hundred yards from Union troops who were hidden in a cornfield. His brigade charged the position, even before the Confederate artillery unit realized that it was in danger, and drove the federals off.

Early was singled out for special commendation by both Jackson and his top aide, General Richard Ewell, both for his charge to save the guns and his work on holding the Confederate right when the opposite wing was in danger of being turned.

He had an even greater opportunity to impress his superiors later that month during the crossing of the Rappahannock River. Early's brigade was the first

After leaving the military, Early studied law and served in the Virginia legislature. He opposed secession, but after it became a reality, he joined the state militia as a colonel. ***Library of Congress***

Early received special commendation for helping to hold the Confederate right and protecting exposed artillery at Cedar Mountain. ***Library of Congress***

across, but when it got to the far side of the rain-swollen stream, the bridge went out, and Early was stranded there, surrounded by federal troops.

Fearing annihilation as soon as the Union command realized how isolated he was, Early kept calm. Shrewdly shielding his movements he managed to stay in touch with Jackson, who told him to move along the river to the next bridge. He would cover him with artillery fire from the opposite bank in case he was attacked.

As it turned out, Union General John Pope was in the process of bringing up his whole force to attack Early, in the mistaken belief that it was Jackson's entire army. Early managed to get out of the situation without losing a man.

"The skill and presence of mind of General Early was favorably displayed," wrote Jackson approvingly. His reputation for impetuous behavior was starting to lift.

He followed this up with a strong performance at Second Manassas, protecting Jackson's left at a critical time from a stiff blow directed by Major General Philip Kearny. There was now talk that he would be promoted to major general and sent to the Western campaign. Ewell expressed reluctance to let him go, but wrote a friend in Tennessee: "Early is very able and very brave and would be an acquisition to your part of the world."

Early expected promotion, especially after being commended by Lee, Jackson, and Jeb Stuart for his work at Antietam, in September 1862. He was praised for his resolution, judgment, and vigor in the reports of these three commanders.

Early himself wrote proudly of his brigade, which had come under attack from three sides during the battle: "It has never been broken or compelled to fall back or left one of its dead to be buried by the enemy." But he had also become seriously taken with the idea of becoming a major general.

Ewell was seriously wounded during the Antietam campaign, losing a leg and leaving the army for nine months. It was supposed that Early, who was now commanding Ewell's division, would be given the rank that went along with the job. Lee accordingly placed his name on the list of recommended promotions.

But when it went through the political grinding machine in Richmond, where Early had few supporters because of his tart tongue and strong previous affiliation with the Whigs, he was passed over.

Early was deeply disappointed, but in this instance wisely held his peace. There was one indication of his snappish frame of mind, however, and surprisingly it was directed towards Jackson, with whom not many took liberties.

On the movement back towards the Rappahan-

General Richard Ewell was badly wounded at Antietam, and Early took over command of his division. *Library of Congress*

nock, Jackson sent a note to Early inquiring why he noted "so many stragglers in rear of your division." Early responded that these stragglers came mostly from other divisions ahead of him, then added: "The reason the Lieutenant General saw so many stragglers in rear of my division today is probably because he rode in rear of my division."

Jackson's response, if any, is lost to time. But Early continued to exercise the role of a division commander at Fredericksburg, in December, with Jackson's approval.

Ewell's recovery was not going well, and he recognized that one of the factors delaying Early's promotion was the possibility of an early return to his division. The wounded major general graciously wrote Early from his bed that "the injustice you ... have suffered has been a source of constant anxiety to me. I intend to go to work to have it corrected as soon as I am able.

"An officer of high rank in your division," he concluded, "told me the other day they just discovered they had a trump and the country is fast arriving at the same conclusion."

With this sort of support, the long-awaited promotion came through on January 19, 1863.

At the start of the spring campaign, it was obvious that Early had earned Lee's confidence. He was placed in the critical position of guarding the heights at Fredericksburg at the start of the Battle of Chancellorsville. Holding these heights protected the entire Confederate rear. As Douglas Southall Freeman notes in *Lee's Lieutenants*: "To this post of military trust in less than two years had risen the former Commonwealth's Attorney of Franklin County, Virginia!"

Despite being told mistakenly to withdraw from the position by a member of Lee's staff who had misunderstood the orders, Early was able to fight a delaying action against his old West Point classmate, Sedgwick. He held on long enough for Lee to rejoin him, drive Sedgwick back, and complete the sweeping Confederate victory.

Lee's report said his performance "reflected credit upon himself and his command."

Ewell returned to action at the end of May and was given the fallen Jackson's old command, with Early's division attached to him. But, as it turned out, this was a different Ewell. He had become cautious and indecisive. Whether it was because of his grave wound or his recent marriage, no one could guess. But it became apparent, in the most critical moments at Gettysburg, that the man in Jackson's post was neither Jackson nor the Ewell of former times.

On the first day of battle, when it was essential for the South to take control of Cemetery Ridge, Ewell would not commit the forces to do it. Lee had given him discretionary orders, telling him to make the assault "if possible." Ewell decided it wasn't.

Moreover, he persuaded the normally combative Early that this was the right course. Early indicated later that he had wanted to make the attack, but at the critical hour he did not argue forcefully for it and acquiesced to Ewell's decision.

At a conference with Lee that evening, moreover, Ewell remained strangely silent while Early, his subordinate, made a strong argument for an attack on the Union left, at the Round Tops, on the following day. To Lee's consternation, Early opposed an attack by his division on Cemetery Ridge, intended to relieve the pressure on Longstreet's planned movement against the Round Tops.

This change of temperament has puzzled historians for decades. Why the usually aggressive Early argued for caution on his front and resisted any suggestion that his division be shifted to support the attack of Longstreet's corps has never been properly understood. But his version of these events and what he said was Lee's response to them would eventually produce the most bitter dispute arising from the war: Early's grudge match with Longstreet.

Early did end up making an attack on Cemetery Ridge, but it was not well coordinated and failed to hold the position. It came close enough to succeeding,

At Chancellorsville, Early was given the critical task of guarding the heights at Fredericksburg, protecting the rear of the Confederate force. *Library of Congress*

however, that it also raises the question as to why he had argued against it so strongly.

After the defeat at Gettysburg and the ensuing fall-back of Lee into Virginia, Early was dispatched briefly to the Shenandoah to deal with troublesome Union raiders. When he returned, early in 1864, it was obvious that his relationship with his old friend and mentor, Ewell, had changed. Whether it was attributable to Ewell's shaky performance at Gettysburg or to Early's rising ambition, it soon became apparent that he was looking to replace him.

Leczinska Campbell Ewell saw the change at once and may have alerted her husband, who was still physically infirm. At one point, in late April, Ewell had Early placed under arrest for conduct "subversive of good order and military discipline." Lee dismissed the charge but also made the odd statement that he considered Early at fault, although no specifics were ever made public.

Freeman says that Early was in "a strange, confident, perhaps overbearing state of mind," which he later describes as "arrogance." But by the end of May, Lee agreed he had to make a move in view of Ewell's failing health. Ewell was transferred to command of the Department of Richmond, and Early succeeded to his position as lieutenant general.

All through May and early June, however, the overwhelming numerical strength of U. S. Grant drove Lee inexorably back towards Richmond. It was now that Lee sought to repeat the same strategy employed two years before. Jackson had been turned loose in the Shenandoah in May 1862, preventing General George McClellan from obtaining reinforcements in his drive against Richmond.

Lee's hope now was that Early could raise enough commotion in the Shenandoah to compel Grant into releasing several thousand troops to deal with him. That would relieve the mounting pressure on Richmond and give Lee some breathing room.

Early opposed an attack by his division on Cemetery Ridge, despite the fact that General James Longstreet's hard-pressed troops needed relief in their assault on the Round Tops. *Library of Congress*

The immediate instigation for sending Early was the damage being done by Major General David Hunter. He was raiding at will through the upper Valley. His burning of the Virginia Military Institute and several other buildings in Lexington, Virginia, had outraged the state, and by the middle of June, he was threatening the important rail center at Lynchburg.

Early left the Richmond lines with 9,000 men on June 17 and on the following day engaged Hunter's force. The Union attack on the city was repelled, and Hunter, surprisingly, decided to retreat into West Virginia. He explained later that he feared going up against

General Lew Wallace opposed Early's troops as they headed toward Washington. Early sent him into retreat, but the delay gave the capital time to reinforce. *Dictionary of American Portraits*

Jackson's old corps and that the devastation he had spread across the Valley would not enable him to sustain his men in hostile country.

But his removal left the entire Shenandoah suddenly open to Early. He wasted no time in taking advantage of it. By July 4, he had reached Harpers Ferry and compelled the retreat of the small Union force there into the nearby heights. Early then crossed the Potomac and entered Maryland.

The Union high command still had no inkling as to his whereabouts. Grant's intelligence reports indicated, in fact, that Early was still at Richmond. The first indication that something was afoot came from the president of the Baltimore and Ohio Railroad, John Garrett. He had received reports of Confederate raiders all across his stations in western Maryland and wanted the army to do something about it.

The officer he went to was Major General Lew Wallace, who was in charge of the Baltimore District. The future author of the best selling novel of the nineteenth century, *Ben-Hur*, was placed in this military backwater because he had annoyed Grant earlier in the war. He misread orders at Shiloh, and Grant blamed him for nearly losing the battle. Besides, the Indiana native was regarded as a political appointee, not worthy of serious consideration by professional soldiers.

So Wallace was on the outs with Washington and wrote later that he expected to be removed at almost anytime. But now that Early had been located and his intentions were becoming clear, Wallace was all the Union command had to save the capital.

Lee was correct in assuming that Grant had stripped the Washington defenses almost clear in order to achieve the highest possible numerical advantage at Richmond. There was supposed to be a 37,000-man garrison stationed there permanently. Instead, there were barely 9,600, and these were mostly inexperienced soldiers. Wallace had another 5,800 men at his disposal.

But no one in Washington knew exactly what was coming at them under Early. He had about 14,000 men with him, but it was feared that his force was almost twice as large.

Dispatches were urgently relayed to Grant for troops to defend Washington. He responded by sending parts of two federal corps to the city by boat. But it was doubtful that they could reach Washington before Early did, and there was a strong possibility the capital would fall if they didn't.

There were strong indications that the North was sick of this endless war. Grant had run up 28,000 casualties in his horrific spring campaigns at The Wilderness and the Spotsylvania Court House. He was also inflicting massive losses on Lee because Grant knew that the North was capable of replacing its fallen, while the Confederacy was not.

But public opinion was not behind this strategy. With the death toll mounting and a standoff developing at both Richmond and Atlanta, Lincoln was in a precarious position for the presidential election of 1864. There was strong appeal among a sizable portion of Northern voters to listen to the Democrats and make peace. If the government now had to flee Washington ahead of Early, that would almost certainly tip the scale.

This was better than Lee had ever hoped for and, on July 8, Early was at Frederick, Maryland, less than 50 miles from Washington.

But his progress was slowing down. There had been looting of captured Union supplies, especially food, at Harpers Ferry and Martinsburg, West Virginia. Early's troops were ravenous, and he lost a day as they gorged and clothed themselves.

When he arrived in Frederick, Early spent more time negotiating with local officials on a ransom for the town. He was demanding $200,000 to spare Frederick from burning, and its leaders said they couldn't possibly come up with that much. Finally, Frederick agreed to borrow the money from its banks—a loan it took the town 87 years to repay, the last installment being made in 1951.

While all this was going on, Wallace and his small force had arrived at Monocacy River, two miles south of Frederick, and started preparing defensive works at

General Philip Sheridan took on Early in earnest, defeating him at the Battle of Winchester. *Library of Congress*

the railroad bridge there. On the morning of July 9, Early suddenly realized that he had a fight on his hands.

In his later report, Early explained that "I could not leave this force in my rear," and so he had to engage it, despite his battle against time.

If Early had a major flaw as a general, it was his dislike of cavalry and his inability to employ it properly. That came back to hurt him now. His cavalry, under Brigadier General John McCausland, advanced too quickly and ran into a Union ambush in a cornfield across the Monocacy.

The chance of sweeping away Wallace's greatly outnumbered force was gone, and Early now had to regroup for a sustained attack. Not until 3:30 P.M. was he in a position to send the seasoned troops of Major General John B. Gordon against the Union forces. The fight took an hour, and Gordon later described it as "desperate and at close quarters."

Wallace was finally sent into full retreat, and the engagement was clearly a victory for Early. But he had lost the greater battle. Wallace had taken out about 700 of Early's best men and held him up for a full day. By the time he reached the outskirts of Washington, on July 11, the city was reinforced. He might have still been able to fight his way in but almost certainly his army would have been destroyed in the process.

He stopped in front of Fort Stevens, on Georgia Avenue, near the grounds of what is now Walter Reed Hospital. His advance troops there were driven back from their positions, but not before they fired a few times at a tall figure on the fort's walls. That turned out to be Lincoln, and with some annoyance the fort's commanders had to tell the president to stay down.

Early had to be content with burning down the house of Postmaster General Montgomery Blair, at Silver Springs, Maryland, and knowing, as he told his officers, "we scared hell out of Abe Lincoln." Washington was safe, but Early wasn't quite finished, and the war was about to enter a much meaner phase.

The Union command knew that Early was lingering nearby, threatening to cut off Washington from the west. But there was no consensus about what to do about it. There was poor coordination among the various forces sent out to stop him, and Early was more than a match for their second-rate commanders.

He defeated a Union force outside Winchester, Virginia, at Kernstown, where Jackson once had been driven off by a far larger Northern concentration in 1862. This again left the Valley clear of federal arms, and Early decided to send another quick message into Union territory.

As Early retreated from the Shenandoah Valley, Sheridan followed, employing a scorched earth policy as he passed. ***Library of Congress***

At the end of July, he dispatched two cavalry brigades under McCausland and General Bradley Johnson to Chambersburg, Pennsylvania. Their orders were to collect $100,000 in gold or $500,000 in greenbacks. If the town failed to pay, they were to burn it.

Early explained that he gave these orders in response to what Hunter had done earlier in Virginia. He had seen "evidence of the destruction wantonly committed by troops under his orders," wrote Early, and he decided "it was time to try and stop this mode of warfare by some act of retaliation."

If that was his intent, it backfired badly. Chambersburg had been captured before, during the Gettysburg campaign 13 months earlier. It was just 25 miles west of the former battlefield. But Lee had given strict orders then that there would be no "unnecessary or wanton injury to private property." "We make war only on armed men," he said. "We cannot take vengeance for the wrongs our people have suffered without lowering ourselves in the eyes of all."

He was severely criticized in the Southern press for taking that stance, and Early was one of those who did not believe in turning the other cheek. When the ransom was not paid, Chambersburg was burned down. Early's written orders had stipulated that it was to be "laid in ashes."

Colonel William Peters refused to follow these orders, telling McCausland that he would "break his sword and throw it away before he would obey them, as there were only defenseless women and children in Chambersburg." McCausland ordered him arrested, and the destruction went on.

The total damage was 400 buildings burned with a total value of $1.5 million. The act shocked public opinion in the North and, if anything, solidified support for the Republicans. Early continued to insist that the burning of Chambersburg "was in strict accordance with the laws of war and was a just retaliation.... I had a duty to perform to the people for whose homes I was fighting."

Johnson, however, said his men were demoralized by what had happened and that "the grand spectacle of a national retaliation was reduced to a miserable huckstering for greenbacks."

The sack of Chambersburg also enraged Grant. He now decided to deal with Early in earnest. Assembling a force of 40,000 men, he placed it under the command of one of his most able subordinates, Major General Philip Sheridan.

He was sent to the Shenandoah with explicit orders to "eat out Virginia clean and clear as far as they go, so that crows flying over it for the balance of this season will have to carry their provender with them."

It was now total war. Just as Sherman's March to the Sea through the Georgia heartland was to be a deliberate campaign to bring the war home to the civilian population, Sheridan's relentless pursuit of Early destroyed the land he passed through.

Sheridan handed Early two quick defeats, at Winchester and Fisher's Hill. As Early withdrew down the Valley, Sheridan followed, burning everything across a 92-mile swath in early October. In the Shenandoah, this is still referred to as "The Burning."

Lee sent in reinforcements, with a message to Early not to be discouraged. Taking this admonition to heart, Early went on the offensive, attacking Sheridan's much larger force at Cedar Creek, near Middletown, on October 19. Sheridan's offensive had already been proclaimed a sweeping success in the North, and the general himself had gone off to Washington to confer with the high command.

But Early designed a night attack, with three columns converging to hit the flank of the totally unsuspecting federal force. The Confederate attack rolled over whatever it encountered. One Union division, however, held up the advance for an hour, making a stand at the town cemetery.

Military historian Joseph W. A. Whitehorne writes that "Early lost full vision of the battlefield and was unable to control all of his forces." While his senior commanders urged him to bypass the cemetery, he insisted on concentrating his force against the one holdout Northern division. It was finally driven back, but at a cost of irreplaceable time lost.

By the time he first got news of this battle, Sheridan had returned to Winchester. Riding furiously to the scene of the fight, he came upon stragglers who were fleeing the apparent defeat. They began to cheer when they saw him, but Sheridan wasn't having any of this. Cursing and bellowing at the men, he got them to turn around and go back to Cedar Creek.

Sheridan's wild ride became one of the most celebrated incidents of the war. It inspired a poem, whose catch phrase—"And Sheridan twenty miles away"—was a classroom recitation staple for decades. His dramatic arrival at Cedar Creek managed to unify his scattered command and drive Early from the field, forcing him to abandon equipment and artillery that could not be replaced.

"The Yankees got whipped," he said in tacitly summarizing the engagement. "We got scared." That was an oversimplification, but it was also an admission. Early was simply not the equal of Sheridan in generalship, either strategic or inspirational.

The defeat ended Early's ability to campaign effectively in the Shenandoah. Instead, he fell back steadily to the south, and Lee returned all but 2,000 of his men

At the end of the war, Early refused to surrender, making his way first to Vera Cruz, Mexico. ***Library of Congress***

to the defensive line at Petersburg. On March 2, 1865, at Waynesboro, Sheridan finished the job that Grant had given him. In a cavalry action led by General George A. Custer, Early's line was shattered, and he lost all but 400 of his men.

Lee had no choice but to relieve him of whatever remained of his command. Early was being bitterly criticized throughout the South as a failure and a drunk, incompetent and intoxicated on the eve of battle. Lee recognized that this was unfair. Early had done everything he could to pull Union troops away from Richmond, allowing Lee to fight on for months longer than would have been possible otherwise.

In his message of dismissal, on March 30, he made a point of thanking Early for his "fidelity and energy . . . courage and devotion." But he said that he could "not oppose what seems to be the current of opinion, without injustice to your reputation and injury to the service."

Lee's war ended at Appomattox 10 days later, but Early's went on. He eluded federal troops and headed west, hoping to link up with General Edmund Kirby Smith and continue the fight beyond the Mississippi River. When he learned that Smith also had surrendered, he traveled on to Mexico by ship, arriving in Vera Cruz in December, 1865.

But Mexico was not to his liking, and in August 1866, he decided to transfer his base to Niagara Falls, in Canada, and then to Toronto. He worked on a history of his campaigns, accepted checks from his family as his only means of support, and scoffed at the idea of accepting a pardon and coming home.

As a final act before leaving office, however, President Andrew Johnson extended a blanket pardon to all

Eventually returning to the U.S., Early remained an unreconstructed rebel, championing the Lost Cause and celebrating the memory of Robert E. Lee. *Dictionary of American Portraits*

former Confederate officers. In May 1869, Early returned to Virginia. His exile had lasted four years, and his bitterness had not ebbed. He still believed in states' rights and published a caustic defense of slavery, arguing that if blacks were truly ready to be given the vote so quickly upon gaining their freedom "what a civilizing influence that institution must have had."

He took up his law practice in Lynchburg and got himself involved in the crooked Louisiana Lottery in an effort to make some money. But for the next 25 years, Early mostly would take up the banner of the Lost Cause.

A group of Virginians, outraged at what they felt were unfair Northern depictions of the war and its issues, formed the Southern Historical Society to present their version of events. Early became its president and most combative spokesman.

It was mostly through the writing of Early and his colleagues that the image of the Lost Cause became engrained in the Southern consciousness. The Confederacy had not really lost the war, they claimed, because it wasn't a fair fight. The North did not have the better leaders or the better generals. It just had more factories and more people. Moreover, the justice of the Southern cause could not be extinguished.

Early became the chief defender of Lee's reputation and more than any other writer elevated him to a demigod. He was infallible, unconquered. He took it upon himself to lead the fund-raising for Lee's memorial statue in Richmond and almost pitched a fit when he heard that part of its base was made of Maine granite. He had to be assured by the governor of Virginia that 19 of 20 parts of the stone were Southern.

Finally, he engaged in a furious battle with Longstreet. When the war ended, it was Early who was reviled in the South and Longstreet admired as Lee's faithful lieutenant to the last. But when Longstreet joined the Republicans and then dared to publish an article critical of Lee at Gettysburg, Early went on the attack.

A skilled advocate and trial lawyer, he was more than a match for the stolid Longstreet. He turned his opponent into a traitor in Southern eyes, a blasphemer who tried to cover his own incompetence by sullying the memory of the sainted Lee.

By the 1880s, the roles of the men had been completely reversed. It was Early who was now hailed as the true hero, and Longstreet who had failed.

Although crusty and sardonic to the end, he also gave large amounts of money to charity, especially widows and orphans of former Confederate soldiers. With his health failing and bothered by his old wounds, he suffered a bad fall down a flight of steps in 1894. He never recovered and died two weeks later, at the age of 77.

The obituaries praised him as a Southern eagle, the defender of the faith. Only after his death did the reputation of Longstreet, who outlived him by 10 years, begin to recover. While Early had lived there was no quarter given.

When his longtime colleague, General Fitzhugh Lee, served in the U.S. Army during the Spanish-American War, another former Southern officer, General Basil Duke, wrote that he was glad Lee survived. Otherwise, said Duke, "what would Jubal Early have said had he met Fitz Lee in the next world wearing a Yankee uniform."

BRAXTON BRAGG

"No one needed friends more than Bragg, but his manner created malignant enemies and indifferent, callous friends."

General St John R. Liddell, in Liddell's Record, *published posthumously*

Taken as a group, the Confederate generals were an unusual bunch. Many of them had their flaws, their quirks, their unpleasant idiosyncrasies. But none was disliked quite so widely, both by contemporaries and by historians, as Braxton Bragg.

His subordinates petitioned repeatedly to have him removed as the commanding general of the Army of Tennessee. The men who fought under him detested him as a heartless martinet who was notorious for ordering the execution of deserters. Some of the South's most able leaders, James Longstreet, Nathan Bedford Forrest, and Pat Cleburne, were disgusted with his leadership style.

One recent biographer, Grady McWhiney, intended to write a two-volume study of Bragg. He gave it up after one book as a bad job and allowed a graduate student to complete the second volume.

The best that McWhiney's successor, Judith Lee Hallock, could say about Bragg is that he had a first-rate mind but was ill suited to in the position of battlefield general. His talents ran more along the lines of administration, and when he was recalled to Richmond in that capacity in 1864, he turned in a more credible performance.

Bragg was a "strange and unfortunate mixture," wrote Stanley F. Horn in his history of the Army of Tennessee. "Nearly all observers, on both sides, give him credit for the highest moral character and for skill in planning and carrying out some military maneuvers. But his execution of his own plans was hampered by an innate vagueness of purpose, and his unpopularity with practically everyone he encountered greatly diminished his effectiveness."

Through most of his career he complained of dyspepsia, migraines, and an assortment of other painful ailments, which may have been brought on by the stress of a job he could not handle. He seemed driven to achieve perfection, and when he or those around him fell short, Bragg could not deal with the strain.

He was also described as argumentative and easily irritated. Tall and ungainly in physique, his most notable physical characteristic was thick, bushy eyebrows.

The classic Bragg story, recounted by U. S. Grant in his memoirs, supposedly occurred when he was a young lieutenant, just out of West Point. He was stationed at an outpost where he was both a company commander and quartermaster. As company commander he wrote out a requisition for some supplies, and as quartermaster he turned it down.

"My God, Mr. Bragg," he was told by the post commander. "You have quarreled with every officer in the army, and now you are quarreling with yourself."

While apocryphal, the anecdote does illustrate the reputation that Bragg carried with him from the start of his military career.

He was a North Carolinian and, indeed, the largest military base in that state still proudly carries his name. He was born in 1817 in the town of Warrenton. His father was a carpenter and a fairly successful one. But he was born into a class-conscious culture, and in Warrenton he was never allowed to forget that he did not belong to the upper echelon.

Even after he was acclaimed as a hero in the Mexican War, the U.S. congressman from the district, David Outlaw, would write to his wife, "It will be awful if the people of Warrenton should fail to make proper

Better suited to administration than to field command, Braxton Bragg angered superiors and subordinates alike.
Museum of the Confederacy, Richmond, Virginia

preparations to receive properly Colonel Bragg, who I am certain must in his heart despise those who were formerly disposed to sneer at his family."

His mother, in fact, had been released from prison in order to give birth to him. She had been awaiting trial on the charge of murdering a freed black man who, she claimed, had "acted biggity" towards her. She was, however, never charged with a crime and was released permanently after young Braxton was born.

His older brother, Thomas, became a successful attorney. He had the political skills in the family and was elected governor and then a U.S. senator from North Carolina. He was also attorney general of the Confederacy for a brief time.

Bragg won appointment to West Point and graduated fifth in the class of 1837, choosing the artillery as his branch. But in the nine years that preceded the outbreak of war with Mexico, he was not a happy man.

While he was fiercely protective of his prerogatives as a general, he was known to be rude and occasionally insubordinate as a junior officer. While stationed at Fort Moultrie, South Carolina, in 1843, he was openly contemptuous of his commanding officer, Lieutenant Colonel William Gates.

Asked by Gates to join him in a drink, Bragg snapped: "If you order me to drink a glass of wine with you, I shall have to do it."

The following year was marked by a far more serious affront. He was court-martialed for openly criticizing the commander of the army, General Winfield Scott, and during the trial he again questioned the competence of his superior.

Bragg was reprimanded in severe terms by the court and reminded that "the disrespectful tenor of his remarks ... is not justified by the facts and is highly disapproved. The Lieutenant is admonished to correct his error lest its too frequent indulgence may become a confirmed and dangerous habit."

He saw action in the Seminole War, in Florida, and was also posted on the western frontier. But it was during the Mexican War that he became, for a time, a national figure.

Capt. Bragg served with General Zachary Taylor at the battle of Buena Vista. American forces there had come under heavy attack and were about to be forced into retreat when Bragg's artillery unit arrived. It withstood a Mexican cavalry charge, despite a lack of infantry support. The barrage it then laid down was credited with turning the tide of battle.

Taylor's supposed order to him, "A little more grape, Mr. Bragg," was repeated around the country and made both men nationally known. What Taylor actually said is a matter of dispute. The general claimed, at various times, that the order was more like, "Double shot those guns and give them hell, Mr. Bragg" or even "Whither the haste, Mr. Bragg?"

Taylor would ride his fame from Buena Vista into the White House in the election of 1848. While Bragg never reached those heights, he made a connection that would affect the rest of his career. Among the officers in the hard-pressed U.S. regiment at Buena Vista was Jefferson Davis. Bragg's supporting fire enabled him, while seriously wounded, to reorganize his faltering troops and successfully continue the fight.

The two men admired one another's courage in the battle and became close friends. But the admiration did not seem to be shared by the men Bragg led. According to some historical sources, one of them planted a shell underneath his cot in the earnest intent of blasting Bragg to eternity. The bed was destroyed, and Bragg emerged badly shaken but unscathed.

Already, indications of the pettiness that would mark his later career were emerging. In the midst of one battle, he insisted on sending a soldier to remove the sword from the body of a dead teamster. It was government property, Bragg said, and he didn't want it lost. The soldier said he also took the dead man's pocketknife, just in case Bragg wanted that, too.

Nonetheless, he was brevetted three times during the war and, despite his previous brush with insubordination, his career seemed promising.

Three years later, however, he married the daughter of a wealthy Louisiana planter. Eliza (Elise) Brooks Ellis would remain devoted to him for the rest of their lives, never seeing him as anything but a romantic hero. His biographer, Judith Lee Hallock, however, described the match as "a set goal that he had managed to accomplish."

Moreover, the routine of army life was losing its appeal for Bragg. Still with the rank of captain, at the age of 39, he resigned from the army in 1856. His wife's wealth enabled him to buy and develop a sugar plantation near Thibodaux, Louisiana.

He went on to become the state's commissioner of public works, a job he held until the outbreak of the Civil War. He apparently was good at it and is credited with helping to design Louisiana's system of levees.

With secession, however, he was named colonel of the Louisiana militia in February 1861. One month later he was appointed brigadier general in the Confederate Army and was placed in charge of Gulf Coast defenses between Mobile and Pensacola.

He did not like what he saw there. In a letter to his old comrade-in-arms, Davis, he said, "Our strength consists in the enemy's weakness." Once the Union army got itself organized, he believed, there wasn't much he would be able do to withstand an attack on these ports.

"Our troops are raw volunteers," Bragg wrote to his wife, "without officers and without discipline, each man with an idea that he can whip the world." But if there was one thing he excelled at, it was whipping men like these into soldiers. His performance at this task was so impressive that by September, before fighting a battle, he was promoted to major general.

Bragg was inclined to rage privately at the poor quality of the men he was called upon to train, a condition he traced to the evil of universal suffrage. He felt granting such rights to the wrong sort of men made it that much more difficult to organize them.

Davis pointed out with pride, however, in announcing the promotion, that Bragg was the only commander in the army who could do this sort of thing while retaining the respect of the men. As Bruce Catton notes, however, in *Terrible Swift Sword*, that was "a judgment which would call for revision before the war was over."

By the following April, Bragg was the fifth ranking general in the army and was sent to Corinth, Mississippi, to join in the preparation for the engagement that would be known as the Battle of Shiloh.

Bragg served under General Zachary Taylor at the Battle of Buena Vista, laying down an artillery barrage that changed the course of the battle. ***Library of Congress***

Once more he was asked to instill discipline in raw recruits, a task he grumpily undertook. The men, he said, displayed "more enthusiasm than discipline, more capacity than knowledge and more valor than instruction." In his official report he said that he doubted most of them "had ever so much as made a full day's march and most of the rank and file had never done a day's work in their lives."

His pessimism was borne out in the advance towards the battlefield, at Pittsburg Landing, Tennessee. With plans that called for speed and efficiency, attributes beyond the grasp of this army, Bragg's corps became hopelessly tangled up behind the troops of General Leonidas Polk.

An exasperated General Albert Sidney Johnston had to personally ride back into the tangle and clear the road in front of Bragg's men to get them where they were supposed to be. The battle itself, which would cost Johnston his life, was a confused free-for-all, which saw Confederate troops firing at each other by mistake at one point.

The army fought well, however, and Bragg was especially effective in his assault on the Union left. But the Southern forces failed in the primary goal of preventing the linkup of the two Union armies opposing it. Their huge manpower losses left the Confederates exhausted, and they had to fall back to Corinth.

When Johnston's successor, General P. G. T. Beauregard, retreated even further, to Tupelo, Mississippi, Davis decided to get rid of him. The departure came sooner than expected. Beauregard left the army in

Bragg first met Jefferson Davis during the Mexican War. They became close friends, though Davis later removed him from command of the Army of Tennessee. ***National Archives and Records Administration***

June, on the advice of his physician, to visit a spa at Bladon Springs, Alabama, to regain his fragile health.

Davis decided this constituted absence without leave and immediately placed his old friend, Bragg, in command. A furious Beauregard sputtered and fumed that by this action Davis had revealed himself as little more than a traitor. But the Confederate president, who was always more comfortable with close friends in positions of top army command, was delighted with the change.

Bragg, a genius at organization, quickly sized up the situation in the west. He decided that if he could move his army to Chattanooga by rail it would position him to carry out an invasion of Kentucky behind the main body of the Union army. He hoped that would relieve pressure on Mississippi by forcing the federal command to move men north to oppose him.

Bragg was also convinced that Kentucky, a slave state that had remained in the Union, wanted to be "liberated." Once he reached it, he was sure that the population would rise up in support of the Confederacy.

The campaign started north on August 28, 1862, with Bragg leading 27,000 men. The plan was to coordinate his movements with those of General Edmund Kirby Smith, who was to seize the Cumberland Gap from the Union with his 18,000 men and then join Bragg to threaten Cincinnati or Louisville.

But Bragg's directives to Smith were vague and, instead of combining, the two forces followed divergent paths into Kentucky. Nonetheless, at the start the plan worked as conceived. General Don Carlos Buell was forced to leave Nashville and follow Bragg and Smith north to defend Louisville. Union forces also retreated from the Cumberland Gap, and when Smith entered Lexington in September, with local son John Hunt Morgan leading the cavalry, the city went wild with joy.

Bragg, meanwhile, was making his way north through Munfordville, Kentucky, where he attacked a federal garrison commanded by Colonel J. T. Wilder. An Indiana businessman, he had no military experience and was entirely nonplussed by Bragg's arrival. He wanted to observe the etiquette of war but wasn't quite sure what that required.

"He did not like the idea of surrendering," wrote Horn, in his history of the Army of Tennessee, "but could see nothing else to do. Finally, he adopted the unorthodox (but probably sensible) expedient of going under a flag of truce to General [Simon Bolivar] Buckner's headquarters and asking his advice."

Wilder said he believed Buckner was a "gentleman who would not deceive him." Buckner, honestly perplexed, said he could not advise Wilder, but he would allow him to count his cannon. Wilder did so and said that had decided to surrender. Thereupon, he was taken to Bragg who accepted the offer.

On this strange note, Bragg's Kentucky campaign began. He moved up to Bardstown unopposed and settled his army there. "My army is in high spirits and ready to go anywhere the 'old general' says," he wrote his wife. "Not a murmur escapes a man.... We have made the most extraordinary campaign in military history."

But this campaign already had wasted its best chance. Bragg was blocking Buell's supply lines at Munfordville but felt that he could not take on the Union army without the support of Smith's troops. And they were celebrating off in Lexington.

So Bragg's withdrawal to Bardstown actually cleared the way for Buell to reach Louisville, reinforce his army, and prepare to take on the two Confederate forces that opposed him.

Moreover, Bragg was not getting the support he expected from the people of Kentucky. Although he had installed a pro-Southern governor in the capital, at Frankfort, there was no general swelling to the Confederate colors as he had anticipated.

He wired the War Department in Richmond that if these ungrateful Kentuckians should "decline the offer of liberty," he would have to alter his plans. "Unless a change occurs soon we must abandon the garden spot of Kentucky to its own cupidity."

On October 8, Buell made the decision for him. The Union general, under severe prodding from Washington, finally came out of Louisville and headed for Bragg with about 22,000 troops. Bragg, having been unable to link up with Smith, was at a numerical disadvantage.

It had been a dry summer, and the Battle of Perryville began over access to drinking water at Doctor's Creek. The furious fight ended in a standoff, but Bragg's casualty rate was almost one in five. Given the overall lack of support in men and material in Kentucky and the fact that Buell had access to reinforcements, he felt that he had no option but a retreat into Tennessee.

His decision met with approval from the Confederate command in Richmond, but it baffled Bragg's troops. The soldiers thought they had held their own at Perryville and could not understand why they had been ordered to fall back. What had been the purpose of the campaign if this was the result?

When Buell declined orders to pursue Bragg and returned, instead, to the safety of Nashville, he was replaced with General William S. Rosecrans. Bragg, however, stayed on the job. During a visit from Davis at the army's new base, in Murfreesboro, Tennessee, he personally assured the president that Tennessee was secure and that if the Union army ventured out of Nashville, he'd take care of it promptly.

At the end of December, he got his chance. Emboldened by reports that both Morgan and Forrest had left Bragg's army to go on wide-ranging raids, Rosecrans came to Murfreesboro to force a battle. The armies met at Stones River, just north of the city. While Bragg had the chance to choose the terrain on which to make his stand, he settled on open country with few natural defenses and a river running through his lines.

The plan of both commanders was to attack the other's right, but Bragg hit first. That gave him the advantage. He had concentrated in overwhelming numbers against the weakened Union right, and the Confederate attack buckled it all the way back to the center of the line, exposing the road to Nashville.

The Federals rallied, however, under the direction of General George Thomas and formed a defensive line in the shape of an arrowhead. The Confederate assault broke down amid heavy thickets of trees where Union forces were clustered. The area came to be known as Hell's Half Acre.

Thomas's artillery pounded the oncoming Southern troops. Many of them stopped to pluck cotton in the fields and stuff it in their ears to deaden the noise. Some reported later that they saw small animals, driven wild with fear from the sound, scampering from the scene.

Bragg tried to bring reserves into the attack, but Major General John Breckenridge's division had been posted across Stones River. When men from Bragg's four brigades came up, they arrived piecemeal and were thrown back with heavy losses.

When the day ended, however, Bragg was convinced that he had won and that Rosecrans was in full retreat. His wire to Richmond on January 1 read: "God has granted us a Happy New Year."

But what Bragg's scouts had seen headed back to Nashville were wagons carrying the Union wounded. The army itself was holding on. In fact, at a meeting of the federal command after the first day of battle, it was Thomas who announced: "This army can't retreat."

"Bragg is a good dog," Rosecrans would crow later, "but Hold Fast is a better." Hold Fast was Rosecrans's favorite name for himself.

Bragg had decided that his army was not capable of following up the attack. On the second day of the new year, however, to his dismay, Rosecrans went after him. In desperation, Bragg ordered a frontal assault on the Union left by Breckenridge, a decision that resulted in 1,700 casualties in little more than an hour.

In the two days of combat, the slaughter had been

Soon after secession, Bragg received the rank of brigadier general and was placed in charge of Gulf Coast defenses between Mobile and Pensacola. *Smithsonian Institution, National Portrait Gallery*

Though the Confederates failed in their primary objective at Shiloh, Bragg proved effective in his assault on the Union left. *Battles and Leaders of the Civil War*

appalling. Bragg had lost 10,000 of his 34,000 men, while Union casualties totaled 13,000. The battle had been fought in an icy rain, and the troops on both sides were sick and exhausted. Moreover, the river at Bragg's back was rising, and he feared that his position would become untenable.

Bragg began to withdraw to the southeast, to Tullahoma, Tennessee, on January 3, and Rosecrans could do little more than repair his battered army in Murfreesboro. About a month after telling Davis how secure Middle Tennessee was for the Confederacy, Bragg had abandoned it to the Union.

Moreover, the collapse of Bragg's strategy to disrupt the Union supply lines secured Grant's advance into Mississippi. In a few more months, he would resume his campaign against Vicksburg and take the last Southern stronghold on the Mississippi River. In the North, despite the terrible losses, Stones River was regarded justifiably as a victory.

The retreat from Stones River was just as frustrating to Bragg's army as the earlier withdrawal from Perryville. Once more, a battle that had seemingly been won was turned, inexplicably, into defeat and retreat. The grumbling which had started as an undercurrent in October, rose to a crescendo by January.

Bragg was of no help to himself in this regard. After Stones River, he decided to seek a vote of confidence from his top officers. "I desire that you will consult your subordinate commanders and be candid with me," he wrote. "I shall retire without a regret if I find I have lost the good opinion of my generals, upon whom I have ever relied as upon a foundation of rock."

As administrative moves go, this was a fiasco. Almost to a man, his generals told him to go away.

Ignoring the fact that he had advised in favor of the retreat, Major General Leonidas Polk turned on Bragg. He urged his replacement, partly on the basis of his carrying out the very policy Polk had suggested. The other senior commander, William J. Hardee, concurred, and Major General Benjamin Franklin Cheatham went even further. He asserted that he would never again fight under Bragg's leadership.

Breckenridge, still furious over what he regarded as the careless slaughter of his brigades, took the opportunity to challenge Bragg to a duel.

A dejected Bragg wrote Davis, inquiring whether it wouldn't be better for all concerned if he were replaced. Davis, in spite of his long friendship with Bragg, was inclined to agree.

"It is not given to all men of ability to excite enthusiasm and to win the affection of their troops," he said in response. Davis then appointed General Joseph E. Johnston, who had previously been named commander of the western armies, to investigate the situation and make recommendations.

Johnston regarded this as far beyond his mandate. How could he recommend Bragg be replaced, knowing that he most likely would be the man named to succeed him? To the Virginia gentleman that Johnston was, that was a dishonorable course, and he wanted no part of it.

At one point, he even wrote friends in Richmond

In Kentucky, Bragg attacked the garrison of Colonel J. T. Wilder. A businessman with no military experience, Wilder elected to surrender. *Library of Congress*

Bragg believed he had prevailed at Stones River, but General William Rosecrans renewed the attack the next day, forcing a Confederate retreat. ***Library of Congress***

that the Army of Tennessee was so vital to Southern interests that Robert E. Lee should be placed in command, with Johnston replacing him in the Army of Northern Virginia. This suggestion was not seriously considered.

In the end, Bragg stayed put. He had come down with boils, his wife had nearly died of a fever, and he had obviously lost the confidence of his subordinates. All of this had made his temper even more fearsome and his tongue more acerbic.

But when Rosecrans finally began moving towards Tullahoma in June, he was no better at fending him off. Rosecrans had put off this movement for weeks, over the protests of Washington, pleading that he needed just a little more time to plan. But his lengthy preparation paid off.

He feinted at Bragg's left at Tullahoma, then had major generals George Thomas and Thomas Crittenden slip around him on the right. The alarmed Bragg, reacting as if Rosecrans wasn't fighting fair by flanking him in this way, ordered another retreat, this time to Chattanooga. When he got there he placed himself in the hospital, saying, "I am utterly broken down."

Rosecrans hesitated again for another six weeks and then repeated the maneuver, slipping two of his corps behind Bragg on the east. Once more, the Confederates fell back, this time into northern Georgia.

By now Davis was alarmed enough to detach the corps of James Longstreet from Lee's army and send it by rail to Bragg's assistance. But Bragg had come up with a plan, the best he developed through the entire course of the war. He had managed to extricate his army from danger with minimal losses and was now awaiting his chance to strike at an imprudent Rosecrans.

Judge Albion Tourgée, in his account of the Battle of Chickamauga, *The Story of a Thousand*, credited Bragg with playing "a game of wits" and of knowing Rosecrans's weaknesses. The Union general wanted very much to believe that Bragg was on the run, and Bragg was determined to give him every encouragement to think so.

He used decoy deserters to convince their captors that Bragg had no intention of stopping. Bragg was known for his harsh treatment, usually execution, of deserters so Union interrogators were inclined to accept their stories.

"The Confederate deserter," wrote Tourgée, "was of far greater value to the Southern cause than the best corps in the Confederate army. He was ubiquitous,

Though the Battle of Chickamauga departed from Bragg's plans, General Leonidas Polk's belated attack and General James Longstreet's advance turned it into a Confederate victory. *National Archives and Records Administration*

Bragg kept his Tennessee headquarters at Missionary Ridge. *Library of Congress*

willing and altogether inscrutable. Whether he told the truth or a lie, he was almost equally sure to deceive."

Tourgée felt that Bragg's employment of this tactic was masterful. Upon hearing their stories, Rosecrans could hardly wait to get after him. But he had to wait until Thomas's corps came up to join him, and that delay gave Longstreet the time he needed to arrive at Chickamauga. Because of detours and torn up tracks, the trip Longstreet thought would take four days for his corps actually took ten. By the time he got there, the fight already had begun.

Bragg hoped to lure the Union army into rugged terrain, broken up by mountain ridges, south of the city. Then he planned to hit its unsuspecting, separated segments with everything he had. His field order closed with the instruction: "The above movements will be executed with the utmost promptness, vigor and persistence."

But he was speaking to men who had lost confidence in his leadership months before. Moreover, they resented him and were not inclined to use their own initiative on the battlefield, knowing that they stood to be second-guessed unmercifully for any failure.

Rosecrans also had become aware of the danger he was in and was shifting his troops, concentrating to meet the anticipated attack. On September 19, Rosecrans was no longer where Bragg thought he was going to be. So all the plans were discarded, and the first day of battle quickly turned into a murderous ambush, with fights breaking out against unseen enemies in the underbrush.

Horn describes the battle plan, apparently with a straight face, as "a masterpiece of strategy.... If one overlooks the fact that Rosecrans had changed the position of his army from where Bragg thought it was, one can find no fault with Bragg's basic strategy."

Although the day had not gone according to plan, Bragg was convinced that he had inflicted severe damage on Rosecrans and could still cut him off from Chattanooga. With Longstreet now available, it was decided that Polk would hit the Union left "before the dawn of day." Longstreet would then deliver a massive strike on the right, coordinated with Polk's advance.

It didn't work out. When no movement was detected on Polk's wing, a staff officer was sent to see about the delay. He found Polk sitting in a rocking chair reading a newspaper. He said that he had wondered about the delay himself, since he had ordered General Daniel Harvey Hill to attack "so soon as you are in position." He had transmitted no time element more urgent than that.

How a fairly direct order could have been so misinterpreted by one of Polk's experience was never satisfactorily explained. But the bungled attack delayed Bragg's plan by more than four hours.

When Polk finally struck, however, it was effective, and Rosecrans began moving troops to support his battered left wing. That's when Longstreet hit him on the right in what may have been the most devastating assault of his distinguished career. He had found the exact spot in the Union line where the gap caused by the troop movement occurred.

Longstreet's five divisions swept through the breach, and most of Rosecrans army, including its commander, were stampeded back to Chattanooga. Only Thomas's resolute stand, which earned him the name of the "Rock of Chickamauga," prevented a complete Union rout.

As it was, this was the most sweeping victory in Bragg's career. Even Rosecrans, in a desperate wire to Washington, described it as "a serious disaster; extent not yet ascertained, enemy overwhelmed us."

Longstreet and Forrest could hardly contain themselves in pressing Bragg to pursue the defeated enemy into Chattanooga and destroy him. Instead, with an opportunity for a decisive victory in the west in front of him, Bragg did not move.

He had taken massive casualties, 18,454 men out of 65,000 engaged. He was convinced his army was exhausted and could fight no more. But Union casualties were placed at 16,170 out of 62,000 men, and Forrest personally reported that the Northern army was in a state of total disorganization. But Bragg refused to advance. Although the war would last another 18 months, the last great offensive opportunity for the South was gone.

Longstreet said later that he was now convinced "nothing but the hand of God can save us or help us as long as we have our present commander." Forrest was so outraged, he threatened to smack Bragg in the face. Polk and Hill were both removed from command by Bragg, who blamed them for the failure to destroy the Union army during the battle.

Davis again considered replacing Bragg. But he now had even less confidence in Johnston than he'd had nine months before because Davis blamed him for losing Vicksburg. So while he seemed inclined to make a move, there was no one to make it with, and Bragg again was left in place.

There was no way the South could win a war of siege, but that's the position Bragg had placed himself in at Chattanooga. He held the heights outside the city with the federal army bottled up inside. But after Rosecrans was replaced with Grant, a steady buildup leading to a Union breakout began.

In November, Bragg wrote his wife, Elise, from his headquarters on Missionary Ridge, sounding almost like a dreamy tourist describing a guidebook attraction.

"At night, all are brilliantly lit up in the most gorgeous manner by the campfires," he said. "It surpasses any sight ever witnessed and ... it is worth a trip of a thousand miles."

He had already reduced his own force by sending Longstreet off to Knoxville on an irrelevant sideshow. Longstreet was thoroughly disgusted, but also relieved to get away from Bragg. "This was to be the fate of our army," he wrote to Buckner, "to wait till all good opportunities had passed, and then in desperation to seize upon the least favorable one."

But soon the opportunities ran out. On November 24, Grant attacked. Despite brilliant defensive work on most of Bragg's line, the center gave way against a heroic uphill federal assault and the slow, steady retreat to Atlanta began.

Bragg, characteristically, blamed his men, saying that the sight of the Bluecoats swarming up the hill broke the resistance of some of the toughest fighters in the Confederate army. It was "bad conduct," he said in a letter to Davis, traceable to the actions of Longstreet, Polk, and Hill. These men were guilty of "sacrificing the army in their effort to degrade and remove me for personal ends."

He also accused two more of his generals of drunkenness, before getting to the point with the president. "I fear we both erred in the conclusion for me to retain command here after the clamor against me," he said.

This time, Davis could not hold back. He inquired about Lee moving to Georgia to replace Bragg, but met determined resistance there. He reluctantly placed Johnston in command on December 2.

Bragg was named general-in-chief of the Confederate armies three months later. All this meant, however, was that he would have an office in the War Department in Richmond and become Davis's military adviser.

Even that was regarded as too much throughout most of the South. Bragg had become the most thoroughly detested man in the Confederacy. "We looked for results that would pay for our losses in battle," wrote the Southern diarist Mary Boykin Chesnut. "But, no. There sits Bragg, a ... dog howling on his hind legs."

According to another story current at the time, a woman announced that she wished Bragg dead and in heaven for the good of the Southern cause. "If the general were near the gates of heaven," admonished a friend, "and invited in, at the critical moment he would fall back."

News of his removal had been met with general approval. In Richmond, it was regarded as accepted fact that only his friendship with Davis protected him for so long. Although Davis still felt that Bragg's talents for organization could be put to use as general-in-chief, the opinion was not widely shared. "This happy announcement," wrote the *Richmond Examiner*, "should enliven the confidence and enthusiasm reviving among the people like a bucket of water poured on a newly kindled grate."

The move had been made without the approval of Secretary of War James A. Seddon. His clerk, Robert Kean, expressed the prevailing sense of uneasiness in the army. "They think that if anything should happen to Lee," he wrote in his diary, "Bragg would be assigned, which they regard with universal assent as the ruin of the army and the cause."

That never happened, but Bragg still had a chance for some mischief. Davis sent him to Atlanta in June to

With his subordinates pressing for his removal and President Davis realizing his inability to score significant victories, Bragg was removed from command. *Dictionary of American Portraits*

assess the performance of his successor, Johnston. He had been waging a defensive campaign against Sherman in an effort to lengthen his supply lines so he, eventually, could attack his rear.

Davis disapproved of this strategy, and Bragg was only too happy to reinforce his suspicions. "There is but one remedy," Bragg wrote Davis. "Offensive action." That encouraged Davis to name Hood as Johnston's replacement, with wholly disastrous results.

Most of his eight months in Richmond was spent dealing with internal management problems: mediating between quarreling generals (which seems like an odd assignment for him), trying to keep the railroads functioning, and helping prepare the defense of Petersburg and Richmond. He had a direct hand in replacing General George Pickett, who gave evidence of nervous collapse, with Beauregard at Petersburg.

In November, he was sent off to North Carolina with instructions to maintain the defense of Wilmington, the last port open to Confederate blockade runners. When a Union force attacked Fort Fisher, the installation at the mouth of the Cape Fear River, in January, the approach to Wilmington was cut off. The fort's commanding officer, Colonel William Lamb, pleaded with Bragg to send the infantry division based in the city to assist him.

Sent to North Carolina to defend the port of Wilmington, Bragg delayed in sending infantry to Fort Fisher, allowing it to be captured. Wilmington fell a month later. *Library of Congress*

But the maddening tendency to delay that haunted him throughout the war plagued Bragg here, as well. He refused to commit the division, and the fort fell in fierce hand-to-hand fighting. One month later Wilmington was gone, as well, severing the South's last sea link to the outside.

The former commander at Wilmington, General William Whiting, was wounded in the battle at the fort and later captured. While still a prisoner, he sent a report to Lee denouncing Bragg's performance.

"I think the result might have been different ... if the commanding general had done his duty," wrote Whiting. "I charge him with this loss.... In all his career of failure and defeat, from Pensacola out, there has been no such chance missed and no such stupendous disaster."

Bragg, for his part, wrote that he was "tired and sad." But there was just a bit further to go.

His former command, the Army of Tennessee, with Johnston once more at its head, had been driven back into North Carolina. Bragg now found himself fighting under the general whose replacement he had suggested nine months before at Atlanta.

Even in his final engagement, at Bentonville, on March 19, 1865, Bragg is blamed for delaying his advance so long that the units he was to support ran out of momentum. His own men suffered heavy casualties in the poorly timed assault.

Within a few weeks, Bragg and his wife joined the flight of the defeated Confederate government. He caught up to Davis in South Carolina. While Davis still harbored hopes of continuing resistance in the west, Bragg convinced his old friend that it was useless and is credited with finally getting the Confederate president to accept reality.

The group separated in May, and in a few days the Braggs were captured by some Pennsylvania troops near Concord, Georgia. They were paroled immediately, although Elise Bragg scolded her captors severely for their insensitivity.

Their former Louisiana plantation had been seized and sold at auction. Bragg was reduced to living with one of his brothers in Alabama, besieged by debtors, having lost all of his possessions. "Not a human being has ever called to see us," he complained to friends.

Jobs as a civil engineer, insurance salesman, and superintendent of the New Orleans waterworks did not last. He was hired as chief engineer at the port of Mobile in 1871, and two years later was employed by the Gulf, Colorado and Santa Fe Railroad in Texas. But just as with his military career, he ended up being embroiled in arguments with the company's directors and was terminated.

At Bentonville, Bragg's final engagement, his delayed advance destroyed the momentum of the units he was supposed to support. His own troops suffered heavy losses. ***Library of Congress***

In the last few months of his life, he worked as chief railroad inspector for the state of Texas. While in Galveston, he collapsed on the street on September 27, 1876, and died in a matter of minutes of a massive stroke. He was buried in Mobile.

Bragg's career and his inability to follow up on any successes he achieved is taken by some historians as a parable of the Southern experience in the war. In more recent years, a few medical researchers have concluded that some of his hazy indecisiveness at critical times could be traced to the opium-based medicines that doctors prescribed to treat his various painful maladies.

Almost to the last, he railed against the "old, trading politicians and demagogues" in Richmond who, he was convinced, had sold out the cause. When asked about reconciliation with the North, he replied: "The war is over but there is no peace, and there can never be between two such people."

The saddest summation, however, was offered by one of his soldiers, Samuel R. Watkins, in the book, *Company Aytch.*

"None of General Bragg's soldiers ever loved him," wrote Watkins. "They had no faith in his ability as a general. He was looked upon as a merciless tyrant.... He loved to crush the spirit of his men. The more a hang-dog look they had about them the better was General Bragg pleased. Not a single soldier in the whole army ever loved or respected him."

ROBERT A. TOOMBS

"He was no soldier and had no business in the Army, but he took good care of his men and did the best he could, and was deserving much more credit than some who have a higher name in history for their war record."

Capt. J. C. Haskell, Army of Northern Virginia

Irascible might be a gentle way of describing Robert Toombs. One might also try argumentative, immoderate, and intolerant.

"Bob Toombs disagrees with himself between meals," wrote Southern diarist Tucker DeLeon.

"Had he been less surely entrenched as a member of the ruling class, he would have been a demagogue," wrote historian Douglas Southall Freeman. "If he had been more patiently tolerant, he would have been a statesman."

But one must always add that he was brilliant, talented, and ferociously intelligent. "One of the South's tragedies was the fact that it never quite found out how to put his undeniable talents to work," wrote Bruce Catton, in *The Coming Fury.*

That failure was not through lack of trying. Toombs was the man Jefferson Davis beat out for president of the Confederacy. He was then named secretary of state, a job for which he was temperamentally unsuited. After that he was made a brigadier general. But he quarreled with everyone around him and challenged a fellow general to a duel before achieving a degree of military distinction amid the carnage at Antietam.

When Davis refused to promote him, he resigned from the army and spent the rest of the war complaining and undercutting the government. Ultimately, he was a tragic figure, losing his family and his country, and living to see the South change beyond his understanding.

Toombs also drank a little, and that may have cost him more than all his other weaknesses. It certainly was a decisive factor in his loss of the presidency to Davis. During the nominating convention in Montgomery in 1861, he was observed tippling a bit more heavily than many delegates thought was proper in a national leader. That convinced them to back Davis as the more serious man.

He was born into the privileged world of a Georgia plantation and grew to manhood convinced of the superiority of the white race and the necessity for defending slavery. An ardent supporter of the Union in his early political career and an ally of Abraham Lincoln in Congress, he turned into one of the most impassioned of the Fire-Eaters, demanding secession when he became convinced that Lincoln would trample on states' rights as president.

Toombs was born in 1810 in Wilkes County, a few miles north of his lifelong home of Washington, Georgia. His forebears had moved from Virginia and in the generation before his birth established themselves as prosperous slaveholding plantation gentry.

He was enrolled at the University of Georgia as a precocious 14 year old. His three years there were marked by brawls and insubordination, punctuated by flashes of brilliant scholarship. He was expelled as a sophomore for attacking two tormentors with a pistol, hatchet, and knife—although no harm was done in the altercation. Both of the university's literary societies, however, submitted petitions calling for his reinstatement. That expulsion was rescinded, but in his senior year he was permanently thrown out of school for an assortment of offenses, including drinking.

Toombs, eventually, graduated from Union College, in Schenectady, New York. He then entered the

University of Virginia Law School and earned a degree in 1829, but finished at the bottom of his class.

Undaunted, he returned to Georgia and quickly gained a reputation as one of the best attorneys in the state. A gifted orator, his appeals to juries were regarded as masterful by his contemporaries. His best friend, fellow Georgian and future Confederate vice president, Alexander Stephens, said he had "never seen his superior before judge and jury."

Varina Howell Davis, wife of the future Confederate president, described him in her memoirs as "an agreeable companion ... his wit keen, and his audacity made him equal to anything in the heat of debate. His coloring was good, and his teeth brilliant white.... His eyes were magnificent, dark and flashing, and they had a certain lawless way of ranging about that was indicative of his character."

In 1830, the 20-year-old Toombs married Julia Ann DuBose, a match that would last for 53 years and give him three children, all of whom preceded him in death. They moved into a fine home seven years later on Washington's main street, which is now named after him. Toombs remained in this house for the rest of his life. It is now a state memorial.

With his considerable legal income added to the wealth of the land he had inherited, Toombs had a solid financial base on which to enter politics. In the South of the 1830s, men of property who could not stomach the Democratic Party of Andrew Jackson joined the Whigs. They stood for financial conservatism and, in the party's Southern wing, the preservation of slavery through guarantees that were understood to lie within the Constitution.

Toombs was elected to the state legislature in 1836 on this platform. Even during the severe depression of the 1830s, he insisted on sound finances coming ahead of debtor relief.

He spoke rarely on national affairs, but unlike most Southerners, he opposed the annexation of Texas. It was generally felt throughout the region that the addition of this vast territory would give slavery room to expand and enable Southern interests to control the federal government. But Toombs foresaw that the sectional conflict such an expansion would cause was too high a price. He did not like the idea of forcing a national debate on slavery, a debate that would surely arise in the aftermath of any such territorial war.

Moreover, he was not eager for war. "A people who go to war without just and sufficient cause, with no other motive than pride or love of glory, are enemies to the human race and deserve the execration of all mankind," he wrote at the time of the Texas debate.

After seven one-year terms in the state legislature, he was sent to Congress in 1845. His first four years there were spent quietly, following the same conservative financial agenda he had backed in Georgia. He also opposed the Mexican War, partially because it was sponsored by President James K. Polk, a Democrat, and partially because of his old fears of what would follow large-scale territorial acquisitions.

The argumentative Robert A. Toombs lost to Jefferson Davis for president of the Confederacy, served as secretary of state, and commanded as a brigadier general. *National Archives and Records Administration*

At war's end, Toombs's misgivings proved justified. The Wilmot Proviso, attached to the treaty ending the war, tried to prohibit the expansion of slavery into the new territories. As a practical matter, it was highly unlikely that any of the new lands were suitable to a slave-based agricultural economy. But the debate over the Proviso, which passed the House but was never considered by the Senate, was weighted with symbolic explosives.

Toombs did not want slavery expanded, but he also didn't want the government telling the South that it could not be expanded. He felt that denial of the right to spread slavery was a threat to the Constitutional

Toombs lived in Washington, Georgia, just south of his birthplace in Wilkes County. His home is now a state memorial. ***Library of Congress***

privileges that protected the "peculiar institution" where it already existed. Erosion of any piece of that protection threatened the whole.

The issue of slavery's expansion refused to go away, though, and by 1850 many Southern states were considering secession to protect their rights. In the historic debate over the Compromise of 1850, which would delay the Civil War by another decade, Toombs emerged as a vigorous defender of the Union, but not if its preservation came at the expense of the South. On February 27, he delivered one of his most effective speeches in Congress, outlining his position.

"In this emergency," he said, "our duty is clear; it is to stand by the Constitution and laws ... until the act of exclusion is put in the statute books. It will then be demonstrated that the Constitution is powerless for our protection. It will then be not only the right but the duty of the slaveholding states to resume the power which they have conferred upon this government and to seek new safeguards for their future security. When the argument is exhausted, we will stand by our arms."

Toombs's speech was well received in the South. As the long debate, featuring some of the greatest names in the history of Congress—Henry Clay, Daniel Webster, and John Calhoun—wound on through the spring, Toombs emerged as the emotional voice of the entire region. When he rose to speak on June 15, 1850, he was about to become a national figure.

He repeated his insistence that Southerners be allowed to enter the new territories with all the rights they now enjoyed in their own states.

"Deprive us of this right," he said, "and appropriate the common property to yourselves, and it is then your government, not mine. Then I am its enemy, and I will then, if I can, bring my children and my constituents to the altar of liberty, and like Hamilcar I would swear them to eternal hostility to your foul domination. Give us our just rights and we are ready, as ever heretofore, to stand by the Union, every part of it.... Refuse it and I for one will strike for independence."

The Hamilcar speech (named for its reference to the father of Hannibal, the Carthaginian leader in the Punic Wars against Rome) caused a sensation. Even his friends were alarmed at its combative tone, and the first insinuations of a drinking problem began finding their way into print (although there was no evidence of intoxication when he gave the speech). Toombs was now a hero throughout the South, but regarded as a dangerous man elsewhere.

His biographer, William Y. Thompson, writes that the speech provides a critical insight into Toombs's character. "Basically a man of conservative instincts," says Thompson, "he could in moments of commotion explode in any direction, after which he would assemble the pieces and resume his former character."

But as the breakup of the Union neared, the explosive Toombs, the fire-eater, was the one who took control.

Toombs was one of the final architects of the Compromise of 1850. After it was ratified, however, he no longer felt there was a home for him with the Whigs. He led in the formation of a new party in Georgia, the Constitutional Union, and was elected from it in 1852 to the U.S. Senate. Eventually, he went over to the Democrats. It was a reluctant move, but formation of the new Republican Party, with the anti-slavery Northern wing of the Whigs at its core, offered him no alternative.

Toombs still saw himself as a Unionist in 1859 but events were rushing past him. After a September speech in Augusta, urging moderation and opposing a specific plank in the next Democratic platform that would protect slavery, he was denounced in his own state as having gone soft.

"We do not say that Senator Toombs is an Abolitionist in feeling or in principle," wrote the Macon Telegraph, in a fairly typical response. "...But we do say, and say it deliberately and we believe it when we say it, that he is an unprincipled traitor to the rights and interests of the South ..."

After that, Toombs was never anything less than a fire-eater, and with the election of Lincoln in 1860 the flames rose steadily higher. He was convinced the spirit that had enabled Congress to weave a compromise 10 years before was now dead.

Toombs was appointed in December to a bipartisan Senate Committee of Thirteen, which tried to formulate a set of principles by which the South could remain in the Union. But there was no chance that a declaration of slaveholding rights would be approved by the Committee's Republican members or by Lincoln.

Earlier in this congressional session, when complimented for his more moderate tone, Toombs had responded: "I always try to behave myself at a funeral." But now the corpse was well and truly buried. After the final Committee of Thirteen vote, Toombs wired a message to Georgia newspapers that "secession should be thundered from the ballot box" and that remaining in the Union was "fraught with nothing but ruin for yourselves and your posterity."

On January 7, 1861, he rose on the Senate floor for

Alexander Stephens, Confederate vice president, was Toombs's best friend and political ally. *National Archives and Records Administration*

the final time to announce his resignation and fire off one last salvo at the North. First denouncing the Republican anti-slavery wing, he affirmed that "we want no Negro equality, no Negro citizenship; we want no mongrel race to degrade our own.

"Restore us [our] rights as we had them ... redress these flagrant wrongs seen by all men. Refuse them and what then? We shall then ask you: Let us depart in peace. Refuse that and you present us with war. We accept it."

Cheers and hisses filled the chamber as Toombs sat down. Three days later, he nearly got into a fistfight with General Winfield Scott, in an argument over a Northern ship sent to relieve the besieged Fort Sumter. Then he departed Washington, D.C., forever.

When Toombs returned to Washington, Georgia, he had every reason to expect that he would be named president of the Confederacy. He was a national figure, and his speeches had made him a familiar name across the South. Moreover, he wanted the job. Davis,

Toombs entered politics in the 1830s, joining the Whigs and spending seven years in the state legislature before being elected to Congress. ***Dictionary of American Portraits***

regarded as the only other man in the South of comparable stature, had made it clear that with his West Point training he anticipated a military commission. When delegates from the seceding states met in Montgomery, in February 1861, to choose a leader, Davis stayed home in Mississippi.

But things were in disarray within the Georgia delegation. It was assumed by many of the other states that Georgia wanted former secretary of the treasury and U.S. Representative Howell Cobb as its candidate. That was not a popular choice outside of Georgia. So several delegations, many of which would have preferred Toombs, rallied around Davis to block Cobb. When the Georgia delegates realized what was happening, they did get behind Toombs, but by that time it was too late.

Toombs had remarked acidly that Cobb had done more for the South in President James Buchanan's cabinet than anyone else. As secretary of the treasury, Toombs said, Cobb had been such a free spender that he had nearly bankrupted the federal government and "did not even leave old Buck two quarters to put on his eyes when he died."

It was the sort of witticism that made men laugh but left them wondering if the speaker had the necessary gravity for the new nation's highest office. Stephens wrote in a private letter that two nights before the balloting Toombs "got quite tight at dinner and went to a party in town tighter than I ever saw him—too tight for his character and reputation by far. I think that evening's exhibition settled the Presidency where it fell."

As compensation to Georgia, Stephens was named vice president, and on February 24, Toombs was sworn in as secretary of state, a job he did not want and for which he had no calling.

If Toombs had been given a choice of cabinet posts, his preference would have been Treasury. His public career had been based on advocating sound money, and he was greatly disturbed by an overreliance on credit to finance the war.

He endured the State Department for five months, but the position lacked any meaning. Toombs was given two goals. The first, to arrange a peaceful departure from the Union, was impossible. The second, to arrange a treaty with Britain, was illusory. Britain was not as dependent on imported cotton as the South wanted to believe, and public opinion there was firmly set against support of a nation that was going to war for the right to own slaves. Arguments over states' rights were lost on the British. They were not about to offer comfort to slavery.

Toombs's frustrations mounted. The post had nei-

Though he long argued for preservation of the Union, Toombs opposed new restrictions on slavery. With Abraham Lincoln's election, he saw no alternative but secession. ***Library of Congress***

Toombs lost control of his force at Malvern Hill, but the Confederate loss there concerned him less than General Daniel Harvey Hill's insult of his generalship. ***Library of Congress***

ther stature nor depth. When a job applicant confronted him, Toombs took off his top hat in exasperation and said: "Can you get in here, sir? That's the Department of State, sir."

Almost alone among Davis's cabinet members, he argued against bombarding Fort Sumter. In an echo of the speech he had given 24 years before on the issue of going to war to annex Texas, he said that he did not feel competent to advise anyone on touching off "a civil war greater than the world had ever seen." As the cabinet meeting went on, Toombs paced the floor, hands behind his back. Finally, he could keep silent no longer.

"Mr. President," he said, "at this time it is suicide, murder and will lose us every friend in the North. You will wantonly strike a hornets' nest which extends from mountains to ocean, and legions now quiet will swarm out and sting us to death. It is unnecessary, it puts us in the wrong; it is fatal."

But Lincoln was just as determined to force the issue of Fort Sumter as Davis was, and in the end Toombs's advice, which was right on the mark, was disregarded.

While he had been reluctant to begin hostilities by firing the first shot, once the conflict was underway, he wanted eagerly to carry it to the North. He regarded the South's defensive strategy as self-defeating and felt the only war it could win was a short one, in which it took the offensive immediately.

The Confederate generals were too closely tied to the lessons they had learned at West Point, he insisted, and they were the very same lessons being employed by their Union counterparts. Toombs felt the South possessed a distinct elan and could not win a struggle in which it simply mirrored its opponent.

"Set this down in your book," he would write later to Stephens. "Died of West Point. We have patched a new government out of old cloth; we have tied the living to the dead."

In July 1861, Toombs resigned from the cabinet and was given the rank of brigadier general, commanding a Georgia infantry brigade, by the highly reluctant Davis. He had no military training, but plenty of self-confidence. However, he was 51 years old, rather portly, accustomed to good living. His family was against the change because they feared he could not stand up to the rigors of camp life.

At Antietam, Toombs had orders to hold the only Confederate-controlled bridge over the creek. ***Library of Congress***

But they had little to worry about for a while. He spent most of his first 11 months quarreling with General Joseph E. Johnston, whom he called a "poor devil, small, arbitrary and inefficient ... who a few months ago I could have made or ruined by a word and who as soon as this little war is over and I go back to the Senate will be so much below me that my sense of magnanimity will forbid my ever getting even with him."

He saw some action at Yorktown at the start of the Peninsula Campaign, in the spring of 1862. His first serious engagement, however, was at Golding's Farm, on June 27, during the Seven Days Battles east of Richmond. It did not go well.

Toombs's disparaging attitude towards caution was well known in the army, and he was given written orders because his superior, General John Magruder, did not trust him to follow verbal ones. In a move that was only supposed to ascertain enemy strength and intentions, he was told to feint towards the Union lines in concert with Colonel G. T. Anderson.

When Anderson encountered resistance, he halted. But Toombs, disregarding the plan, kept plunging forward, and was thrown back with heavy losses. Upon hearing the report of this engagement, General Robert E. Lee ordered a cessation of any offensive action until further notice.

On the following morning, however, Toombs attacked again. Because of a lack of coordination, Lee's orders got to Anderson but not to Toombs. His attack carried to the federal lines, but because the anticipated support from Anderson never came, he had to fall back. Toombs, in a letter to Stephens, called Magruder "an old ass" and blamed him for the defeat.

There was worse to come. On July 1, as the series of battles continued, Toombs was sent to Malvern Hill, which was ringed with federal artillery and supported by gunboats on the James River. It was a confusing, chaotic battle. At one point, during the peak of the thunderous naval bombardment, Confederate General Theophilus Holmes, almost completely deaf, came out of his headquarters, cupped a hand to his ear and said: "I thought I heard firing."

Toombs, from most accounts, lost control of his force, which at one point was lined up aimlessly behind a fence. General Daniel Harvey Hill came by and ordered it to charge, but it soon was repulsed and scattered by fire coming from the top of the hill. Hill then rounded on Toombs.

"For shame," he cried, "rally your troops. Where were you when I was riding up and down your line rallying your troops?"

Malvern Hill was a Confederate disaster, shattering

the last illusion that the Yankees would wilt under fire. Hill was in despair over what he had seen there and later said: "It was not war—it was murder." But for Toombs the main concern was the blow to his honor.

He wrote Hill and demanded an apology for the remarks he had made about his brigade. Hill replied that his remarks had not been intended for the brigade but for Toombs.

"It is notorious," wrote Hill, "that you have a thousand times expressed your disgust that the commanding general did not permit you to fight. It is equally notorious that you retired from the field."

This was too much. Toombs demanded a duel. Hill refused, on the grounds that "we have a battle to fight and a country to defend ... and it would be abhorrent to my principles and character." The dispute soon fizzled out, but again Toombs had come across as a bumbler and malcontent.

Then on August 18, he was arrested for once more disregarding orders. He left a road unguarded near Verdiersville, Virginia, almost resulting in the capture of J. E. B. Stuart. Toombs wrote Stephens that he was being persecuted and that his reason for leaving his position was to make sure that his hungry men would have cooked rations on their advance north.

He was released in time to fight at Second Manassas and led his brigade, which cheered his arrival vigorously. There are differing accounts on how large a role Toombs played in this victory, but it was enough to restore him to the good graces of the Confederate command.

On September 17, Lee's advance to the north reached Antietam Creek, outside the town of Sharpsburg, Maryland. The Battle of Antietam would be the single bloodiest day of the war. There were 22,700 casualties on both sides. Political commentator George Will once wrote that if television had existed in 1862 and sent back images such as those it caught in Vietnam, the Civil War would have ended on this day.

Lee had intended to force a battle on Northern soil and inflict a decisive defeat on the Union army. But a courier lost a copy of his strategic plan, and it fell into the hands of the Union commander, Major General George McClellan. Even with this advantage, McClellan, as was his wont, moved too cautiously and gave Lee the time to array his vastly outnumbered forces in an excellent defensive position.

Still, an important segment of the Confederate forces, under General Ambrose P. Hill, was still many miles to the south, at Harpers Ferry, and could not get to Sharpsburg before the battle began. The Federals also controlled two of the three bridges across Antietam Creek.

The third bridge was held by Toombs, on the far right of the Southern line. It was imperative that he hold this position or the entire army would be turned.

The battle opened on the Confederate left, a fierce, horrific struggle that left 13,000 men dead or wounded in four hours. Then the center came under assault, with Daniel Harvey Hill barely able to hold on before the Union onslaught.

Finally, the pressure began to build on Toombs. Facing him were the forces of General Ambrose Burnside, and at 9 A.M. they started a tentative thrust at the bridge. But Toombs's force occupied the heights on the far side of the creek and had a clear shot at the road leading to the bridge.

For four critical hours, while the rest of the Confederate line was fighting for survival, this bridge held on. Finally, at 1 P.M., Burnside brought up reinforcements in overwhelming numbers, and Toombs was forced to fall back from the bridge to defensive positions further up the hill.

By 3 P.M., Burnside had pushed the Confederates back into the town of Sharpsburg and was within 1,200 yards of breaking the Southern lines. It was at this moment that Ambrose P. Hill's troops arrived at last and smashed into the Union advance. Toombs, seeing his opportunity, attacked the Union flank at the same instant. The double blow broke the federal advance and sent them in retreat down the hillside and back to the creek.

The bridge held during the critical hours by Toombs is now called the Burnside Bridge and is used by the National Park Service as the visual signature of Antietam National Battlefield.

Lee had barely survived, but McClellan, cautious as always, refused to renew the attack the following day, allowing the Confederates to slip away back to Virginia. Despite the bloody price, Antietam ended as an indecisive engagement. But since it had blunted Lee's offensive, it gave Lincoln the opportunity he was awaiting to issue the Emancipation Proclamation.

Toombs had grown increasingly disgusted with what he had seen of the army, and, it must be said, vice versa. He had written his wife that he would not leave, however, until he had distinguished himself in battle. "The day after such an event, I will retire, if I live through it," he said.

On the day following Antietam, while riding on a still-contested portion of the battlefield, he came upon a Union cavalry patrol and in an exchange of gunfire was shot through the hand. He returned home to recover from the wound and to await a promotion from Davis that he was sure would follow his valiant efforts at the bridge. Lee himself had described his actions there as "marked by distinguished gallantry."

But no such word came from Richmond, and Toombs decided that what Davis really wanted was to drive him out of the army. He returned to his troops in

General Ambrose Burnside (above) opposed Toombs at Antietam, mounting an assault to cross what is now know as Burnside Bridge (top). Toombs held the bridge for four hours, but Burnside came close to breaking the Confederate line. *National Archives and Records Administration/Library of Congress*

March 1863, and a few days later told them that he was resigning his commission.

"Under existing conditions," he stated in explanation, "I can no longer hold my commission under President Davis with advantage to my country, or to you, or with honor to myself."

With that, he returned to Georgia. Neither Lee nor Davis lamented his departure. As a general, he had been far more trouble than he was worth, and there was no inclination by anyone in the army to promote him further. Toombs never believed that, however, and felt it was only personal animosity by Davis, whom he took to referring to as "that scoundrel," that held him back.

Once back home, Toombs spent the rest of the war sulking and bitterly criticizing Davis's policies. He was against the military draft. He was against the use of credit and paper currency to finance the war, suspension of habeas corpus, impressment of supplies, Lee's military strategy. Toombs and his old friend Stephens became a two-man chorus of rising discontent, fracturing Confederate solidarity, and Davis fully returned their contempt.

In June, Toombs refused to join a voluntary program to switch from cotton to foodstuffs on his plantations, thundering that no government could tell him what he could raise on his own land. As a result of this anti-government attitude, his popularity began to plunge in Georgia, and when he ran for a seat in the Confederate senate, he was defeated in the state legislature, which made the selection. At one point, he was arrested after making a speech in Savannah, which rehashed all his grievances against Davis, and threatened with a court-martial. But the proceedings were dropped.

He volunteered to raise a militia unit to help defend Atlanta in the battle for that city, but could do little to slow the inexorable Union advance across the state in late 1864. Stephens wrote to him with the suggestion that Georgia salvage a hopeless situation by making a separate peace. But Toombs responded by advising his friend to forget the idea, because "it will place you in a wrong, very wrong position."

Even in the North, his activities were noted. His bitter speeches came to the attention of Lincoln's Secretary of the Navy Gideon Welles. He wrote in his diary that "scarcely a man has contributed more than Toombs to the calamities that are upon us and I am glad to see that he is aware of the misery that he and his associates have inflicted upon the country. I have always considered him a reckless partisan ... an unfit leader in public affairs."

When the end came, a detachment of Union cavalry arrived at his home in Washington, Georgia, on May 11, 1865, and announced they had come to arrest him. Toombs, having been forewarned, slipped out the back door and escaped. The house was confiscated a few months later. The former U.S. senator and general became a fugitive, hiding in his own homeland, before finally reaching New Orleans in November and boarding a ship for exile in Cuba.

He and his wife moved on to Paris. But overcome with loneliness and a sense of estrangement, he began to consider a return home, even though he had sworn he would never live in a defeated land. In October 1866, he received the crushing news that his last surviving child, Sallie, had died in Georgia, leaving four small children.

He set out for America three months later, "my hopes buried in the grave." He shrugged off the possibility of being imprisoned. "I don't see much to choose between my present condition and any decent fort," he wrote his wife, who had preceded him to Georgia.

He found that the desire for retribution that blazed up at the end of the war had passed, and he was allowed to return home without interference. However, he refused to apply for a pardon and, under the laws of Reconstruction, was not considered an American citizen.

This didn't seem to bother him much. He took up his law practice and began to rebuild the fortune he had lost in the war. He regained much of his zest for political combat, opposing the policies of the radical Republicans and campaigning for Democratic candidates in the election of 1868. Georgia was one of the few states the party won.

After the war, Toombs escaped to Cuba and moved to Paris. He eventually returned home to establish himself as an elder Southern statesman. ***Battles and Leaders of the Civil War***

Slowly, the popularity that he had squandered by his behavior during the war was regained. He was perceived in the state as a fearless campaigner against the abuses of the Carpetbaggers and a defender of Southern rights. He also gained a reputation as a fighter against railroad profiteering and other corporate excesses.

But he had become mired in the past. Toombs angrily rejected talk of a New South, insisting that the future of the region must rely on the agricultural values of the prewar era and not industrialization. So while he awakened nostalgic enthusiasm in his speeches and public statements, he was increasingly regarded as an anachronism.

Another call for a duel, this time with an old political enemy, Governor Joe Brown, did nothing to enhance his standing. As Reconstruction ended and Georgia regained its full political rights, his role once again diminished.

Toombs did play a major part in the state's constitutional convention of 1877. He had called for such a meeting for several years, primarily to repudiate the constitution imposed by the Republicans in 1868. With his unrepentant racist beliefs, Toombs wanted to severely restrict the black vote. In fact, some of his wilder pronouncements on this issue ("I can make you a convention in which the people will rule and the nigger never be heard of") almost succeeded in killing off the meeting before it began.

Once it convened, however, Toombs chaired two key committees and got much of his agenda passed. With that, however, his public career ended.

Insisting that he be addressed as General Toombs, he stepped into the role of colorful elder statesman. Sitting in his home or in the lobby of his favorite Atlanta hotel, he met reporters and politicians and issued quotable, inflammatory statements that no one took seriously. "I am not loyal to the existing government of the United States," he told all who would listen, "and do not want to be suspected of loyalty."

He also insisted for years that his hometown of Washington need not build a hotel. "If a visitor is a gentleman, he is welcome to stay with me," said Toombs. "If he isn't a gentleman, we don't want him in Washington."

He continued his feud with Davis and the advocates of the New South. But he was drinking to excess and becoming increasingly careless in matters of dress. The death of his wife in 1883 seemed to sap most of his energy and spirit.

His last public appearance came upon the election of the Democratic candidate, Grover Cleveland, as president in 1884. This was a victory celebrated in the South as the end of Republican political dominance. A crowd gathered in front of his home in Washington and chanted his name. The old man came out and delivered a short, emotional address and then invited everyone inside for refreshments.

He died little more than a year later, in the pillared mansion he had occupied for 47 years, almost blind and not often lucid. "He is the most remarkable man in many respects the South ever produced," wrote the Atlanta Constitution, "and it is doubtful if the records of a lordlier life than his can be found in the history of our republic."

Assessments were less generous in the Northern press, which reminded readers of his past as a fire-eater and his continued appeals to racial bigotry.

His biographer, William Y. Thompson, concurred. Toombs "missed the stature of greatness" he wrote. "He could have done much more. Robert Toombs, unfortunately for himself and his country, will live mainly as a legend."

The Eccentrics

PIERRE GUSTAVE TOUTANT BEAUREGARD

"An ardent heart, a fine-looking soldier, a mediocre strategist, an able engineer."

E. Grasset in A History of the War of Secession *(French)*

Had he been born in the previous century, in the homeland of his ancestors, he might have been one of Napoleon Bonaparte's commanders. As it was, Pierre G. T. Beauregard admired the Corsican general above all other military leaders and modeled his own behavior and thinking after Bonaparte.

In the flowery, overwrought language of his dispatches and in the dramatic exhortations to his soldiers and citizens of the Confederacy, Beauregard seemed to come from another time and place. While he shared many attributes with the chivalric cavalry leader Jeb Stuart, Beauregard lacked that general's self-deprecatory sense of humor. He was quick to take offense at anything touching his sensitivities, which encompassed an astonishingly wide array of comment.

"I know that if I succeed I only increase the irritation of certain persons against me," he wrote moodily to a friend, "and if I fail, their satisfaction and ire. Without intending to flatter myself, I feel like Samson shorn of his locks."

But he did intend to flatter himself and did it endlessly, so that his pen became his worst enemy. He also fought with Jefferson Davis and his abrasive secretary of war, Judah P. Benjamin, and opposed the strategies of General Joseph E. Johnston and Robert E. Lee.

"The history of war is full of buried feasibilities that might have been brilliant realities," he wrote in criticism of them all. "If it were not for this 'I dare not' waiting upon 'I would.'"

His greatest joy was planning. Right up to the final hopeless months of the war, Beauregard was full of grand theories and magnificent strategies to win it. It was his greatest disappointment that no one ever seemed to share his sweeping visions. Davis, indeed, described them as "driveling on possibilities."

What makes this all the odder is that in the two major battles he did plan, First Manassas and Shiloh, his overly complicated schemes collapsed at the very outset, and the fight went on in spite of them. But that never seemed to deter him.

He was a small man, about five foot seven, but quite muscular and proud of his physical strength. With his olive complexion and carefully groomed mustache, he was one of the finest looking generals in the Confederacy. But even when he was a cadet at West Point, observers could not help noticing a deep sadness that marked his eyes.

The troops called him "Old Bory" and admired him, even when he addressed them in the lavish rhetoric he favored. "Soldiers," began one typical flourish, "untoward events saved the enemy from annihilation. His insolent presence still pollutes your soil, his hostile flag still flaunts before you. There can be no peace so long as these things are."

The voice is the voice of Old Bory, but the words are an echo of Bonaparte.

P. G. T. Beauregard modeled himself after Napoleon Bonaparte. His passion for grand battle plans seemed undiminished by their frequent collapse. ***National Archives and Records Administration***

He was born into the Creole aristocracy of Louisiana, on Contreras Plantation in St. Bernard Parish. He proudly traced his French ancestry to the thirteenth century. Around 1600 it was combined through marriage with Welsh nobility and assumed the name Toutant de Beauregard.

His great grandfather came to Louisiana during the reign of Louis XIV and grew rich there. His father, Jacques, married a de Reggio from the Italian ducal family of Este. The life they made on their plantation was more Mediterranean in style than it was American. Most of his biographers believe that young Pierre, born in 1818, did not even speak English until he reached the age of 12.

He was educated in the French language schools of New Orleans and went on to yet another such institution in New York City. The headmasters there, brothers named Peugnet, were veterans of the army of Napoleon. Beauregard listened to their tales and dreamed of emulating their hero.

There were stories told later that presaged a military career. How as a nine year old he picked up a stick and chased away an adult who was teasing him about his skill as a hunter. And how he dashed away from his First Holy Communion when he heard drums on the street outside the cathedral.

Still, his parents were taken aback when he announced his desire to enter West Point in 1834. The Creoles stood aloof from the U.S. government and the army. They were in this country but not really of it. But when the father saw how determined his son was, he pulled the right political strings, and the appointment was made.

His career there was brilliant, and Beauregard graduated second in his class, although he was never popular. He also decided that his name sounded too Gallic. For a while, he simply called himself Gustave, then used just his initials, P. G. T., a form he favored the rest of his life.

His class rank entitled him to choose the branch of the service he favored. In those years, most ambitious young officers picked the engineers, and Beauregard was sent in that capacity to Newport, Rhode Island. The genteel social life in the resort, favored at the time by many Southern planters in summer, appealed to him. But a chronic throat condition, a malady that would plague him throughout his career, kicked up during winter. He was transferred to balmier posts in Florida and then, to his delight, Louisiana.

His assignment there was to make a topographic map of the state's mysterious Barataria region, onetime haunt of the pirate Jean Lafitte. Within two years, in 1841, he also had married Marie Laure Villere, daughter of another old Creole family.

Aside from nearly engaging in a foolhardy duel that would have involved shotguns (the sheriff arrived before anyone could start blasting away), his career in his home state passed uneventfully. But when war with Mexico broke out in 1846, Lieutenant Beauregard was sent to Puebla to join the staff of General Winfield Scott.

There had been rumors of an earlier love affair with Scott's daughter, which ended when the young lady was sent off to Europe by her disapproving parents. If that was true, however, no trace of it seemed to cloud the early relationship between the two men in Mexico.

Beauregard distinguished himself especially on the April 1846 advance inland. At the mountain pass of Cerro Gordo, his commanding officer, General David

Twiggs, brushed aside Beauregard's reconnaissance report. It recommended taking a hill adjacent to the Mexican entrenchments and avoiding a frontal assault.

Historians of the war have described Twiggs as a first-rate fighter but "not possessing the highest intellect in the Army." Fortunately, Scott overruled his battle plan, and Beauregard's advice was taken, resulting in an American victory at a much lower cost.

"Young man," said Scott after the battle, "if I were not on horseback I would embrace you."

Beauregard won even greater satisfaction at the climactic battle at Chapultepec, the fortress guarding the approach to Mexico City. Scott chose Beauregard's suggested route of attack rather than the one recommended by his trusted chief of staff, Captain Robert E. Lee.

Nonetheless, Lee was awarded a new brevet, and Beauregard, twice wounded in the fight, was passed over. He nursed his resentment against Scott for the rest of his life, later criticizing him for undertaking the campaign inland from Puebla because it violated military principle by abandoning his base.

Historian Robert Leckie argues that Beauregard's position illustrates one of his major flaws as a strategist. "The book-swallowing Beauregard never did develop political acumen and thus could not understand Scott's real reasoning...He [left the base] because he feared that at any moment an order might arrive from the jealous and hostile President Polk recalling him to Washington. Although Beauregard had seen war, books, not experience, remained his guide and a solution of a situation not arising in print always eluded him."

There were more personal disappointments, as well. His wife died in childbirth in 1850. He remarried another member of the Creole elite, Caroline Deslonde, but it appears to have been a match made as much for political advantage as passion. Her family was related to U.S. Senator John Slidell, and, using some of his connections, Beauregard briefly entered politics.

He was a fervent supporter of the Democratic candidate, Franklin Pierce, in the 1852 presidential election. Pierce's victory gave Beauregard special satisfaction because he defeated the hated Winfield Scott. Beauregard ran for mayor of New Orleans in 1858, but he was identified too closely with the Creole establishment and went down to defeat.

His full-time occupation, however, was as an engineer. For most of the 1850s he was superintendent of federal projects in the New Orleans area, improving navigation on the lower Mississippi River and building a new U.S. Customs House.

While he did not take an active role in the critical election of 1860, he made no secret that his sympathies

To the surprise of his Creole parents, Beauregard elected to attend West Point. He was ranked second in his class. *Library of Congress*

As a young engineer officer, Beauregard was sent to Rhode Island. A chronic throat ailment prompted a later transfer to his native Louisiana. *Missouri Historical Society*

General David Twiggs disregarded Beauregard's reconnaissance report that argued against a frontal assault at Cerro Gordo. Fortunately, General Winfield Scott overruled him. *Center for American History, University of Texas at Austin*

rested with the South. In a final defiant gesture, however, his in-law, Slidell, and outgoing Secretary of War John B. Floyd, a future Confederate general, secured Beauregard the appointment as superintendent of West Point.

Given the deteriorating political situation, it remains baffling why he took the job. Beauregard, now a major, knew that Louisiana was close to seceding, and when it left the Union, he would go with it. Nonetheless, he arrived at the U.S. Military Academy on January 23, 1861, to take up his new post.

When cadets from southern states approached him for advice, he responded: "Watch me, and when I jump, you jump. What's the use of jumping too soon?"

He never got the chance to jump. After five days, his appointment was rescinded, establishing a mark for brevity in the job which probably will never be equaled. Later, he billed the U.S. government for travel expenses and even while serving with the Confederacy insisted that he was entitled to the money.

The crafty Slidell had the situation wired, however. He had anticipated what would happen at West Point but wanted Beauregard sent there as a career move to build up his reputation. He still lost out to Braxton Bragg as commander of Louisiana's armed forces, but Slidell saw an even better opportunity shaping up.

The U.S. Army was refusing to surrender its fort in the harbor at Charleston, South Carolina. Although a minor post which could not possibly withstand an extended siege, it was a major political chip for President Abraham Lincoln. If there was to be a war, he understood the necessity of maneuvering the Confederacy into firing the first shot somewhere. Fort Sumter was the most likely candidate to be on its receiving end.

The South also recognized the political importance of Sumter, and Slidell lobbied hard to place his relative in command of the campaign to take it. On February 26, Beauregard was appointed the Confederacy's first brigadier general and sent off to Charleston.

He arrived to a tumultuous welcome. Charleston had been the very epicenter of secession, and if eagerness for war blazed anywhere in the South, it was here. Beauregard himself was charmed by the city and its people. The courtliness he found there was so much like New Orleans, he wrote family members, "that I see but little difference."

The garrison at the island fort was commanded by Major Robert Anderson, a native of Kentucky who was married to a woman from Georgia and considered in the army to have strong pro-slavery sympathies. He had also been Beauregard's artillery instructor at West Point. Anderson was a 36-year veteran of the army and a man who understood what was expected of him.

"We shall strive to do our duty," he wrote in his

Beauregard briefly entered politics, supporting presidential candidate Franklin Pierce and running unsuccessfully for mayor of New Orleans. *New-York Historical Society*

official report, "though I frankly say that my heart is not in the war which I see is thus to be commenced." Anderson knew that his situation was impossible, that the fort could not stand up to concentrated shelling. Yet it could not be surrendered without a fight.

Beauregard inspected the artillery configuration that the gentlemen of Charleston had made to batter the fort. Trying not to give offense, he set these unprofessional plans aside and began to realign the shore batteries so that the entire harbor was sealed off by what he called "a circle of fire."

The situation dragged on through the month of March 1861 with the Charleston home guard conducting military drills on the waterfront and Anderson doing what he could to shore up his defenses. But by April 10, two decisions had been made that would lead directly to war.

A supply ship left New York to provide Anderson with food, and the Confederate cabinet voted to move on Sumter before it could land there. Davis understood that Lincoln was forcing his hand but felt a forceful response was justified. Beauregard was instructed to ask for Sumter's surrender and, if it was refused, to open fire.

The general confidently sent out two members of his staff by boat under a white flag on April 11 to meet with his old teacher. Beauregard's note outlined the reasons for his surrender demand in two paragraphs and then came to the point in the third.

"All proper facilities will be afforded for the removal of yourself and your command, together with company arms and property, and all private property, to any post in the United States which you may select. The flag which you have upheld so long and with so much fortitude, under the most trying circumstances, may be saluted by you upon taking it down."

Anderson understood that he could not accept the offer, and his written answer was that "my sense of honor and of my obligations to my government prevent my compliance." However, as the two emissaries turned to leave, he blurted out, "Gentlemen, if you do not batter us to pieces, we shall be starved out in a few days."

Beauregard wired this information to Montgomery, and for a few hours it seemed that Anderson's offhand remark might give Davis a way out of the impasse. But the supply ship was approaching, and when Anderson refused to give a specific hour for his surrender, the messengers were again sent out to the fortress.

It was 3:20 A.M. on the morning of April 12 when Anderson was informed that bombardment would begin within an hour. "If we do not meet again in this world," he replied. "I hope that we may meet in the better one."

Major Robert Anderson commanded Fort Sumter, which Beauregard asked him to surrender to the Confederate government. ***National Archives and Records Administration***

The orders from Beauregard were clear, and the Southern emissaries rowed directly to nearby Morris Island where Confederate batteries were standing ready. Roger Pryor, a Virginia Congressman who had urged Charleston two days before to "strike a blow," was offered the honor of doing so. He could not bring himself to fire the first shot of the war, however. So it was probably a private named Henry S. Farley who sent the first shell towards Sumter in the predawn gloom.

There was no way Anderson's little garrison of 86 men and 40 guns could offer much resistance. Beauregard had spotted his batteries with skill. After taking a pounding that lasted 33 hours and with all but six guns knocked out of the battle, Anderson hoisted a white flag. Although 4,000 rounds had been fired, no one on either side had been killed.

But as Anderson was allowed to fire off a final 50-

After a 33-hour bombardment, Fort Sumter finally surrendered. The incident made Beauregard a Confederate national hero.
National Archives and Records Administration

gun salute to the flag before leaving the fort, a store of powder blew up and killed Private Daniel Hough. He was the first casualty of the Civil War.

The news from Sumter enflamed the North and, as Lincoln had hoped, unified it for the start of the long ordeal ahead. In the South, it made Beauregard a national hero.

At the end of May, he was summoned to Richmond, placed in charge of the army, and instructed to repel the Northern force that had crossed the Potomac and entered Virginia. Almost unknown outside of Louisiana before Sumter, Beauregard was now cheered at every stop on the train ride north, hailed as one of the greatest military geniuses in the world. He was, indeed, given the ultimate satisfaction of being saluted as the new Napoleon.

The Richmond papers reported that he had warned Lincoln to remove all noncombatants from Washington because of his intention to take the city. On May 31, cheering throngs accompanied his carriage from the station to his hotel, although the general modestly declined to make a speech.

Beauregard was sent to inspect the troops gathered at the rail junction of Manassas. He knew that he needed more than the 6,000 men that were on hand there but felt it was just as important to rouse Virginians to the coming crisis.

"A restless and unprincipled tyrant has invaded your soil," his ringing declaration began. "Abraham Lincoln, regardless of all moral, legal, and constitutional restraints, has thrown his abolition hosts among you, who are murdering and imprisoning your citizens, confiscating and destroying your property and committing other acts of violence and outrage too shocking and revolting to humanity to be enumerated. All rules of civilized warfare are abandoned, and they proclaim by their acts, if not on their banners, that their war cry is 'Beauty and booty.'

If that wouldn't get the state ready to fight, nothing would.

Within 10 days, Beauregard had drawn up his first battle plan. Many more would follow, all of them ambitious, including a grand strategy for turning the army of Union General Irwin McDowell and capturing Washington. "My troops are in fine spirits and anxious for a fight," he said. "They seem to have the most unbounded confidence in me."

General Joseph E. Johnston, who had slipped away from his base in the Shenandoah Valley to join Beauregard, was actually the senior general. But when their two armies combined at Manassas, Johnston deferred on the grounds that he was unfamiliar with the terrain and Beauregard already had a plan in place.

Actually, the plan was the mirror image of that drawn up by his former West Point classmate, McDowell. Both generals envisioned a classic turn of the opposition's left wing and an ensuing encirclement. If it had worked, the opposing armies would have wheeled around together in a choreographed embrace. But this early in the war, with both troops and leaders green and untested, nothing much worked according to plan. This battle on July 21 would be proof of that.

Beauregard's orders to his generals on the right, where the attack was to begin, were vague and open to misinterpretation. After crossing the stream of Bull Run, the Southern force was then to proceed towards the town of Centerville. "The order to advance will be given by the commander-in-chief." But no one knew what that meant. Which advance? How would the order be given?

So while Beauregard and Johnston waited for the sounds of combat that would signal the opening attack of the grand plan, they heard only silence. Meanwhile, the Confederate left had come under massive, unexpected assault.

"My heart for a moment failed me," Beauregard wrote in a subsequent letter. "I felt as though all was lost and I wish I had fallen in the battle ... but I soon rallied, and then I solemnly pledged my life that I would that day conquer or die."

Actually, it was Johnston who first recognized the urgency of moving to the left wing to oversee the battle. Beauregard was right behind him and managed to brace up the faltering Confederate line. With Stonewall Jackson making his celebrated stand at Henry Hill, Beauregard and Johnston gathered their reserves and built up the left wing for a counterattack.

Screaming the Rebel yell, the first time it was heard in the war, the Confederate forces streamed across the field and turned the closely-fought battle into a rout. Panicked federal troops fled towards an undefended Washington, but the Southern army was too exhausted and disorganized to pursue.

Ironically, the failure to execute Beauregard's original plan had given the South the leverage and manpower it needed to break through the Union lines. At the critical moment, moreover, it was Johnston who had taken charge of the battle.

Beauregard, however, was popularly acclaimed as an even greater hero than before. He was promoted by Davis to the rank of "General in the Army" on the following day. Newspapers across the South competed for words of praise. It was regarded as a certainty that, with this victory, the war would soon be over.

But it was not, and soon the less appealing side of Beauregard's temperament revealed itself. He quibbled with Johnston about who deserved the credit for the victory. "General Johnston came to Manassas beset with the idea that our united force would not be able to cope with the Federal army," he wrote later, "and that we should be beaten—a catastrophe in which he was not anxious to figure on the pages of history as the leading and responsible actor."

Both General Irwin McDowell and Beauregard planned to turn their respective opponent's left wing at Manassas. Neither plan worked, but the Confederates carried the day. ***National Archives and Records Administration***

So Johnston's gesture to go ahead with Beauregard's battle plan was now seen as an act of self-preservation. Worse was to come, because Beauregard now stumbled into the political arena.

As the South's greatest military hero, it was inevitable that his name would be mentioned as a rival to Davis for the presidency in the November 1861 election. He did, after all, have some campaigning in his

After Manassas, Beauregard garnered great acclaim. His seeming attempts to undercut Jefferson Davis, however, resulted in his being transferred to the West. ***National Archives and Records Administration***

background. Beauregard disavowed such intentions. But as Davis read the general's communications, which kept making their way into public print, his suspicions grew that Beauregard was seeking to undercut him.

Beauregard complained that jealousy was keeping supplies from him. His vast, impractical plan to take Washington, drawn up before Manassas, was now presented as a missed opportunity by Davis. So was the failure to pursue the defeated Federals afterwards.

He then wrote an insufferable letter to the *Richmond Whig* accusing unspecified enemies of "slanders and calumnies aimed at me. If certain minds cannot understand the difference between patriotism, the highest civic virtue, and office-seeking, the lowest civic occupation, I pity them from the bottom of my heart."

Beauregard explained later that his darts were directed at Secretary of War Benjamin, with whom he had begun a bitter and losing feud. Benjamin ultimately would maneuver Beauregard into making rash statements that made it appear as if he considered himself above the law. That gave the unforgiving Davis the opportunity to finish him off. Davis terminated his command in January 1862, and sent him to serve under General Albert Sidney Johnston in the West.

Within six months, he had gone from brightest star in the sky to near eclipse. To his credit, however, Beauregard took up his new assignment in Tennessee with undiminished enthusiasm.

He put out a call for all plantations in the area to send him their bells, so that they could be melted into cannon. His plea found very few takers and earned him the scorn of the *Louisville Courier*. "The rebels can afford to give up all their church bells, cow bells and dinner bells to Beauregard," wrote the pro-Union paper, "for they never go to church now, their cows have all been taken by foraging parties and they have no dinner to be summoned to." But he was ready to try.

The fall of forts Henry and Donelson in February had opened the way for a Union invasion of the Confederate heartland down the Tennessee and Cumberland rivers. Albert Sidney Johnston was forced to evacuate Nashville and fell back into Alabama.

But Beauregard moved his headquarters to the rail center of Corinth, Mississippi, and urged Johnston to join him there. His hope was that in rapidly concentrating their two armies the Confederacy could strike at the advancing U. S. Grant and destroy him before he had the chance to build up his own numbers.

Just as Joseph E. Johnston had allowed Beauregard to draw up the battle plan at Manassas, Albert S. Johnston deferred to his junior officer before the Battle of Shiloh. Beauregard, completely smitten with Napoleon, drew up an ingenious, complicated plan modeled after the master's design at Waterloo.

Once again, however, Beauregard neglected to consider that Bonaparte had been fighting with veterans who had years of combat behind them. His Confederate troops were almost totally green and incapable of the sort of close coordination the plan required. He also didn't seem to notice that Waterloo had been Napoleon's downfall.

His troops were late in starting, travel was slow on muddy roads, and some of the Southern boys almost gave away their approach by firing their weapons to see if they still worked after being rained on.

At that point, a despairing Beauregard wanted to go back and start all over again, but was overruled by Johnston. Despite his misgivings, the Confederates did achieve surprise on April 6 and nearly overran the Union position in a confused combat of separate skirmishes that soon bore no relationship whatever to the general's elaborate plans.

Only a stand by Union troops at the Hornets' Nest held up the Confederate advance, and, in the course of assaulting this area, Johnston was killed. Beauregard assumed command and decided to keep the news of the general's death from the troops.

He renewed the attack on the Union position the following day and, after two hours, finally broke through. But it had taken too long. By now Grant had been reinforced, and the Confederate Army could not hold the field.

Beauregard tried repeatedly to rally his exhausted troops, but Tennessee's Governor Isham G. Harris, leading his state's forces, finally convinced him that it was pointless. "General," asked Harris, "do you not think our troops are very much in the condition of a lump of sugar thoroughly soaked in water—preserving its original shape but ready to dissolve? Would it not be judicious to get away with what we have?"

Beauregard finally agreed and retreated to Corinth. Although the battle ended in a stalemate, it was actually a Southern defeat. It had only slowed Grant. He was still coming on with even greater numbers than before.

Or rather his army was still coming on. Major General Henry Halleck, commander in the west, had decided after Shiloh that Grant could not be counted on and took control of the Union armies in the field. He reorganized them, shuffled the commanders, and placed Grant under his own supervision. By the end of April, he had assembled a force of 120,000 men, with no clear idea of what to do with them.

Beauregard, meanwhile, had fortified Corinth, but knew he could not survive a prolonged siege. His fighting strength was only about half the size of Halleck's. So he decided to play mind games with his opponent.

He sent out "deserters" who were instructed to get themselves captured and warn of an impending Confederate attack. Beauregard ordered his troops to cheer as empty trains clattered into town, as if reinforcements were arriving daily. He sent out diversionary parties to attack Halleck's rear.

Finally, in the morning hours of May 25, he ordered a retreat. All signposts were taken down, campfires were left burning, stick figures placed in blankets in the trenches. More empty trains arrived. By the time Halleck figured out what was happening, Beauregard had safely fallen back to Tupelo and left the Union forces to occupy a deserted town.

Halleck was ridiculed in the Northern press, and two months later he was recalled to Washington to serve in an administrative capacity for the rest of the war. But Beauregard, despite saving his army, fared even worse. When his chronic throat condition began acting up again, he took a medical leave and went to a

Beauregard devised a complicated battle plan at Shiloh. It fell apart, but the Confederates nevertheless advanced, slowing down only in the hazardous terrain of the Hornet's Nest. *Battles and Leaders of the Civil War*

After Beauregard led the Army of Tennessee through a successful strategic retreat, Davis removed him from command. Later, he returned to Charleston. *Battles and Leaders of the Civil War*

Beauregard directed the defense of Charleston, even experimenting with torpedo boats and a prototype submarine.
National Archives and Records Administration

resort in Alabama. No sooner had he left Tupelo then Davis, who had not wanted a single foot of Mississippi soil given up to the invaders, removed him from command for being absent without leave and replaced him with Bragg.

While sending a correct letter of congratulations to his successor, Beauregard was humiliated and furious. In letters to friends he referred to Davis as "demented or a traitor to his high trust." In fact, mere words seemed inadequate to convey the contempt he felt for the president. "That living specimen of gall and hatred," he sputtered. "That Individual."

For five months, Davis let him sit. Even a petition by 59 Confederate members of Congress to restore Beauregard to his command failed to move Davis. "If the whole world were to ask me," he said, "I would refuse it."

Finally, in September 1862, he was appointed to return to the scene of his first glory, Charleston. Although this was truly one of the war's backwaters, Beauregard once again took up his duties with vigor.

"I have no preference to express," he said to those urging him to decline the assignment. "Will go wherever ordered. Do for the best." He admitted privately that because he was in Charleston he "may think it more important than it really is."

But the city still stuck in the throat of the Union. The war started here, and the symbolic importance of retaking Fort Sumter was a strong consideration. Beauregard was a man who understood the importance of symbolism and worked diligently to ward off the blow he knew was coming.

Issuing one of his typically florid proclamations, he urged all Carolinians and Georgians "to prove your devotion to your country's cause.... Come share with us our dangers, our brilliant success, or our glorious death."

More practically, he built up the shore defenses and also procured two rams, armored hulks to take the offensive against Union attackers. His chance came in April 1863, when a fleet of Union vessels, two of them ironclads, under Rear Admiral Samuel Du Pont appeared outside the harbor to take the city. They were driven off by floating mines and the shore batteries, which inflicted heavy damage.

Beauregard was ecstatic. In his report, he pointed out that these ships were thought to be invulnerable. But his men had "vanquished the iron-mailed, terribly armed armada, so confidently prepared and sent forth by the enemy to certain and easy victory."

That is vintage Beauregard.

Still, as the great events of 1863 unfolded, he remained in Charleston. He sent plans for another bold strategic thrust to his old commander, Joseph E. Johnston. It was ignored. But he beat off a land-based attempt to capture Charleston. And the Confederate flag still flew over Sumter.

For his defense of the city, he was given a commendation by Congress. But when Davis visited Charleston in October, he barely mentioned Beauregard in his speeches and did his best to ignore his presence. For his part, the general turned down an invitation to dine with the president because, he informed his host, "My relations with [Davis] being strictly official, I cannot participate in any act of politeness which might make him suppose otherwise."

Beauregard contented himself in the next few months by experimenting with torpedo boats and even a prototype submarine against the blockading Union ships.

At last, in the spring of 1864, he was summoned to Petersburg, Virginia, to take up the campaign to halt Grant's advance on the city. His assignment was to prevent General Benjamin Butler from cutting off the railroad to Richmond. Butler commanded a 39,000-man army and was advancing up Bermuda Hundred, the neck of land between the James and Appomattox rivers.

Beauregard relished the job. He detested Butler for the brutal reputation he had acquired while heading up the occupation of his beloved New Orleans. He was referred to there as "Beast." Moreover, Butler was a political appointee, with virtually no military talent.

Instead of advancing with his clear superiority in numbers, Butler chose to entrench and delay. When he finally started to move on Petersburg, Beauregard was prepared and met him on May 12 at Drewry's Bluff, just outside the city. The initial Union attack drove the Confederates from their line. They fell back to previously prepared positions.

An overly cautious Butler concentrated so heavily on his defensive strategy that he didn't have enough troops left to press the attack. Instead, Beauregard ordered a devastating counterassault, which was partially shielded by rain and fog (and stopped in part by the first use of wire as a defensive impediment).

A demoralized Butler with 4,000 casualties, accounting for one of every four men he engaged in the battle, retreated to Bermuda Hundred. In Grant's sarcastic phrase, he stayed there "bottled up."

But by June 15, Grant had managed to slip away from Lee, north of Richmond, and was facing Beauregard outside of Petersburg with a manpower advantage of more than five to one. A desperate Beauregard urged Lee to come to his assistance or else "the last hour of the Confederacy has arrived."

"Unless reinforcements are sent before forty-eight hours, God Almighty alone can save Petersburg," he said. Responded Lee: "I hope God Almighty will."

The Bermuda Hundred line was abandoned to free up all available troops for the defense of Petersburg, although an exasperated Beauregard had to make that decision himself when his superior, Bragg, demurred from offering any guidance.

Beauregard managed to withdraw before an overpowering federal assault and concentrate his forces on shorter lines. In the ferocious fighting of June 18 in front of the city, the First Maine Heavy Artillery lost 632 of its 900 men, the highest casualty rate of any Union regiment in any battle of the war.

Beauregard held on until Lee's arrival. The staggering losses, around 10,000 casualties overall, convinced Grant that he could not take the city by direct assault, and he settled in for the start of a 10-month siege that lasted for the rest of the war.

The defense of Petersburg may have been Beauregard's finest performance. But his command was soon merged into the Army of Northern Virginia, and in October he cheerfully accepted a transfer to head the Army of Tennessee, the post he had lost to Bragg more than two years before.

Since John Bell Hood had assumed command of this force, in July, it had been severely beaten by William T. Sherman in front of Atlanta and reduced to a spectator's role in the destruction of Georgia. But in a meeting at Hood's headquarters in Gadsden, Alabama, Beauregard found the general had a plan. He would head north through Tennessee into Kentucky, forcing Grant to remove some of the pressure on Richmond by shifting troops to the west.

Called on to defend Petersburg, Beauregard successfully held the city against attacks by Generals Benjamin Butler and Ulysses S. Grant. ***National Archives and Records Administration***

Variations of this scheme had been suggested for months, by Beauregard and others, and its grand strategic sweep deeply appealed to him. But the manpower available to Hood was not deep enough to support it. Moreover, Hood did not have the ability to carry it through.

Nonetheless, Beauregard gave his approval. The result was a horribly mismanaged campaign, culminating in a terrible loss at Franklin, Tennessee, and the retreat of the force into Mississippi. It was now a dazed and beaten army. Beauregard joined it at Tupelo, in January 1865, and described it as "if not in the strictest sense of the word a disorganized mob."

Hood resigned, sparing Beauregard the necessity of removing him. But the army was in such terrible shape that he realized it would be of minimal help in trying to hold off Sherman, who was heading north through South Carolina.

Beauregard's health began to fail once more. As he retreated to Charlotte, North Carolina, it became clear to Lee that he was not capable of stopping Sherman. "General Beauregard makes no mention of what he proposes to do or what he can do or where his troops are," he wrote Davis. "He does not appear from his dispatches to be able to do much."

Instead, he was still forwarding plans for great strategic thrusts, moves for which the means and the will were now totally lacking. On February 23, he was replaced by Joseph E. Johnston. Beauregard immediately gave his support, although both men understood there was little that could be done.

The two men soon concurred that the only course

Beauregard returned to his home in New Orleans after the war, holding a number of prestigious jobs and writing extensively about his campaigns. ***Library of Congress***

possible was to seek terms. He did have the satisfaction, at the very end, of telling Davis to his face that his plans to continue the war were nonsense. He would blame the president for the rest of his life for removing him from command three times. In Beauregard's mind, he had been blameless on each occasion, and his bitterness towards Davis never subsided.

At the end, it greatly outweighed the emotions he felt towards the North. When he heard some of his troops celebrating news of Lincoln's death, he sent an aide with instructions to "shut those men up. If they won't shut up, have them arrested. Those are my orders."

In the years after the war, Beauregard continued to have his admirers. In 1866 he was offered command of the Rumanian army, and three years later Egypt made him the same offer, which was repeated the following year. He turned them all down, spending the last 28 years of his long life as a civilian, trying to justify his career during the war.

He returned to New Orleans as a widower, his second wife having died in 1864, and spent five years as a railroad president. He then was named president of the Louisiana Lottery, a position that left him open to severe criticism for the public abuses that were uncovered in its operation.

With his background as a civil engineer, he became commissioner of public works in the city and, finally, the adjutant general of Louisiana. He also wrote extensively: rehashing the campaigns he had participated in, finding fault with all of his contemporaries, and justifying his grand, discarded schemes. The plans that Davis had dismissed as "driveling on possibilities" were by now in Beauregard's mind the imaginative opportunities that could have won the war but were carelessly thrown away.

"There still remains, of course, the hazard of accidents in execution," he admitted, "and the apprehension of the enemy's movements upsetting your own." But that was as close as he ever came to admitting that there had been any chance of failure. He died in 1893 still convinced that he had been robbed of a Napoleonic destiny.

An early Civil War historian, R. M. Johnston, wrote that Beauregard was "strong in fortification and of unquenchable courage, but weak in strategy and wanting in coolness, insight and method on the battlefield. His dispatches lack clearness and at times candor, while rhetoric is a pitfall he rarely resists."

That verdict has stood up over the years. Yet his popularity remained so high in Louisiana that years later an anonymous resident of that state was quoted as saying: "Lee? Lee? Yes, I've heard Beauregard speak well of Lee."

LEONIDAS POLK

"The first glance revealed him as a man to be obeyed. A closer scrutiny showed him to be a man whom noble men might love and meaner men might fear."

W. S. Perry, History of the American Episcopal Church, *1885*

He seemed almost like a figure out of the Crusades, a warrior in priestly vestments. But Leonidas Polk was far too good-natured ever to be mistaken for a religious zealot.

What he may have lacked in military skills was more than compensated for by a beaming Christian benevolence that endeared this general to his men and even, some claim, to his enemies.

The only man he couldn't get along with, unfortunately, was the man he served under for most of the war, General Braxton Bragg. Utterly dissimilar in temperament, the two simply could not tolerate each other. Bragg felt, with some justification, that Polk was trying to undercut him, while Polk, for his part, felt that Bragg simply was not fit for command.

By the end of their relationship, they could not stand the sight of one another and were barely on speaking terms. They ended up blaming each other for the failure to attain a complete victory at Chickamauga.

Such acidity was totally out of character for Polk, a man who had given over his life to working for the Episcopal Church and educating the young. It was only a twist of fate, an old friendship with Jefferson Davis, that led him into the Confederate army. For a man whose entire military experience consisted of four years at West Point, Bishop Polk acquitted himself fairly well as a general.

He would have much preferred the path of peace, however, and worked for it earnestly right until the very outbreak of the war. But when it came and sides had to be chosen, there was no doubt where he stood. As much as his Virginia heritage bound Robert E. Lee to the Southern cause, Polk's roots reached far too deep in Southern soil to let him choose otherwise.

One of his cousins, James K. Polk, of Tennessee, had been the 11th president of the United States. Another of his forbears founded the University of North Carolina. The Polk plantations in Maury County, Tennessee, were showplaces of that state. Polk himself had been Bishop of Louisiana, and his missionary work took him all across that state and Texas.

The South was his homeland, and he regarded the war as a political conflict that was to be fought with religious fervor.

The Polks had arrived in America from northern Ireland in the 1680s and by the 1750s were established in North Carolina. Both the grandfather and father of Leonidas had been active in the political affairs of the colony and dedicated themselves to the Revolutionary cause. His father, William, had spent the bitter winter with George Washington at Valley Forge, was wounded fighting Loyalist troops in South Carolina, and was a prominent political leader in the first days of statehood.

William was a close friend of Andrew Jackson and managed his campaign in North Carolina. He was also an astute investor who saw that the future would lie in the west. He bought up Tennessee land and, while never leaving his home in North Carolina, came to own 100,000 acres of rich farmland south of Nashville.

With his second wife, Sarah Hawkins, whom he married at the age of 41, he had 12 children. Leonidas came along seven years into this marriage, in 1806. The Hawkinses were also a politically active family, and Sarah's brother was governor of North Carolina. As a young man, therefore, Leonidas had all options and doors open to him.

He attended the University at Chapel Hill, but after two years felt the call of military life. So he won an

Leonidas Polk, a bishop by trade and temperament, accepted a position with the Confederate army in deference to his Southern sympathies and friendship with President Jefferson Davis. ***University of the South***

appointment to West Point and began his studies there in 1823.

Polk was described then as being "full of life," a high-spirited young man from a wealthy and well-connected family. His roommate, who would also be a lifelong friend, was a physician's son from Kentucky, Albert Sidney Johnston. It was through Johnston that Polk befriended the young Davis.

At about this time the Military Academy appointed a new chaplain, Dr. Charles P. McIlvaine. He was a charismatic figure, a man who believed in an evangelical form of the Episcopal religion. He would later become Bishop of Ohio, president of Kenyon College, and an outspoken supporter of the Union cause during the Civil War.

During his tenure at West Point, however, he completely won over the heart of the young Southerner. Polk experienced a religious conversion of the most profound sort. "At length the whole corps was aroused as by a thunderbolt," wrote Polk's son, William M. Polk, in the biography of his father, "at the announcement that Leonidas Polk and others had been converted and that Polk was to lead a praying squad."

By the time he graduated, Polk had become convinced that he would make the church and not the military his career. This was not quite the effect that the U.S. Army intended the chaplain to have on its cadets, and McIlvaine was dismissed by West Point after three years. But by then the course of Polk's life was set.

He resigned his commission six months after graduating in 1827, having ranked eighth in his class. He immediately enrolled in the Virginia Theological Seminary, and in 1830 was ordained as a deacon in the Episcopal Church.

He had become active in the American Colonization Society, an organization dedicated to removing freed black slaves to Africa. Polk was troubled by slavery but could never bring himself to call for its abolition. He was, instead, a gradualist, believing that "in the course of not many years one state after another will be willing to abolish slavery," as he wrote his father in 1829.

As a religious man, he believed it was his duty to educate the slaves he owned and prepare them for eventual freedom. But exactly when "eventual" was supposed to be, he wasn't prepared to say.

Polk married his childhood sweetheart, Frances Devereux, shortly after his ordination and in 1833 took his wife and infant son and moved to Tennessee. He began work on Ashwood Hall, a plantation house built on land that his father had acquired, near the town of Columbia.

Ashwood was surrounded by a 200-acre park, and those who knew it called the place the finest home in the vicinity. The house was sacked during the Civil War and then abandoned before fire claimed it in 1874.

Polk also built the nearby St. John's Episcopal Church for the use of the neighborhood, and he served as its rector. It was modeled after the Gothic parish churches of England and much of its interior wood came from the trees of Ashwood. In later years, General Patrick Cleburne remarked that the site was so beautiful that "it is almost worth dying to be buried in such a place."

Cleburne was granted that wish after falling at the nearby Battle of Franklin in 1864, although his remains were later removed to his hometown in Helena, Arkansas. The church still stands as a local shrine.

In 1838 Polk was appointed missionary bishop of the Southwest. In those days, that meant the states of

Louisiana, Arkansas, Mississippi, and Alabama as well as the Indian Territory. It was a vast chunk of land and on his first tour of the area, according to his son's biography, he "traveled 5,000 miles, preached 44 sermons, baptized 14, confirmed 41, consecrated one church and laid the cornerstone of another."

This was largely Catholic territory and his reception was not always friendly. When he ventured into Texas, he said in later years, he was greeted by a man who advised him to "Go back; we are not worth saving."

Polk was overwhelmed by the sheer size of the job. He felt it would take two years of "incessant labor" merely to visit it all. "It is in extent about equal to all of France, the surface exceedingly rough and the facilities of communication off the river wretched," he wrote to another churchman.

The experience did make him an ardent advocate of a transcontinental railroad. He felt such a project might even forestall the civil war that many of his contemporaries feared was coming. In his book, *Polk's Folly*, his descendant, William R. Polk, quotes Leonidas in a letter to a former friend at West Point, as believing that such a project "would so unite all parts of the country in the bonds of a common interest as to make a disintegration of the Union difficult, if not impossible."

He printed up 5,000 copies of an essay that promoted such a plan and distributed them wherever his duties as bishop took him.

James K. Polk, Leonidas Polk's cousin, was the 11th president of the United States. ***Library of Congress***

Under the influence of the school's chaplain, Polk underwent a religious conversion while at West Point. By 1830, he was ordained as a deacon in the Episcopal Church. ***University of the South***

The burden of travel was eased somewhat in 1841 when he was permanently assigned as Bishop of Louisiana. He purchased a sugar plantation, Leighton, near the town of Thibodaux, with the idea that he could best serve the state by being part of its economic culture.

To this end he brought almost 400 slaves with him. Only one-third were field hands, and Polk was eager to put his theories about educating slaves into effect. He started a Sunday school for them and earnestly felt that he was an enlightened master.

But the demands of running a plantation of this size were simply not consistent with his church duties. In the end, he lost Leighton and turned his attention to other pressing problems: education and war.

Religious education had always concerned him. While living at Ashwood he helped found the Columbia Institute for Women. His wife would go on to teach there after his death.

But the greater need was a great Episcopal university for the Southern states. This again tied in, to his way of thinking, with the question of emancipation. He thought that such a university would educate the children of the Southern aristocracy to take the steps that would end slavery. He also wanted it to be a conservative force to help hold back the rising tide of modernization.

After moving from Leighton in 1854, this school

Seeing a need for a great Episcopal university for the Southern states, Polk campaigned to raise funds to found the University of the South. *Library of Congress*

Despite his philosophical opposition to war, Polk agreed to accept a position as a Confederate general at Davis's urging. *Library of Congress*

became his passion. He traveled tirelessly raising funds for such an institution, along with the Bishop of Tennessee, James Otey. Land was donated near the town of Sewanee, Tennessee, and more than $500,000 was raised.

On October 9, 1860, less than one month before the election that would sweep the nation into war, the cornerstone was laid for the new University of the South.

Polk still felt that war could be averted. More than that, it had to be. In December 1860, he wrote President James Buchanan, imploring him to find a way to stop the oncoming conflict.

"The want of accurate and reliable information as to the true state of feeling and determination of the Southern states," he wrote, "might cause you to interpret your obligations to your oath of office differently from what you would if you were in full possession of the facts as they are.

"This feeling is deepening and widening every day, and no difference exists as to the mode of effecting it. To attempt to prevent it by force of arms would instantly extinguish that difference and unite the whole population as one man."

But Polk was talking to the wrong man. Buchanan's term of office was drawing to an end, and he was eager to get out. Moreover, he had no idea how to stop the momentum towards war. His four years in office had proven that.

Even the Polk family was divided. His cousin, William Hawkins Polk, the brother of the late president, ran unsuccessfully for governor of Tennessee in 1860 on a pro-Union ticket. But Leonidas Polk and his immediate family stood with the South.

In the early months of 1861, the secessionist tide

At the battle of Shiloh, Polk commanded one of the four Confederate corps, personally leading four charges. ***Library of Congress***

swept across the area. Although he must have known somewhere in the back of his mind that his work could not continue, Polk went on making plans for the construction of his treasured university at Sewanee.

In the spring, Tennessee Governor Isham G. Harris asked Polk to use his friendship with Davis to drive home the fact that the west must not be scanted on troops. To his surprise, Polk was invited to Richmond for a meeting with the president.

His surprise turned to astonishment when Davis asked him to take command of an army based along the central Mississippi River. Polk immediately refused, believing that Davis could not possibly be serious. He had, after all, no military experience in the field and was philosophically opposed to war.

But Davis persisted, reminding Polk of his duty to his home state and promising that their mutual friend, Albert Sidney Johnston, would soon be in command of the western army. On June 22, Polk finally acquiesced and was made a general.

He described it as "buckling the sword over the gown." To another friend, he said he felt like "a man who has dropped his business when his house is on fire to put it out; for as soon as the war is over I will return to my calling."

But to his wife, in a more somber tone, he asked that "the Lord have mercy upon me and help me to be wise, to be sagacious, to be firm, to be merciful."

Davis knew that this appointment would cause a sensation. The Northern press was outraged at the idea of a man of God at the head of an army, even though its own "Battle Hymn of the Republic" was filled with warlike religious imagery. Davis was more concerned with Southern morale, however, and in this region, where Polk was a well-known figure, his appointment was met with approval.

He was sent to the river town of Belmont, Missouri. Recognizing the vulnerability of the outpost, he ordered his troops across the Mississippi to take the 148-gun fort at Columbus, Kentucky.

Until that time, Kentucky had taken a stand of neutrality in the war. But it was a neutrality heavily weighted towards the Union side. Polk knew that Union forces under U. S. Grant were poised to enter the state from Illinois and that when they did Columbus would certainly be a primary objective.

But members of Davis's cabinet still hoped that Kentucky could be kept out of the war, blocking the federal invasion route to Tennessee. Even after Polk entered the state, he was urgently requested by Governor Jones to withdraw immediately. But Davis backed the move, wiring Polk that "the necessity justifies the

At Stones River, General Benjamin Cheatham encouraged the troops to "give 'em hell." Polk seconded with, "Give them what General Cheatham says, boys." ***Library of Congress***

action." Some historians feel that he should have gone even farther and seized the Ohio River port of Paducah, too.

Polk's move gave Kentucky's unionist-controlled legislature the excuse it needed to invite in federal troops to repel the invasion. But it was a certainty that when Grant was ready to move he would have violated the neutrality anyhow.

In early November, Grant finally was ready. He came down the Mississippi, landed his force of 3,000 men below Belmont, and captured the place. He was told that Polk had sent a good part of his command further south to the New Madrid area to assist Jeff Thompson, a Confederate guerilla leader. After defeating a small Southern force at Belmont, his men started looting the supplies stored there.

But Grant's information was wrong. Polk still had 14,000 men with him and was just waiting to see what Grant intended to do. Once he landed in Missouri, Polk sent part of his force across the river to cut Grant off from his boats. Then he opened fire with the big guns from the fort in Columbus.

Grant, fighting in his first action of the war, found himself in a trap. "Well," he told his aides, "we must fight our way out as we fought our way in."

He managed to do that, but he left behind the looted Confederate supplies, a good deal of his own, and 607 casualties, about the same number as Polk. Both sides chalked it up as a victory, although not much of anything had been accomplished. Polk did get a resolution of thanks from the Confederate Congress, and Grant's men had been given their first taste of combat.

Grant was the last man to board the Union ships on the retreat, and the story is told that when Polk spotted him on the riverbank, he called to his men: "There is a Yankee. You may try your marksmanship on him if you wish."

Luckily for the Union cause, Polk's men had not yet refined their accuracy.

The two men met personally a few days later to discuss a prisoner exchange. It was a cordial encounter, with a toast raised by Grant to George Washington and accepted by Polk with the statement, "Good! The first rebel."

In a subsequent letter to his wife, Polk described the Union commander as "second rate, though I dare say a good man enough."

True to his promise, Davis had named Albert Sidney Johnston as commander of the western forces. He was given the thankless task of trying to defend a line that stretched 500 miles, from Arkansas across to the Cumberland Gap. Polk was to protect the Mississippi River route from invasion, and with the fort at Columbus in Confederate hands that seemed secure.

But in February 1862, Grant breached the center of this line, at Fort Donelson, Tennessee. Johnston had to reformulate his plan and concentrated his forces at Corinth, Mississippi, to stop the Union advance. Polk was brought there from Columbus in March with about 10,000 men.

At the ensuing Battle of Shiloh, the bloodiest fight of the war so far, Polk was in command of one of four Confederate corps. The action at Belmont five months before had given Polk's men more battle experience than most of the others in this army.

The meticulously planned battle at Shiloh fell apart into a series of disorganized melees. Polk found himself in the middle of the attack on William T. Sherman's brigade, on the Union right. It drove Sherman back late in the first morning of battle, and only the strength of the Hornets' Nest, a small but deadly pocket of resistance on the Union left, prevented a Southern encirclement of the federal army.

But Johnston was killed at the Hornets' Nest, Grant was able to hang on long enough for Union reinforcements to reach him, and on the afternoon of the following day the Southern army had to fall back to Corinth. Polk had acquitted himself well, personally leading four charges and even raising concern among his men for exposing himself to danger.

The assault at Chickamauga was set to begin with Polk, but he was four hours late due to a communications problem. *Library of Congress*

Beauregard succeeded Johnston as commander of the western army. But after he ordered a further fall-back to Tupelo, Mississippi, and then took leave of the army to visit a spa, an impatient Davis sacked him. He was replaced with Bragg, thus beginning one of the more tumultuous relationships in the war. Polk and Bragg were destined to clash, and it didn't take many months for that to occur.

Polk led one of the two corps that Bragg took on the late summer invasion of Kentucky, a move that began with great promise. While Bragg went to the state capital, at Frankfort, to inaugurate a pro-Southern governor, he split his army, leaving Polk in charge of just about half of the 32,000-man force. So when Union commander, Don Carlos Buell, moved out of Louisville with 60,000 men, in early October, he was dealing with a scattered opponent.

Bragg was convinced that the main body of Buell's army was heading towards Frankfort, and he ordered Polk to attack it on the flank. Polk learned from his cavalry, however, that the move towards Frankfort was only a feint, and Buell was actually heading south, towards Harrodsburg. He ordered a movement that would, instead, combine with Bragg near the town of Perryville, to meet Buell there.

The willingness of Bragg to order a move that would have committed half his forces on the basis of incomplete and inaccurate information gave Polk his first serious doubts about the man's abilities.

The struggle at Perryville was another confused engagement, with all order of battle breaking down and men fighting in small, desperate encounters. In the gathering autumn dusk, units on both sides became intermingled, and it became difficult to distinguish which uniform anyone was wearing. Polk himself captured a Union brigadier who wandered across his lines.

In the midst of the confusion, Polk came under fire from a position that had been occupied by a Southern brigade. Riding over to the place, he ordered it to cease firing. When an officer insisted that he was sure he was firing on the enemy, Polk asked him to identify his unit.

"Twenty-second Indiana," came the reply. "And who are you?"

Although he had made a potentially fatal blunder, Polk thought quickly. "Who am I?" he blustered. "I'll soon show you who I am, sir. Cease firing at once!"

Polk then rode slowly across the federal line, repeating the order, expecting to be shot at any moment. When he reached a group of trees, he suddenly wheeled and made for his own lines as hard as he could go.

"I have reconnoitered those fellows pretty closely," he joked later.

Polk and his fellow corps commander, General William J. Hardee, were satisfied that their men had fought well enough to win this battle. But Bragg was unable to make a decision. The two subordinates watched in alarm as they met at Bragg's headquarters that night and saw their commander pacing in nervous uncertainty. To their shock, he decided to withdraw.

That decision was a morale-breaker for the army and another indication to Polk that he was fighting under a man unfit for command. Nonetheless, Bragg commended him in his official report, and later that month Polk was promoted to lieutenant general.

An idyllic interlude followed. With the Southern army comfortably based in Murfreesboro, Tennessee, Polk was called upon to perform his religious duties. Wearing his bishop's robes over his uniform, he officiated at the wedding of General John Hunt Morgan to local belle, Mattie Ready. Most of Bragg's staff attended the December ceremony, a welcome reminder of normal life in the midst of the gathering inferno.

The final break with Bragg came after the Battle of Stones River, which began on the last day of 1862. Polk

General Braxton Bragg dismissed Polk after Chickamauga, and soon the clergyman-turned-soldier went to Georgia to serve under General Joseph Johnston. ***University of the South***

was at the center of the Confederate line on the first day of this engagement. He was unsuccessful in breaking a strong Union position in the Round Forest and, when reinforcements were sent to him, he made the mistake of sending them in as they arrived, rather than waiting for a concentration. As a result, he took exceptionally high casualties.

The battle was renewed in an icy rain on January 2, and the slaughter began again. Of the 78,000 men on both sides involved at Stones River, 23,000 became casualties.

Although he again had not been driven from the battlefield, Bragg felt that he could not maintain his position. He ordered another retreat, this time to Tullahoma, Tennessee.

During the thick of the first day's fighting, one of Polk's divisions, commanded by Major General Benjamin Franklin Cheatham, prepared to go in. Cheatham, standing beside Polk, tried to rally his men. "Give 'em hell, boys," he shouted as they moved forward.

Polk appreciated the sentiment but, as a bishop, could not quite bring himself to echo it. "Give them what General Cheatham says, boys," he cried. "Give them what General Cheatham says."

Polk had agreed initially that the army could not continue the fight at Stones River. "I greatly fear the consequences of another engagement in this place..." he advised Bragg. "We could now, perhaps, get off with some safety and some credit, if the affair is well managed."

After the army did withdraw to Tullahoma, Polk took a short leave to visit his family, which had moved for safety to North Carolina. When he returned, he found that an open revolt against Bragg was stirring. Bragg had brought it on himself, asking for what amounted to a vote of confidence from several of his generals. Instead, he was given stinging criticism and told he should resign.

Polk at first declined to join in the criticism. But when Hardee told him that his attitude made the other generals appear to be insubordinate, the bishop decided to drop a note to his old friend, Davis.

"I feel it is my duty to say to you," he said, "that had I and my division commanders been asked to answer our replies would have coincided with those of the officers of the other corps.... My opinion is he had better be transferred."

Polk suggested that Bragg be moved to Richmond and generously added that "his capacity for organization and discipline, which has not been equaled among us, could be used by you at headquarters with infinite advantage to the whole army." He closed with the suggestion that Joseph E. Johnston be named as Bragg's replacement.

This left Davis perplexed. He respected Polk, but he had made a deep commitment to Bragg. Moreover, Johnston, as Bragg's superior, did not feel it proper that he recommend himself to succeed him.

Davis decided that he would just leave things alone. But Bragg, knowing that Polk had indeed agreed to the withdrawal from Stones River, now marked him as a man who could not be trusted. Polk had changed his opinion after the fact and behaved as if that had been his view all along. From this point, the relationship between the two generals would poison morale throughout the Army of Tennessee.

When General William S. Rosecrans's flanking movements made the Confederate position at Tullahoma impractical, Bragg as much as jeered openly at Polk when he recommended a further retreat towards Chattanooga.

This set the stage for the final break between the two at Chickamauga. Bragg had drawn up a masterful plan to trap Rosecrans's army where it could not concentrate, in the hilly country south of Chattanooga, and then cut it to pieces. On September 20, 1863, the final morning of this three-day battle, he prepared a rolling assault against the entire Union line. It was to begin with Polk on the Confederate right and culminate with General James Longstreet smashing into a gap on the federal right.

Polk was four hours late getting started. Nonetheless, the battle ended in a complete Southern victory, with only the brave stand of General George Thomas preventing a rout. The defeated Union army fled back to Chattanooga. But Bragg did not follow up on his victory. An immediate attack had a good chance of dislodging the confused Federals from Chattanooga. Instead he besieged Chattanooga, enabling the opposing army to be reinforced and playing right into the Union's hands. The strategy could not possibly succeed.

Then the finger pointing began. Many of the Confederate generals, Longstreet and Nathan Bedford Forrest especially, were almost beside themselves at Bragg's failure to pursue Rosecrans. But Bragg, as was his wont, looked for others to blame. He fastened on Polk.

In Bragg's view, it was Polk's delay on the morning of the third day that had denied him a complete victory. A staff officer had reported to Bragg that two hours after the attack was to have begun, Polk was seen sitting on the porch of a nearby farmhouse having breakfast and reading a newspaper.

Bragg was nearly apoplectic when he heard that and rode off himself to confront the bishop. He was told that Polk had just gone to the front and left a message for Bragg that "my heart is overflowing with anxiety for the attack."

It was explained later that General Daniel Harvey Hill had been unable to find Polk during the night. Hill was unaware of the orders for him to attack at 6 A.M. He understood that he was to attack when "in position" and that was how he had proceeded.

With criticism of him rising again, and Polk joining those who urged an immediate move on Chattanooga, Bragg made his decision. He fired Polk, Forrest, and Hill and later sent Longstreet on a pointless assignment to Knoxville.

"The truth is, General Bragg has made a failure," Polk wrote to Davis, "notwithstanding the success of the battle, and he wants a scapegoat."

To his closest aides he was even more direct. "I feel a lofty contempt for his puny effort," he said, after being sent back to Atlanta, "to inflict injury upon a man who had dry-nursed him for the whole period of his connection with him and kept him from ruining the cause of the country by the sacrifice of its armies."

In his report to Davis, Longstreet was just as blunt. "I am convinced that nothing but the hand of God can save us or help us as long as we have our present commander."

Nonetheless, Bragg stayed and Polk went. There was no court of inquiry, as Polk demanded. He was, instead, sent to Demopolis, Alabama, and placed in charge of recruiting. But even in this comparative backwater, the war soon found him again.

Sherman had been dispatched on a raid through Mississippi in February 1864. A primary objective was to destroy $12 million in Southern supplies at Meridian. But by skillfully managing the railroads, Polk emptied out the warehouses and removed the stores to Demopolis before Sherman could reach Meridian.

At Pine Mountain, Polk was killed by an artillery barrage intended to drive away the Confederates overlooking Sherman's positions. ***Library of Congress***

By May, Bragg was gone from the Army of Tennessee, and Polk was returned to Georgia to join Joseph E. Johnston at Resaca. One of his first acts there was to baptize Lieutenant General John Bell Hood. It was to be his final official duty as a clergyman.

The tireless British observer, Colonel Arthur J. L. Fremantle, had linked up with the army and left a description of Polk. "A good-looking, gentleman-like man with all the manners and affability of a grand seigneur..." wrote Fremantle. "Tall, upright and looks much more the soldier than the clergyman. He is much beloved by his soldiers on account of his great personal courage and agreeable manners."

In early June, rain had become incessant as the two armies maneuvered through northern Georgia. Sherman was constantly trying to turn Johnston but, instead, found his opponent always had managed to

Originally buried at St. Paul's Church in Augusta, Georgia, Polk's body was reinterred at Christ Church Cathedral in New Orleans forty years later. ***Library of Congress***

defend his flanks and entrench, falling back towards Atlanta all the while.

On June 14, Johnston was in front of Marietta and established a new line in hilly terrain. One of the elevations along his front was called Pine Mountain.

The morning was clear after 11 consecutive days of rain, and Johnston, Polk, and Hardee took the opportunity to go up to the heights and examine their position. Sherman had decided to make the same sort of inspection on a rise directly opposite the one occupied by the Confederate generals. He wanted to dislodge Johnston while avoiding a frontal assault.

The two positions were little more than half a mile apart, well within range of the other's guns. The generals on both sides had been warned of the possibility of coming under fire at any time.

The foul weather had hampered his operations and put Sherman in a foul mood. As he stood on the hilltop and noticed the Southern officers directly across from him, he grew even more annoyed.

"How saucy they are," he remarked. He ordered his artillery to send some shells their way to drive them from the vantage point, which commanded a view of the Union deployments.

At the first shot, most of the generals immediately ducked for cover. Whether Polk's formidable girth prevented his moving quickly enough or whether he simply refused to show any sign of fear, he took his time about getting to shelter. The second shot struck him in the chest and killed him instantly.

Sherman mentioned it as a passing incident in the day's events. "We killed Bishop Polk yesterday and today the fighting goes well," he reported.

When he wrote his memoirs several years later, however, Sherman took pains to disavow the story that he had knowingly fired the shot that killed Polk.

"The fact is at that distance we could not even tell that the group were officers at all," he wrote. "I was on horseback, a couple of hundred yards off, before my orders to fire were executed, had no idea that our shot had taken effect and continued my ride down along the line."

Not until he returned to his headquarters that evening was Sherman told by a signal officer, who had broken the Confederate code, that "he had translated a signal about noon, from Pine Mountain to Marietta, 'Send an ambulance for General Polk's body…' From this we inferred that General Polk had been killed, but how or where we knew not."

In *Polk's Folly*, William R. Polk writes that one of the Union soldiers standing beside the gun that fired the fatal round was William Harrison Polk, a distant cousin of the bishop. He later wrote Leonidas's son a letter describing his father's death from his viewpoint.

The death moved General Johnston, who had been baptized by Polk earlier in the campaign, to tears. There was mourning throughout the Army of Tennessee. According to a story repeated for years afterwards at the University of the South, the soldier who fired the shot that killed Polk was so filled with remorse that he committed suicide.

According to William Harrison Polk's account, however, the gunnery commander who sighted the gun said simply, "Thank God! They killed my brother yesterday and I have killed a lieutenant general." The commander was killed in action two days later.

Polk's body was taken to Augusta, Georgia, and interred there at St. Paul's Church. Forty years later it was removed to Christ Church Cathedral, New Orleans, for permanent burial.

His beloved University of the South was badly damaged during the war but reopened in 1865 and is now regarded as one of the region's foremost educational institutions. Its carillon was dedicated in his memory, 95 years after his death.

A memorial shaft was erected in 1902 on the spot where he was killed. It is on private land, adjacent to the Kennesaw Mountain National Battlefield Park. The last line of its inscription, betraying, perhaps, a sly reference to Polk's noteworthy girth, reads: "And surely the gates of heaven never opened wider to allow a more manly spirit to enter therein."

GEORGE E. PICKETT

"Are these abject wretches about us, whom our men are now disarming and driving together in flocks, the jaunty men of Pickett's Division, whose steady lines and flashing arms but a few moment's since came sweeping up the slope to destroy us? We know, but so sudden has been the transition we can yet scarce believe."

First Lieutenant Frank A. Haskell, The Battle of Gettysburg, *1863*

Were it not for the action of an hour in the hot July sun on the fields of Gettysburg, the name of George Pickett would be a footnote to the Civil War. He would have remained an obscure figure who never quite made it to the center of the action and spent his career, ineffectually, in the wings, while the great show went on without him.

He did not even participate in the historic charge that bears his name, but instead was an observer from a rear position. That was where a major general should properly have been positioned, although there are those who criticize him for it.

But the aspect of heroic failure that defines Pickett's Charge has, over time, become attached to the man himself. Commentators have searched for meaning in the character of the individual.

It is pointed out that he finished last in his class at West Point, perfumed his hair and wore it in long ringlets, became infatuated with a teenaged girl, and courted her in the midst of the war.

He was "dapper and alert," according to one admiring description; "a desperate-looking character" in the words of British observer Arthur J. L. Fremantle. The information is turned over carefully and examined, as if it contained the germ of a clue as to why the charge failed.

As the years passed and Robert E. Lee was elevated to the status of martyred saint, it was forgotten that Pickett and his men were simply instruments of the desperate, doomed action that Lee had ordered. Or, if not forgotten, ignored.

Ironically, in the war's final days, it was Pickett's dereliction of duty that enabled the Union army to finally turn Lee's flank outside Richmond and bring the war to an end. But that event is barely remembered. Only the brave slaughter of Pickett's Charge summarizes his career.

Both life and career have become thickly encrusted with legend. After his death, his young widow, La Salle Corbell Pickett, became the keeper of the flame. She invented incidents, forged documents, did whatever she could to enhance her husband's reputation for a generation after his death. She succeeded admirably.

Even in the 1990s, the long-dead general was still making news. A legal battle was fought between his descendants and a Pennsylvania museum over the ownership of several Pickett artifacts. They were prized so highly because even those who know next to nothing about the Civil War recognize his name.

It is a name almost as old as Virginia. The Picquetts arrived there in the seventeenth century and by the time of George's birth, in 1825, were well established as landowners and merchants in the Richmond area. He was educated in exclusive schools, explored his grandfather's estate on an island of the James River, and breathed in the military heritage of a family that rushed to take up arms in defense of Virginia in the Revolution and the War of 1812.

The boyhood idyll ended in the Panic of 1837. His family suffered severe reversals in the resulting depression. He was forced to drop out of Richmond Academy and was packed off to join his mother's brother in Quincy, Illinois, to prepare for a career in the law.

Pickett's uncle, Andrew Johnston, was well connected politically in Illinois, a close friend of the rising

Although for most of the war true greatness eluded him, George E. Pickett achieved immortality when his division made a doomed charge at Gettysburg. ***National Archives and Records Administration***

young Whig politician, Abraham Lincoln. When it became apparent to Johnston that his nephew had no interest or aptitude for law, he asked another friend, U.S. Rep. John T. Stuart, to secure an appointment to West Point for the young man. It came through in 1842 and the 17-year-old Pickett was on his way to the Military Academy.

Stuart had once been Lincoln's law partner, and a story grew up that it was indeed the future president who had obtained the appointment for Pickett. But Edward G. Longacre, in his 1995 biography of Pickett, points out that Lincoln was not a congressman at the time and could not have nominated him.

Longacre believes the story was the invention of Pickett's widow. She also insisted that when Lincoln visited Richmond in April 1865, he paid a special visit to the Pickett home to express his concern for his former protégé. No Union officers accompanying the president ever mentioned such a visit.

Pickett's academic career was unimpressive, placing 59th in a 59-member class that also included George McClellan and Stonewall Jackson. He did well in French, but ran afoul of the Academy's disciplinary system, which figured into his overall grades.

Immediately after graduation, however, he was sent off to Mexico and served with distinction in the advance from Vera Cruz to Mexico City. He was cited for gallantry at the battles of Contreras and Churubusco and promoted to first lieutenant in August 1847.

At the Mexican War's climactic battle, at the fortress of Chapultepec, Pickett won greater acclaim for being the first man to reach the parapet and raise the American flag. Right behind him was Lieutenant James Longstreet, who handed off the colors to Pickett when he went down with a wound. Their friendship would endure through the years to come.

Within months after leaving West Point, Pickett had found himself in the middle of furious combat and thought it glorious. It would be almost 16 years before he found that taste again.

After the Mexican War, he was sent to Texas in the campaign to secure the frontier from Comanche raiders. It was tedious, lonely duty for the young officer and over Christmas, 1850, he went home to Richmond and wed Sally Minge, whom he had courted through letters.

They did not return to the isolation of the frontier, at Fort Gates, until July. Four months later, his bride of less than a year died of complications during childbirth, along with their infant son. Pickett lapsed into a deep depression and in 1852 returned home on extended leave.

While resting on the seawall near Old Point Comfort, he struck up a conversation with a four-year-old child from nearby Chuckatuck. The precocious young girl sensed the hurt in him. In an effort to cheer him up she promised that she would write to him and that he would always be "her soldier."

The correspondence went on for 11 years, and in September 1863, despite the 23-year difference in their ages, the two were married.

Pickett was promoted to captain in 1856 and sent to one of the most remote corners of the country: Washington Territory in the Pacific Northwest. His mission, as in Texas, was to pacify local Indian tribes. Again, except for some sporadic engagements, the duty was dull and the conditions unsatisfying. Then suddenly he found himself in the middle of an international incident.

San Juan Island in Puget Sound was disputed territory, with both Americans and British claiming it, although its strategic importance was virtually nonexistent. In 1859 an American settler shot a pig belonging to Britain's Hudson Bay Company and was threatened with arrest and trial.

Sensing a chance to confirm American rights to the island, the local U.S. military commander dispatched Pickett there to establish a beachhead. The British sent in warships to compel a withdrawal. "I am here by virtue of an order from my government and shall remain until recalled by the same authority," he responded.

By August, about 4,000 troops, almost equally distributed on both sides, had landed on the island. The two forces glared at each other while diplomats looked for a way out of this "pig war." Some even suspected that the administration of President James Buchanan was trying to promote a small war with Great Britain. It would divert attention from the worsening domestic situation that seemed headed for disunion—a nineteenth century version of "Wag the Dog."

Finally, the situation was defused without violence and, eventually, in 1872, American claims to the island were upheld. But for a time the name of Pickett was once more placed before the American public—although in far less inspiring circumstances than in Mexico.

But the time for more serious matters was quickly approaching. Remote as Washington Territory was, echoes from Washington, D.C., still made their way there. In June 1861, two months after the outbreak of war, Pickett turned in his resignation from the U.S. Army to return to Virginia.

He left behind a three-year-old son, James Tilton Pickett. He had fathered the boy with an Indian woman who had died in childbirth. From all evidence, he never saw his son again.

His trip home was a circuitous journey, made by way of Panama, New York City, and Canada, in an effort to evade detection and possible arrest. He didn't reach Richmond until September 13, 1861. His greeting was rather chilly. His family felt he had been something of a slacker in delaying so long before taking up arms for his state.

But he was quickly commissioned a colonel and stationed along the Rappahannock River. Within five months he had made enough of an impression to be promoted to brigadier general. He was reunited with his old friend Longstreet, and their bond soon became stronger than ever.

When three of Longstreet's children died during an outbreak of typhoid in Richmond, Pickett was immediately at his side to offer comfort. The often-dour Longstreet seemed to genuinely enjoy the company of the high-spirited Pickett.

Pickett was given command of a brigade formerly led by Philip St. George Cocke. Consequently, it was nicknamed the Game Cock Brigade and prided itself

At the climactic Battle of Chapultepec, Pickett was the first to arrive at the castle's parapet to raise the American flag. ***Library of Congress***

After the Mexican War, Pickett found himself posted to the frontiers of Texas and the Washington Territory. ***Valentine Museum, Richmond, Virginia***

In the Pacific Northwest, Pickett established a beachhead on San Juan Island when a dispute formed with Britain over ownership of the island. *National Archives and Records Administration*

on its spirit and elan. This fit perfectly with Pickett's own image of how a fighting unit should conduct itself.

Other officers in Longstreet's Division noted that he took special care with orders he gave to Pickett, making sure they were understood.

Pickett had missed the first big battle of the war at Manassas and chafed during the long lull that followed. But when McClellan opened the Peninsula Campaign against Richmond, in the spring of 1862, Pickett soon found himself in the middle of it.

The Game Cocks acquitted themselves well at the battles of Williamsburg and Seven Pines in May. But at the latter fight, they suffered a casualty rate of 20 percent, although Pickett was commended in the official report for holding his ground "against the odds of ten to one for several hours, and only [retiring] when the Yankees had ceased to annoy him."

Because of its heavy losses, Longstreet decided that the brigade would be held in reserve during the Confederate counteroffensive in late June. But on June 27, Lee's strike at McClellan at Gaines Mill, along the Chickahominy River, started to bog down. According to the report of Colonel Eppa Hunton, Lee requested a brigade that would carry a federal position on a wooded hill.

"I have a brigade that will carry it," replied Longstreet, "but it had been in the thickest of all the fights and has lost heavily. I don't like to send it in." Lee's response: "This is no time for sentiment. I must carry the place."

Pickett was then called upon to advance with three of his regiments. As they neared the Northern lines, he was knocked from his mount by a wound to his right shoulder. Refusing to leave the field until the issue was decided, Pickett watched as his men swept through the Union position.

"There was more individual gallantry displayed upon this field than any I have ever seen," Longstreet wrote in his official Report. It was the first major victory since Lee took command of the Army of Northern Virginia, although it came at a cost of 8,750 casualties (almost 2,000 more than Union losses). Gaines Mill had made McClellan's position untenable, and he began making plans for evacuating his army.

But while Lee then went on the offensive in his first major drive north, Pickett had to spend the next three months recuperating from his wound. He was now considered one of Longstreet's most effective generals, and his absence was felt by the army. Accordingly upon his return to duty, in late October, he was promoted to major general and placed in command of Longstreet's former division.

He held the center during the brilliant Longstreet defense of Marye's Heights, at Fredericksburg. Afterwards, Pickett wrote his young admirer, La Salle Corbell, that the bravery of the Union troops in making their impossible assault against his position was "beyond description."

"Why, my darling, we forgot they were fighting us," he wrote, "and cheer after cheer at their fearlessness went up along the line."

Within a few months, he had the opportunity to tell his war stories and express his ardor first hand. He accompanied Longstreet on his campaign into southern Virginia in the spring of 1863. La Salle's home at Chuckatuck was just a few miles from headquarters, and Pickett frequently made the ride.

Finally, Longstreet had to tell him, even considering their friendship, that he could not grant him any further authorization to leave camp. He went anyhow, and his absence was noted with disfavor by other officers. "I don't think his division benefited by such carpet-knight doings in the field," wrote Gilbert Moxley Sorrel, adjutant general of the corps, in his memoirs.

No matter. Pickett, now 38, was deeply in love with his teenaged admirer. He called her "the charming Sally," which was also the name of his first wife. When he was unable to make the ride to Chuckatuck, he wrote her letters, signed "Your soldier."

The campaign itself was a drawn-out, inconclusive affair that left Longstreet's corps, aside from the smitten Pickett, bored and restless. Meanwhile, Lee had started north again in May, won his sweeping victory at Chancellorsville, but lost Jackson in its course. Longstreet was summoned north to join the main body of the army on its advance towards Gettysburg.

When the battle began, Pickett was in Chambersburg, 25 miles to the west. He didn't arrive at Gettysburg until the end of the second day of fighting, when Longstreet already had been given the order by Lee to assault the federal lines at Cemetery Ridge.

Longstreet had been thrown back with massive losses at the Round Tops on the federal left on the second day, and he believed that this attack on the center had even less of a chance.

"I do not want to make this charge," Longstreet would say on this terrible day. "I do not see how it can succeed. I would not make it now but that General Lee has ordered it and expects it."

He knew that the Union forces had been given the entire night to entrench. A frontal assault on that strong a position ran against everything Longstreet believed as a soldier. He wrote later that "never was I so depressed" as when the day began.

Pickett's division was one of the smallest in the army, numbering 4,500 men. But they were battle-tested veterans, and they were rested. Pickett himself was hardly able to contain his excitement. If he knew of Longstreet's misgivings about what was to come, there wasn't any evidence of it in the early morning hours.

His men were roused from sleep at 3 A.M., allowed a quick breakfast, and then marched in the gathering dawn to their positions on Seminary Ridge. There they stared across the open field to the Union lines and for the first time had some sense of what lay ahead.

The plan was for 180 Confederate cannon, under the command of Colonel E. P. Alexander, to open a barrage at about 1 P.M. It was intended to silence the Union artillery and clear the way for the advance of Pickett's men. Longstreet and Alexander exchanged anxious notes before it began, with the general making clear he wanted some assurance that the Union guns had been "driven off" before he ordered the attack.

Alexander replied that he would only be able to judge that from the return fire. Longstreet still did not want to give the order and felt that "if the artillery did not produce the desired effect, I would be justified in holding Pickett off."

The barrage, which concentrated on the center of the federal line, and the answering salvo lasted about 90 minutes and could be heard 150 miles away. No one who lived through it ever forgot the sheer thundering volume of it.

"A tornado of projectiles," one of Pickett's men would write later. A Union sergeant would describe it as "the most terrible the New World has ever seen, and the most prolonged ... terribly grand and sublime."

There would be no artillery duel to compare with it for more than 50 years, until the Western Front of World War I. To the federal troops at whom it was directed, the infantry assault that followed came almost

At Gaines Mill, a bullet struck Pickett in the shoulder, but he remained on the field to watch his men push through the Union lines. ***Library of Congress***

After returning from his recuperation, Pickett was placed in charge of Longstreet's former division. ***Library of Virginia, Richmond, Virginia***

Pickett arrived at Gettysburg at the end of the second day of fighting, after Longstreet had been thrown back at the Round Tops. *Library of Congress*

as a relief, although when it began the defenders were outnumbered by two to one.

At its conclusion, Alexander sent a note to Longstreet. "If you are coming," it read, "you must come immediately or I cannot give you the proper support; but the enemy's fire has not slackened materially and at least 18 guns are still firing from the cemetery itself."

Pickett was at Longstreet's side. The Union guns were now falling silent, but there was uncertainty about what this meant. Had they been sufficiently damaged or was it a tactic to give a false sense of security to the infantry assault the North knew was coming? Longstreet couldn't be sure.

"General, shall I advance?" asked Pickett. Observers noted how finely turned out Pickett was on this day—mounted on a black charger, blue cap, buff gauntlets, perfectly tailored uniform, golden spurs. There had been talk in the army that Pickett was all show and no go, promoted only because of his long friendship with Longstreet.

Even his three brigadiers, all of whom had started the war as his superiors, were sometimes less than taken with him. None of them liked what they saw on this field, nor did they share any of Pickett's eagerness for the fight ahead. Among themselves they agreed that it was "a desperate thing to attempt." All three of them—Dick Garnett, James Kemper, and Lewis Armistead—would fall in the hour ahead.

For long moments, Longstreet did not respond to Pickett's question. Then he gave a barely perceptible nod. "I shall lead my division forward, sir," Pickett said. Again there was only silence from his commander. Longstreet then mounted his horse to confer with Alexander, and Pickett returned to his troops to give the order to advance.

Alexander was encouraged by the long silence from the Union lines, but told Longstreet that he had insufficient ammunition to continue to protect Pickett. "Go and stop Pickett right where he is," the general cried out. But he was told that if he waited until the Confederate guns were resupplied, the attack would be too late.

"Up, men and to your posts," Pickett was saying to his soldiers. "Don't forget today that you are from old Virginia."

"Sergeant," called Armistead to one of his men, "are you going to put those colors on the enemy's works today?"

"I will try, sir," was the response, "and if mortal man can do it, it will be done."

Armistead then placed his hat on his sword, held it

After a 90-minute artillery barrage, Pickett's men began their charge, deliberately advancing on the Union position. ***Library of Congress***

high over his head and deliberately began to lead the way forward.

The Confederates were never noted for their precise alignment as they marched into battle. General Daniel Harvey Hill described the Southern soldier as "more of a free lance than a machine." It was their abandon, the sound of the rebel yell as they advanced, their sense of elan that characterized this army.

But on this day they marched in perfect order, row after row of silent men, moving at about 100 yards a minute. The Union soldiers watching the advance were temporarily awestruck. But almost as soon as Pickett's brigades had cleared the line of Confederate guns, the Union batteries again opened fire.

Men began to fall and gaps opened in the line. Still, the gray line advanced. Fallen standards were picked up from the hands of the dead and moved forward again.

Pickett's three brigades were on the right, flanked by those of J. Johnston Pettigrew and Isaac Trimble. The line stretched one mile wide across the valley.

While history records this as Pickett's Charge, there is nothing to suggest that he actually considered advancing with his troops. After leading his soldiers out on horseback and coming under heavy fire, Pickett wheeled around and returned to the rear. He felt his role was to direct the advance from behind the lines, and within the army the sense was that it was the proper place for him. Pettigrew chose to do the same.

But as his biographer Longacre points out, "the assault ... would play a major role in setting the standards of Confederate iconography. From the very first, those who suspected that Pickett had not gone in with the troops condemned ... his behavior."

Indeed, the artillery chief, Alexander, when asked if he knew Pickett's whereabouts, responded: "I know where he ought to be," with a jab of his finger at Cemetery Ridge. "He ought to be there."

Still, the Southern line came on. Then it halted, and the order came to close the gap that had developed between Pickett's and Pettigrew's brigades.

"My God," cried out those who were watching in the Union infantry. "They're dressing the line."

They were under constant and direct fire now, cannons and rifle and canister shells. Garnett fell dead from his horse, and Kemper went down with a fatal wound. Elsewhere on the field, brigades were left leaderless as all the officers fell in the fatal hail.

Alexander had asked an infantry officer before the assault began if it was possible to reach the opposite ridge. He was told that it was entirely possible. It had been done the previous day at the Round Tops. The key

The Federals were momentarily awestruck at the mile-wide line approaching them, but soon opened fire with their artillery. Pickett lost nearly 70 percent of his men. *Battles and Leaders of the Civil War*

was to reach it with enough numbers to hold it. That would not happen on this day.

Armistead was still on his feet, urging his men on to the Union lines, hat still on his sword. In a few moments, he, too, would be mortally wounded as he reached the federal line.

Fremantle, the British observer, was watching from Longstreet's side. He called it "a magnificent charge" and said "I wouldn't have missed it for anything."

"The devil you wouldn't," answered Longstreet. "I would like to have missed it very much. We've attacked and been repulsed."

His worst fears had been confirmed. In a display of courage rarely equaled in the history of warfare, a portion of Armistead's brigade reached the federal lines and grappled briefly with the Union gunners. But they were quickly overwhelmed, and no reinforcements came to help them. They had been held back to prepare for the federal counterattack Longstreet was sure would follow.

After a few long moments, the survivors began to straggle back to the Confederate lines. They were dazed, exhausted, disbelieving. No one yet knew that this charge would come to be known as the "high water mark of the Confederacy," or that from this point on the blue tide would roll inexorably south. But it was already clear that for the first time Lee had been beaten, and the psychological effect on these men was stunning.

There has never been a conclusive number given for the casualties in Pickett's Charge. Estimates range from 5,600 to 7,500 men in all the brigades involved, with a rate of nearly 70 percent in Pickett's three. Only one officer in his brigades above the rank of captain was not wounded.

Although horrified by what they had seen, Longstreet and Lee desperately tried to organize their defenses for the anticipated Union onslaught, an attack that would never come. Lee came upon Pickett, dejected and distraught, slowly riding back to Longstreet's headquarters.

"General Pickett," said Lee, "place your division in rear of this hill and be ready to repel the advance of the enemy should they follow up their advantage."

Pickett answered in tears. "General Lee, I have no division now."

"This has been my fight and upon my shoulders rests the blame," Lee told him mournfully. "The men and officers of your command have written the name of Virginia as high today as it has ever been written before. Your men have done all that men can do. The fault is entirely my own."

A Virginia captain in a letter home put it another way. "We have gained nothing but glory," he wrote, "and lost our bravest men."

Pickett's bitter report, prepared in the following weeks, was highly critical of other units that participated in the charge for their failure to support him. Lee refused to forward it to Richmond and told Pickett to destroy it.

"You and your men have covered yourself with glory," he said. "But we have the enemy to fight and must carefully, at this critical moment, guard against dissension which the reflections in your report would create."

On the retreat from Gettysburg, Pickett was 38 years old and had another 12 years of life left to him. He would enjoy personal happiness in his marriage to La Salle Corbell, which took place in Petersburg in September after her high school graduation. They spent much of their honeymoon on Turkey Island, the family estate of his boyhood memories. But as a soldier he never recovered from this battle.

Lee thoughtfully transferred Pickett to the Department of Southern Virginia and North Carolina, which enabled him to be with his bride. He was also allowed to build up the strength of his shattered brigades. But the recruits were of uneven quality because as Southern manpower waned age limits were raised.

Pickett acknowledged that "it will not be the crack division it was and I decidedly would not like to go into action with it."

Then, in February 1864, came the first of the events that marred his later years in the military. The area around New Bern, North Carolina, contained many Union sympathizers and Confederate deserters. During Union raids they had assisted the invaders. Pickett was furious over the damage caused by these raids and by his own failure to take New Bern.

Among the prisoners captured during the campaign, 22 were identified as turncoats. Pickett convened a court-martial and, after hasty deliberations, all the accused deserters were taken out and hanged, including a 14-year-old drummer boy. The executions were not sanctioned by the Confederate government and were held against Pickett after the war.

In May, it became apparent that Union General Benjamin Butler was planning to move out of Bermuda Hundred, the neck of land between the James and Appomattox rivers, with a force of 39,000 men. His goal was to try to cut the Petersburg and Weldon Railroad running between Petersburg and Richmond. To oppose them, Pickett had, at best, 3,500 men and had received no clear directives from the War Department—aside from a rebuke by his superior, Braxton Bragg, for allegedly overestimating the Northern forces.

With his enormous advantage in manpower, Butler could have walked right into Petersburg. But the combination of his overcautious planning and general incompetence enabled Pickett to protect the city. But he paid a high price. He went without sleep for several days and was also greatly worried about his wife's health in her advanced pregnancy. He had, after all, lost his first wife to complications during childbirth.

As the immediate military crisis passed and General P. G. T. Beauregard arrived to take charge of the Petersburg defense, Pickett suffered a nervous collapse. For 10 days he stayed in his room, unable to function. His division was heavily engaged at Drewry's Bluff, the first major action the reconstituted force had seen since Gettysburg, but its commander was too ill to join his men.

Throughout the remainder of the war, the general

Pickett married La Salle Corbell in September 1863 after her graduation from high school. ***Library of Congress***

Pickett managed to contain General Benjamin Butler in the Bermuda Hundred until General P. G. T. Beauregard arrived to take command of the Petersburg defenses. ***Library of Congress***

At Five Forks, Pickett's men made their final stand. While trying to defend the junction, they were overwhelmed by the forces of General Philip Sheridan. *Library of Congress*

was frequently taken ill with intestinal disorders, often followed by severe attacks of hemorrhoids.

It was rumored in Richmond that Pickett had lost his nerve, had grown too attached to his young wife, or had been taken drunk, a weakness that had long been whispered about him but was never proven.

Whatever the fact, he was passed over for important assignments upon his recovery. In fact, a growing tension between Lee and Pickett had developed, stemming from the destruction of his division at Gettysburg, and it would never be satisfactorily resolved.

La Salle gave birth to a healthy son in July, and Pickett's command settled down to the deadly dull routine of guarding a backwater, the line opposite Butler at Bermuda Hundred. It was now a war of siege. Morale disintegrated as winter set in, and the rate of desertions soared. There was insufficient food for the Southern troops while it was apparent that the federal forces across the way were well fed and warm.

All a soldier had to do was walk across the line, and the war was over for him. According to one report, the defection rate in Pickett's command was the highest in the army.

Finally, as spring began, U. S. Grant was in position to break the stalemate and administer the final blow. He began extending his lines further and further west, forcing Lee to match him to avoid being turned, which stretched his manpower to the breaking point.

On March 29, Pickett's brigades were moved to a road junction called Five Forks on the farthest Confederate right. He was told to hold on to it "at all hazards" by Lee. If Philip Sheridan's cavalry turned him here, there would be nothing left between the Union force and Lee's rear. The railroad would be cut and both Petersburg and Richmond would fall.

The assignment was an honor. But Pickett was no longer a commander who could accept the responsibility that came with it. The handsome vigor that once characterized his appearance had left him long ago. He was now a sickly, aging man.

Moreover, he accepted this critical task with shocking indolence. It may be that he was sick of the war and no longer could see the point of it. It may be that his dislike of Lee had left him indifferent to his strategy.

Historian Douglas Southall Freeman writes of this final job for Pickett's men that "the descent of those Virginia soldiers from their furious charge up Cemetery Ridge to their pathetic defense of a wooded crossroads was the epitome of their army's decline."

Pickett's force did engage Sheridan on March 31 and pushed him back to the south. But Sheridan was reinforced during the night. Realizing that he was now badly outnumbered, Pickett decided to withdraw to Five Forks.

A better defensive position would have been across the nearby creek, Hatcher's Run. But Pickett had been told to hold Five Forks, which was almost indefensible against the numbers aligned against him. Moreover, the entrenchments he built there were of poor quality and offered little protection from attack.

Pickett apparently expected Lee to send him more men, and this Lee was in no position to do. There were simply no more men to send. Pickett also did not grasp the seriousness of the situation nor Sheridan's intention to move on him immediately.

In the early afternoon of April 1, Pickett and his chief of cavalry, Fitzhugh Lee (nephew of the commanding general and later a U.S. congressman) accepted an invitation to attend a fish bake at the headquarters of General Tom Rosser, two miles away. Incredibly, while the Union forces prepared the assault that would finally break Lee's defenses, Pickett was off eating shad.

When Sheridan struck that afternoon, no senior officer was in command. Even had there been, it was unlikely that anyone could have held Sheridan off. The federal forces outnumbered Pickett's by a margin of three to one. But Pickett's absence was regarded as scandalous in the army.

When Pickett finally arrived at his front lines, after gunfire broke up the picnic and alerted him to the disaster, there was nothing to be done. The rout was complete. Those who did not surrender, including Pickett, escaped across Hatcher's Run. He lost 3,000 men in the battle, compared to 830 on the Union side.

By nightfall, the railroad was in Union hands, and Lee understood that the final collapse was upon him. In eight more days, he would surrender at Appomattox Court House.

Pickett, with his force shattered, was relieved of command. There is some dispute about whether Lee made this decision because there were no longer any troops for Pickett to command or as a rebuke because of his dereliction of duty at Five Forks. Whatever the reason, Pickett decided to remain through the final surrender. It is reported, however, that when Lee saw him at his headquarters near Appomattox, he remarked coldly: "I thought that man had left the army."

Five months later, Pickett went into exile in Canada. An investigation into the executions at New Bern had begun, and there was some fear that he would be put on trial as a war criminal. But he returned home after two months with assurances from Grant, an old friend from prewar days. He took up Pickett's cause, recommending against any action. The personal appeal from this greatest of Union heroes ended the proceedings, and Pickett was granted amnesty.

He was now an ex-soldier, faced with the challenge of making a living for his young family in an impoverished part of the country. Following the example of a few other former generals, he went into the insurance business, selling policies for Washington Life out of its Richmond office.

Pickett went into the insurance business after the war. In failing health, he came down with a fever and died at age 50. ***Library of Virginia, Richmond, Virginia***

But he found the work demeaning, and his health continued to deteriorate. At the age of 50, he was already an old man. On a visit to Norfolk, he was taken sick with a fever and chills, and with La Salle and his son, George Jr., at his side, he passed away.

His wife's uncle, who had served with him in the Army of Northern Virginia, was also present, and in his last moments Pickett turned to his old colleague. "Well, colonel," he said, "the enemy is too strong for me again. My ammunition is all out."

He was buried in Norfolk, but three months later, in October 1875, was reinterred in Richmond's Hollywood Cemetery with full military honors.

There had been one final meeting with Lee. When the former commanding general paid a visit to Richmond in 1870, Pickett called upon him at his hotel. He had not seen Lee since Appomattox and was nervous about the meeting, unsure what sort of reception he would receive.

The conversation, unfortunately, turned to Gettysburg and quickly became, in the words of a witness, "cold and formal."

Afterwards, as Pickett left the room, he turned to a companion and said: "That old man destroyed my division."

The ghosts of Gettysburg would never leave his side.

BIBLIOGRAPHY

Bauer, H. Jack. *The Mexican War.* New York: Macmillan Publishing Co., 1974.

Boatner, Mark Mayo III. *The Civil War Dictionary.* New York: David McKay Co., Inc., 1959.

Bowers, Claude G. *The Tragic Era: The Revolution After Lincoln.* Boston: Houghton Mifflin, 1929.

Bradford, Gamaliel. *Confederate Portraits.* Boston: Houghton Mifflin, 1914.

Canfield, Cass. *The Iron Will of Jefferson Davis.* New York: Harcourt, Brace, Jovanovich, 1978.

Catton, Bruce. *The Coming Fury.* Garden City, NJ: Doubleday & Co., 1961.

———. *Never Call Retreat.* Garden City, NJ: Doubleday & Co., 1965.

———. *Terrible Swift Sword.* Garden City, NJ: Doubleday & Co., 1963.

Chesnut, Mary B. *A Diary from Dixie.* New York: Appleton, 1905.

Commager, Henry S. *The Blue and the Gray: The Story of the Civil War as Told by Participants.* Indianapolis: Bobbs-Merrill Co., Inc., 1950.

Cooke, John Esten. *Wearing of the Gray.* New York: E. B. Treat, 1867.

Davis, Burke. *Gray Fox: Lee and the Civil War.* New York: Rinehart & Co., 1956.

———. *J. E. B. Stuart: The Last Cavalier.* New York: Holt, Rinehart and Winston, 1957.

Davis, George B., Leslie J. Perry, and Joseph W. Kirkley. *The Official Military Atlas of the Civil War.* New York: Arno Press, 1978.

Davis, William C. *Jefferson Davis: The Man and His Hour.* New York: HarperCollins, 1991.

DeVoto, Bernard. *The Year of Decision, 1846.* Boston: Houghton Mifflin, 1942.

Dictionary of American Biography. 125 vols. New York: Charles Scribner's Sons, 1928.

Douglas, Henry Kyd. *I Rode with Stonewall.* Chapel Hill: University of North Carolina Press, 1940.

Dowdey, Clifford. *The Land They Fought For.* Garden City, NJ: Doubleday & Co., 1955.

Duke, Basil. *Reminiscences of General Basil W. Duke.* Garden City, NJ: Doubleday & Co., 1911.

Dyer, John P. *The Gallant Hood.* New York: Konecky and Konecky, 1950.

Eaton, Clement. *Jefferson Davis.* New York: The Free Press, 1977.

Eliot, Ellsworth. *West Point in the Confederacy.* New York: Baker, 1941.

Foote, Shelby. *The Civil War: A Narrative.* 3 vols. New York: Random House, 1963.

Freehling, William W. *The Road to Disunion.* New York: Oxford University Press, 1990.

Freeman, Douglas Southall. *Lee's Lieutenants.* 3 vols. New York: Charles Scribner's Sons, 1944.

———. *Robert E. Lee.* New York: Charles Scribner's Sons, 1935.

Glatthaar, Joseph T. *The March to the Sea and Beyond.* New York: New York University Press, 1985.

Gracie, Archibald. *The Truth about Chickamauga.* Boston: Houghton Mifflin, 1911.

Hallock, Judith Lee. *Braxton Bragg and Confederate Defeat.* Tuscaloosa: University of Alabama Press, 1991.

Hattaway, Herman, and Archer Jones. *How the North Won: A Military History of the Civil War.* Urbana: University of Illinois Press, 1983.

Henderson, G. F. R. *Stonewall Jackson and the American Civil War.* New York: Longmans Green, 1949.

Horn, Stanley F. *The Army of Tennessee.* Indianapolis: Bobbs-Merrill Co., Inc., 1941.

Hurst, Jack. *Nathan Bedford Forrest: A Biography.* New York: Knopf, 1993.

Johnson, Bradley T., ed. *A Memoir of the Life and Public Service of Joseph E. Johnston.* Baltimore: R. H. Woodward & Company, 1891.

Kennedy, Frances H., ed. *The Civil War Battlefield Guide.* Boston: Houghton Mifflin, 1998.

Leckie, Robert. *None Died in Vain: The Saga of the American Civil War.* New York: HarperCollins, 1990.

Longacre, Edward G. *Pickett: Leader of the Charge.* Shippensburg, PA: White Mane Publishing Co., 1995.

Nevins, Allan. *The War for the Union: The Organized War.* New York: Charles Scribner's Sons, 1971.

Osborne, Charles C. *Jubal: The Life and Times of General Jubal E. Early, CSA.* Chapel Hill: Algonquin Books, 1992.

Page, Thomas Nelson. *Robert E. Lee: Man and Soldier.* New York: Charles Scribner's Sons, 1911.

Pfanz, Donald C. *Richard S. Ewell: A Soldier's Life.* Chapel Hill: University of North Carolina Press, 1998.

Piston, William G. *Lee's Tarnished Lieutenant: James Longstreet and His Place in Southern History.* Athens: University of Georgia Press, 1987.

Polk, William R. *Polk's Folly: An American Family History.* New York: Doubleday & Co., 2000.

Riley, Franklin L. *General Robert E. Lee After Appomattox.* New York: Macmillan Publishing Co., 1922.

Robertson, James I. *General A. P. Hill: The Story of a Confederate Warrior.* New York: Random House, 1987.

Snow, William P. *Lee and His Generals.* New York: Gramercy Books, 1996.

Sorrel, G. Moxley. *Recollections of a Confederate Staff Officer.* New York: Neale, 1905.

Symonds, Craig. *Joseph E. Johnston: A Civil War Biography.* New York: W. W. Norton & Co., 1992.

———. *Stonewall of the West: Patrick Cleburne and the Civil War.* Lawrence: University Press of Kansas, 1997.

Taylor, Richard. *Destruction and Reconstruction.* New York: Longmans Green, 1955.

Thomas, Emory M. *Bold Dragoon: The Life of J. E. B. Stuart.* New York: Harper and Row, 1986.

Thompson, William Y. *Robert Toombs of Georgia.* Baton Rouge: Louisiana State University Press, 1966.

Tourgée, Albion. *The Story of a Thousand.* Buffalo: S. McGerald & Son, 1896.

Vandiver, Frank E. *Mighty Stonewall.* New York: McGraw-Hill Book Co., Inc., 1957.

Vatavuk, William M. *Dawn of Peace: The Bennett Place State Historic Site.* Durham, NC: Bennett Place Support Fund, Inc., 1989.

Wallace, Lew. *Autobiography of Lew Wallace.* New York: Harper and Brothers, 1906.

Watkins, Samuel R. *Company Aytch, First Tennessee Regiment.* Nashville: Cumberland Presbyterian Publishing House, 1882.

Wert, Jeffry D. *General James Longstreet: The Confederacy's Most Controversial Soldier.* New York: Simon and Schuster, 1993.

Wheeler, Richard. *The Siege of Vicksburg.* New York: Thomas Y. Crowell Co., 1978.

Wise, John. *The End of an Era.* Boston: Houghton Mifflin, 1899.

INDEX

Numbers in *italics* indicate photos.

Abingdon, Virginia, 30
abolitionists, 115
African Americans
  Forrest's speech to, 78; Fort Pillow massacre and, 74–75; as soldiers, 119–20
Albuquerque, 45
Alcatraz, 94
Alexander, E. P., 48–49, 64, 189
Alexandria, Virginia, 4
American Colonization Society, 174
Anderson, G. T., 154
Anderson, Patton, 120
Anderson, Robert, 164–66, *165*
Antietam, Battle of, 9–10
  John Bell Hood and, 104, 105; Jubal A. Early and, 129; Robert A. Toombs and, 155; Thomas J. Jackson and, 26
Antietam National Battlefield, 155
Arlington mansion, 3, 4, *6*
Arlington National Cemetery, 3–4
Armisted, Lewis, 188–9, 189
Army of Northern Virginia, 9, 26, 48, 52, 106
Army of the Potomac, 48
Army of Tennessee, 40
  Braxton Bragg and, 36, 181; James Longstreet and, 49; John Bell Hood and, 102, 109; Patrick Cleburne and, 113; Pierre Beauregard and, 171
Ashwood Hall, 174
Atlanta Constitution, 158

Banks, Nathaniel, 21, 22
Bardstown, 140
Barksdale, William, 51
Barone, Michael, viii
Beauregard, Pierre Gustave Toutant, 11, 161–72, *162, 163, 164, 168, 169*
  after the Civil War, 172; Battle of Shiloh and, 98–100, 101, 168–69; in Charleston, 170; death, 172; departure from army, 139–40; education, 162; family background, 162; Jefferson Davis and, 167–68, 170, 172; John Bell Hood and, 111; Manassas and, 166–67; marriages, 162, 163; in Mexican War, 32, 162–63; Napoleon and, 98, 161, 168; and Petersburg, Virginia, 170–71; in politics, 163; at West Point Academy, 162, 164; working with Joseph Johnston, 32
Beck, Mariam, 70
Bee, Bernard, 20, 21
Beech Grove, 96
Belmont, Mississippi, 177
Benjamin, Judah P., 21, 30, 33, 108, 161, 168
Bennett Farm, 41
Bentonville, Battle of, 40, 147
Bermuda Hundred, 170, 171
Bill, Alfred Hoyt, 92
Black Hawk War (1812), 31, 92
Blair, Francis P., 8
Blennerhassett Island, 87
Boatner, Mark Mayo III, 49
Bonaparte, Napoleon, 98, 161, 168
Bonham, Milledge L., 46
Bowling Green, Kentucky, 71
Bradford, William F., 75
Bragg, Braxton, 137–47, *145*
  after Civil War, 147; Battle at Stones River and, 141–42; Battle of Buena Vista and, 80; Battle of Chickamauga and, 116–17, 143–45, 180–81; Battle of Shiloh and, 139; at Bentonville, 147; birth/family background, 137–38; death, 147; disliked, 137, 145; Fort Fisher and, 146–47; James Longstreet and, 49, 52; Joseph E. Johnston and, 35–36, 38, 41, 142–43, 145; Kentucky campaign and, 140–41; Leonidas Polk and, 173, 179–80, 181, 182; marriage, 139; in Mexican War, 138–39; Morgan's raids and, 81, 82; Nathan Bedford Forrest and, 73–74; personal characteristics, 138; replacing Beauregard, 170; at West Point Academy, 125–26; withdrawal from Kentucky, 116
Bragg, Elise, 139, 147
Bragg, Thomas, 138
Brandy Station, Battle of, 64–65
Breckenridge, John, 141, 142
Bride Park, Ireland, 113
Brown, Joe, 157
Brown, John (Osawatomie), 7, 19, 59
Bruce, Rebecca, 80
Buchanan, James, 7, 93, 176
Buckland Races, 67
Buckner, Simon Bolivar, 71, 140
Buell, Don Carlos, 72, *82*, 179
  Braxton Bragg and, 140; Morgan's raids and, 81, 82–83
Buena Vista, Battle of, 80, 138
Buffington Island, Ohio, 86
"Bull of the Woods," 52
Bull Run, Battle of, 32, 46
Bull's Gap, 88
"The Burning," 135
Burnside, Ambrose, 155, *156*
  Marye's Heights and, 26; Morgan's raids and, 85; Potomac River and, 48, 49
Burnside Bridge, 155
Butler, Benjamin, 170–71, 191

Calhoun, John, 5
Cameron, Simon, 32
Campbell, Andrew, 88
Carlisle Barracks, 18
Carpetbaggers, 157
Carter, Ann, 4–5
Castel, Albert, 101
Catton, Bruce, 8, 51
  on Battle of Shiloh, 100; on Braxton Bragg, 139; on James Longstreet, 51; on John Bell Hood, 109; on Morgan's raids, 83; on Robert Toombs, 148
Cedar Bluff, 73
Cedar Creek, 135
Cedar Mountain, 23, 128
Cemetary Ridge, 49–50, 130–31
Centerville, 167
Cerro Gordo, 5, 162
Chalmers, James, 75
Chambersburg, Pennsylvania, 125, 134
Champion Hill, 37
Chancellorsville, Battle of, 27, 130
Chapultepec, 163, 184
Chapultepec Castle, 18, 45
Charleston, South Carolina, 164–65, 170
Charleston Mercury, 21
Charles Town, 19
Charlotte, North Carolina, 171
Chattanooga, 35, 38, 74, 181
Cheatham, Benjamin Franklin, 142, *178*, 180
Cheat Mountain, 9
Cherry Grove, 30
Chesnut, Mary Boykin, 32, 106, 107, 108
Cheyenne, 58
Chickamauga, Battle of, 116–17
  Braxton Bragg and, 143–45; James Longstreet and, 51; John Bell Hood and, 107; Leonidas Polk and, 180–81
Christ Church Cathedral, *182*
Christian, Bolivar, 12
Churubusco, Battle of, 184
Cleburne, Joseph, 113
Cleburne, Patrick, 113–22, *114, 120*
  in Atlanta, 120–1; Battle of Chickamauga and, 116–17; birth/youth, 113; on Braxton Bragg, 137; in British military, 113–14; death, 112, 121–22; family origin, 113; in Helena, Arkansas, 114–15; John Bell Hood and, 121; in Perryville, Kentucky, 16; at Richmond, 115–16; at Ringgold Gap, 118; Spring Hill and, 112; on St. John's Episcopal Church, 174; on using African Americans in military, 119–20
Cleveland, Grover, 42, 158
Coahoma County, Mississippi, 76
Coantreras Plantation, 162
Cobb, Howell, 152
Cobb, Irvin S., 122

Cobb, W. G., 32
Cocke, Philip St. George, 185
College of William and Mary, 127
Columbia Institute for Women, 175
Columbus, Kentucky, 177–78
Columbus, Ohio, 87
Compromise of 1850, 151
Confederate flag, vii
Constitutional Union, 151
Contreras, Battle of, 184
Cooke, Flora, 58
Cooke, John Esten, 57–58, 61, 106
Cooke, John R., 59
Cooke, Philip St. George, 59, *61*
Cooper, Samuel, 33
Corinth, Mississippi, 71, 98, 99, 139, 168, 169
Crittenden, Thomas, 143
Cross Keys, Battle of, 22
Cuba, 157
Culpeper, Virginia, 23
Cumberland Gap, 96, 140
Custer, George A., 67, 135
Custis, George Washington Parke, 3
Custis, Mary Ann, 5, *7*

Danville, Virginia, 87
Darrow, Caroline, 8
Davis, Jefferson, *140*
Albert Sidney Johnston and, 91, 94, 98, 101; Beauregard and, 140, 167–68, 170, 171–72; Braxton Bragg and, 138, 139, 142, 145–46, 180; competence as a leader, vii; Jeb Stuart's death and, 68; John Hunt Morgan and, 83; Joseph Johnston and, 30, 32–34, 38, 39–40, 41–42, 108–9; Leonidas Polk and, 177; Pierre Beauregard and, 161; Robert A. Toombs and, 148, 155–56; Robert E. Lee and, 6, 10; on using African Americans in military, 120
Davis, Varina Howell, 32, 149
Day's Gap, Alabama, 73
Decatur, Alabama, 97
DeLeon, Tucker, 148
Demopolis, Alabama, 181
Deslonde, Caroline, 163
Devereux, Frances, 174
DeVoto, Bernard, 10
Diablo Redoubt, 92
Dortch, Helen, *54*
Douglas, Henry Kyd, 62
Dowdey, Clifford, 10–11, 33
Drewry's Bluff, 191
DuBose, Julia Ann, 149
Duke, Basil, 85, 87, 136
Du Pont, Samuel, 170

Early, Jubal A., 125–36, *128*
Battle of Antietam and, 129; Battle of Gettysburg and, 49–50; burning of Chambersburg and, 134; at Cedar Mountain, 128; Cemetary Ridge and, 130–31; criticism of, 135; crossing Rappahannock River, 127–28; defending Robert E. Lee, 53–54; in exile, 135–36; family background, 125; Fort Magruder and, 127–28; as lawyer, 126–27; at Manassas, 127, 129; in Mexican War, 126; personal characteristics, 125, 127, 128; as politician, 126, 127; promotion of, 129–30; relationship with women, 126; Richard Ewell and, 131; on secession, 127; in Seminole War, 126; in Shenandoah Valley, 131–34; Sheridan's ride and, 134–35; at West Point Academy, 125–26
Ebenezer Church, 76
Edgefield, South Carolina, 44
Eggleston, Joseph, 30
Egypt, 172
Eisenhower, Dwight D., 15
Ellis, Elise Brooks, 139, 147
Eltham's Landing, Virginia, 104
Emancipation Proclamation, 119, 155
Emory College, 44
Evelington Heights, 61
Ewell, Leczinska Campbell, 131
Ewell, Richard, vii, 22, *130*
Battle of Gettysburg and, 49–50; Jeb Stuart and, 65, 67; Jubal A. Early and, 128, 129, 131
Ezra Church, 110

Fair Oaks, 35
Farley, Henry S., 165
Fayette County Courthouse, 88
Fisher's Hill, 135
Five Forks, 192–93
Floyd, John B., 97, 164
Foote, Shelby, 12, 37–38, 50, 67
Forrest, Fanny (sister), 70
Forrest, Fanny (daughter), 71
Forrest, Jeffrey, 74
Forrest, Nathan Bedford, vii, 69–78, *70*
after Civil War, 76–77; Braxton Bragg and, 73–74, 137, 145, 181; Brices Cross Roads and, 75–76; death, 78; escaping prison, 97; family background, 70; at Fort Donelson, 71; Fort Pillow Massacre and, 74–75, 77; fortune of, 69; Ku Klux Klan and, 77–78; marriage, 70; murder of A. W. Gould by, 73; at Nashville, 71–72; personal characteristics, 69; racism and, 69, 77; raid by Streight and, 72–73; raids by, 72, 76; slave business of, 70–71; on surrendering, 76; youth, 69–70
Forrest, William, 70
Forrest, William (son), 71
Fort Bridger, 93
Fort Columbus, 18
Fort Donelson, 71, 81, 91, 96, 97, 178
Fort Fisher, 146–47
Fort Hamilton, 5
Fort Henry, 81, 91, 96
Fort Lawson, 18
Fort Magruder, 127–28
Fort Meade, 18
Fort Monroe, 5
Fort Moultrie, South Carolina, 138
Fort Pillow, 69
Fort Pillow, Tennessee, 74–75
Fort Pillow Massacre, 74–75, 77
Fort Pulaski, 5
Fort Stevens, 133
Fort Sumter, 153, 164–66
Fourth Texas Infantry, 104
Frankfort, Kentucky, 179
Franklin, Battle of, 113
Franklin, Tennessee, 121, 171
Frayser's Farm, 23
Frederick, Maryland, 132
Fredericksburg, Battle of, 26
Freeman, Douglas Southall, 30, 49
on James Longstreet, 43, 47–48; on Jeb Stuart, 61; on John Bell Hood, 102, 106; on Pickett's Charge, 192; on Robert E. Lee, 10, 11; on Robert Toombs, 148; on Thomas Jackson, 16
Fremantle, Arthur J. L., 51, 181, 183, 189
Fremont, John C., 22
French, William, 18
Friendly Persuasion (West), 86
Front Royal, 22

Gadsden, Alabama, 171
Gaines Mill, 23, 104, 186
Gainesville, Georgia, 44
Gallatin, Tennessee, 82
"The Gamecock." *See* Johnston, Joseph E.
Game Cock Brigade, 185–86
Garland, John, 45
Garland, Maria Louisa, 45, *46*, 54
Garnett, Dick, 188, 189
Garrett, John, 132
Gates, William, 138
Gettysburg, Battle of
blame for loss at, 53–54; George E. Pickett and, 186–88; James Longstreet and, 43, 49–52, 107, 187; Jeb Stuart and, 57, 66–67; John Bell Hood and, 50–51, 106–7; Robert E. Lee and, 9–10, 15, 53–54, 106–7; Thomas J. Jackson and, 16–17
Gillem, Alvan, 88
Golding's Farm, 154
Goldsboro, North Carolina, 40
Gordon, John B., 133
Goree, Thomas J., 46
Gould, A. W., 73
Govan, Daniel, 121
Grange House, 113
Grant, U. S. (Ulysses), *98*
Albert Sidney Johnston and, 98, 99–100; on Braxton Bragg, 137; James Longstreet and, 53; Jubal A. Early and, 134; Leonidas Polk and, 178; meeting with Robert E. Lee, 12, 14–15; Nathan Bedford Forrest and, 72–73; presidency, 16
Great Salt Lake Valley, 93
Greenville, 88
Gregg, John, 11

Hairston family, 125
Halleck, Henry, 82, 169
Hallock, Judith Lee, 137, 139
Hamilcar speech (Toombs), 150–51
Hanover, Pennsylvania, 66
Hardee, William J., 93, 108, 110, *120*
Braxton Bragg and, 142, 179; marriage, 120
Harper's Ferry
John Brown's raid and, 7; Johnston, Joseph E. and, 32; Thomas J. Jackson and, 25; Jubal A. Early and, 132; Thomas J. Jackson at, 20, 25
Harris, Isham G., 100–1, 169, 177
Harrodsburg, 179
Hatcher's Run, 193
Hawkins, Sarah, 173
Helena, Arkansas, 114
Hell's Half Acre, 141
Hennen, Anna Marie, 112
Henry Hill, 20
Henry, Patrick, 30
Hill, Ambrose P., vii, 23, 25, 64
Hill, Daniel Harvey, *21*
Battle of Chickamauga and, 144, 181; Braxton Bragg and, 145; Fort Magruder and, 128; march from Richmond, 34–35; Robert A. Toombs and, 154–55; Thomas J. Jackson and, 18–19
Hindman, Thomas, *115*
Hobson, Edward H., 86
Hollywood Cemetary, 193
Hood, John Bell, 26, 102–12, *103, 104, 108, 112*
arrested for insubordination, 104, 105; baptism of, 181; Battle of Antietam and, 104, 105; Battle of Chickamauga and, 107; Battle of Gettysburg and, 50–51, 106–7; Beauregard and, 171; birth/youth, 103; death, 112; early Battlefield experiences, 103; family background, 102–3; on

Joseph E. Johnston, 41; Joseph Johnston and, 41, 108–9; marriage, 112; military failures, 109–10, 111–12; physical characteristics, 102; reputation, 102, 105–6; at West Point Academy, 103; William T. Sherman and, 39; wounds, 107–8
Hood, John W., 102–3
Hood, Luke, 102
Hooker, Joseph, 26, 27, 65, 118
Hopemount (mansion), 79, *81*
Horn, Stanley F., 91, 137
Hornet's Nest, 178
Hough, Daniel, 166
Houston, Sam, 5
Howard, Oliver O., 28, 121
Huff, John, 68
Huger, Benjamin, 34–35
Hunt, John Wesley, 79
Hunter, David, 131
Hunt-Morgan House, vii
Hunton, Eppa, 186
Hurst, Jack, 71
Huston, Felix, 92

The Immortals, 17
Indianapolis, Indiana, 85–86
Ingersoll, Robert G., 72

Jackson, Andrew, 173
Jackson, Anna, 16–17, 29
Jackson, Cummins, 17
Jackson, Julia, 27, 29
Jackson, Mississippi, 37
Jackson, Thomas J., 16–29, *17, 19, 22, 26, 27*
attacking forces of General Pope, 23–25; Battle of Antietam and, 26, 105; Battle of Fredericksburg and, 26–27; Chancellorsville and, 27–28; childhood, 17; death, 29; family background, 17; at Harper's Ferry, 25; at Henry Hill, 20–21; James Longstreet and, 49; Jeb Stuart and, 26, 62–63; Jubal A. Early and, 125, 128, 129–30; Manassas and, 20–21; marriage, 19; in Mexican War, 18; personal characteristics, 16–17, 25; religious practices, 17, 18; Robert E. Lee and, 21–22, 25; Seven Days Battle and, 23; in Shenandoah Valley, 21–23; on slavery, 19; at Virginia Military Institute, 18–19; at West Point Academy, 17–18; working with Joseph Johnston, 20; wounded, 28–29, 64
Johnson, Andrew, 135–36
Johnson, Bradley, 35, 134
Johnson, R. W., 82
Johnston, Albert Sidney, 33, 91–101, *92, 93, 94, 95*
Battle of Shiloh and, 98–100, 168–69; birth/youth, 91; in Black Hawk war, 92; criticism of, 97–98; death, 9, 100–1, 169, 178; duel by, 92; farming by, 92; Fort Donelson and, 97, 178; Fort Henry and, 96–97; Jefferson Davis and, 91; Leonidas Polk and, 174; in Mexican War, 92; Mormons and, 93–94; need for military manpower, 94–96; ride across the Southwest, 94; Second Calvary and, 6, 93
Johnston, Andrew, 183–4
Johnston, Joseph E., 9, 30–42, *39*
on African Americans in military, 120; Battle of Bentonsville and, 40; Beauregard and, 166–67, 171; Braxton Bragg and, 35–36, 38, 116, 142–43, 145; criticism of, 30, 33; death, 42; early artillery assignments, 30–31; education, 30; Fair Oaks and, 34–35; family origin, 30; Harper's Ferry and, 32; James Longstreet and, 46–47; Jeb Stuart and, 59; Jefferson Davis and, 30, 32–34, 38, 39–40, 41–42; John Bell Hood and, 108–9; John Hunt Morgan and, 83; John Pemberton and, 37–38; on Lincoln's assassination, 41; marriage, 31; meeting with William T. Sherman, 40–41; in Mexican War, 31–32; military sword of, 30, 35; Pemberton's army and, 37–38; post-war activity, 41, 42; Richmond and, 33–34, 39–40, 127; Robert A. Toombs and, 154; Seminole Indians and, 31; working with Thomas J. Jackson, 20
Johnston, Lydia, 32, 35, 42
Johnston, Peter, 30
Johnston, R.M., 172
Jubal, Joab, 125
Junkin, Eleanor, 19

Kean, Robert, 145
Kearny, Philip, 129
Kemper, James, 188, 189
Kennedy, John F., 4
Kennesaw Mountain, 38
Kentucky Volunteers, 80, 81
Kenyon College, 174
Kernstown, 21, 133
Know-Nothings, 115
Krick, Robert, 24
Ku Klux Klan, vii, 69, 77–78

Lafitte, Jean, 162
Lamb, William, 146
Laurel Hill, 58
Law, Evander, 104
Leckie, Robert, 45, 163
Lee, Capt. Robert E. Lee, 13–14
Lee, Fitzhugh, 6, 28, 57, 106, 136, 193
Lee, George Washington Custis, 6, 9, *10*
Lee, Light Horse Harry, 3, 4, *6*
Lee, Matilda, 4
Lee, Robert E., 3–15, *4, 8, 11, 13, 14, 15, 29*
Albert Sidney Johnston and, 93, 98; Arlington mansion and, 4; Battle of Fredericksburg and, 27; Battle of Gettysburg and, 9, 10, 15, 50–51, 53–54, 66–67, 106–7; Beauregard, 171; birthplace, 3; childhood, 4–5; citizenship of, 15; criticism of, 11, 15; death, 14; education, 5; George E. Pickett and, 183, 192, 193; James Longstreet and, 43, 48, 49; Jeb Stuart and, 62, 66–67, 68; Jefferson Davis and, 10; John Bell Hood and, 103, 104, 105; John Pope and, 47; Joseph E. Johnston and, 39; Jubal A. Early and, 125, 130, 135, 136; Ku Klux Klan and, 77; leadership qualities, 9–10; marriage, 5; meeting with U. S. Grant, 12, 14–15; in Mexican War, 5, 32; Patrick Cleburne and, 122; personal/physical characteristics, 7; Pickett's Charge and, 190; on secession, 8, 9; in Second Calvary, 6–7; soldiers' loyalty to, 11–2; Thomas J. Jackson and, 21–22, 23, 24, 25, 28; Virginia and, 8, 11; Washington College and, 12–14
Lee, Rooney, 9, *10*
Leggett's Hill, 121
Leighton (plantation), 175
Letcher, John, 21
Lexington, Kentucky, 88
Lexington Rifles, 80, 81
Liberty, Tennessee, 85
Lincoln, Abraham
1864 election, 110, 111; assassination, 41; Emancipation Proclamation and, 155; Fort Pillow massacre and, 75; Fort Stevens and, 133; Fort Sumter and, 166; George E. Pickett and, 184; as greatest U.S. president, vii; on Kentucky, 80; on McClellan, 63
Little Round Tops, 50–51
Logan, John A., 110
Longacre, Edward G., 184, 189
Longstreet, Augustus Baldwin, 44
Longstreet, Helen Dortch, 43
Longstreet, James, 11, 43–54, *44, 47, 49, 53*
after Civil War, 52–53, 54; attacking General Pope's army, 25; Battle of Gettysburg and, vii, 49–52, 53–54, 107, 187; Braxton Bragg and, 38, 52, 137, 181; childhood, 44; death, 54; death of children, 46; family background, 44; Fredericksburg and, 48–49; George E. Pickett and, 184, 185, 186; John Bell Hood and, 104–5; Joseph E. Johnston and, 34; Jubal A. Early and, 136; at Manassas, 46, 47–48; march from Richmond, 34–35; marriages, 45, 54; in Mexican War, 45; military successes, 46–47; physical characteristics, 46; as Republican, 53; reputation of, 43–44, 54; Robert E. Lee and, 12, 15, 43, 49, 52; Seven Pines and, 46–47; Thomas J. Jackson and, 23, 26; at West Point Academy, 44–45; wounds, 52
Loring, W. W., 21
Louisiana Lottery, 136, 172
Louisville, Kentucky, 140
Lowndes, William, 35
Lynchburg, Virginia, 127, 136

McCausland, John, 133, 134
McClellan, George, 18, 32, 46, 59–61, 63
McDowell, Irwin, 166, *167*
McDowell, Virginia, 22
McIlvaine, Charles P., 174
McLane, Lydia, 31, 32
McLane, Robert, 31
McNealey, Julia, 126
McPherson, James B., 110, 121
McWhiney, Grady, 137
Magruder, John, 104, 154
Malvern Hill, 154–55
Manassas (First)
Beauregard and, 166–67; casualties, 99; James Longstreet and, 46, 47–48; Jeb Stuart and, 59; Joseph E. Johnston and, 32, 33; Jubal A. Early at, 127; Thomas J. Jackson and, 20–21; *See also* Second Manassas
Martinsburg, West Virginia, 132
Marye's Heights, 26, 186
Meade, George, 32
Mechanicsville, Battle of, 23
Meridian, 181
Mescalero Apache, 45
Mexican War
Albert Sidney Johnston in, 92; Braxton Bragg in, 138–39; George E. Pickett in, 184; James Longstreet in, 45; John Hunt Morgan in, 80; Joseph E. Johnston in,

31–32; Jubal A. Early in, 126; Pierre Beauregard in, 32, 162–63; Robert A. Toombs opposing, 149; Robert E. Lee in, 5; Thomas J. Jackson in, 18
Military Academy. *See* West Point Military Academy
Miller, Mitch, 57
Milton, Tennessee, 85
Missionary Ridge, 118, 145
Monocacy River, 132–33
Monterrey, Battle for, 92
Montgomery, Mary Ann, 70
Montgomery, Richard, 70
Morgan, Alexander, 80
Morgan, Calvin Cogswell, 79
Morgan, Henrietta, 79
Morgan, John Hunt, 79–88, *83*
business of, 80; death, 88; escape from prison, 87; family background, 79–80; home of, vii; marriages, 80, 83; in Mexican War, 80; raids by, 81–82, 83, 84–88; reputation, 79, 87, 88; youth, 79–80
Morgan, Rebecca Bruce, 81
Morgan, Tom, 85
Mormons, 93–94
Mormon territory, 93, 94
Morrison, Mary Anna, 19
Mosby, John S., 62, *64*
Munfordville, Kentucky, 140
Murfreesboro, Tennessee, 72, 116, 141, 179
Napoleon Bonaparte, 98, 161, 168
Narrative of Military Operations Directed During the Late War Between the States (Johnston), 41
Nashville, 94
Nashville, Battle of, 112
Natchez, Mississippi, 112
Nat Turner's Rebellion, 31
Neale, Julia Beckwith, 17
Nevins, Allan, 51
New Bern, North Carolina, 191
Newport, Rhode Island, 162
Niagara Falls, Canada, 135
Nullification Crisis, 31

"Old Blue Light." *See* Jackson, Thomas J.
Old Brigade, 72
Orange Turnpike, 28
Oregon Trail, 93
Osborne, Charles C., 127
Otey, James (Bishop of Tennessee), 176
Outlaw, David, 137–38

Pannill, Elizabeth Letcher, 58
Paris, France, 157
Parkersburg, West Virginia, 87
Pea Ridge, Battle of, 98
Pemberton, John, vii–viii, 37, 126
Pender, Dorsey, 65
Peninsula Campaign (1862), 16, 127
George E. Pickett and, 186; Jeb Stuart at, 59–61
Perryville, Battle of, 116, 140, 179
Peters, William, 134
Petersburg, Virginia, 170, 191
Pettigrew, J. Johnston, 189
Pickett, George E., 183–93
Battle of Gettysburg and, 50, 186–88; death, 193; deserters of army and, 191, 192; education, 18, 183–84; family background, 183; Five Forks and, 192–93; friendship with Longstreet, 184, 185; Game Cock Brigade and, 185–86; illness/nervous collapse, 191; marriages, 190–91; in Mexican War, 184; Peninsula Campaign and, 186; "Pickett's Charge," 188–90; reputation, 183; in Washington Territory, 184–85; wounded, 186
Pickett, James Tilton, 185
Pickett, La Salle Corbell, 183, 186, 190–91, 192, 193
Pickett's Charge, vii, 51, 188–90
Pickett's Mill, 121
Picquett family, 183
Pillow, Gideon J., 97
Pine Mountain, 182
Piston, William G., 43
Pittsburg Landing, Tennessee, 98, 139
Pleasanton, Alfred, 64–65
Polk, James K., 149, 173, *175*
Polk, Leonidas (Bishop), 173–182, *174, 175, 180*
appointed as general, 177; Battle of Chickamauga and, 144, 180–81; Battle of Shiloh and, 139, 178; Battle of Stones River and, 179–80; Braxton Bragg and, 79–80, 142, 145, 173, 181; in Columbus, Kentucky, 177–78; death, 182; education, 173–74; Episcopal university of, 175–76; family background, 173; marriage, 174; opposition to war, 176; religious activity, 174–75, 181; religious conversion, 174; Sherman's raid and, 181–82; sugar plantation of, 175; wedding of John Hunt Morgan and, 83, 179
Polk, William, 173
Polk, William Harrison, 182
Polk, William Hawkins, 176
Polk, William M., 174
Polk, William R., 175, 182
Polk's Folly (Polk), 175
Pope, John, 23, 24–25, *48*
Jubal A. Early and, 129; Thomas J. Jackson and, 47
Port Republic, 22
presidential elections
1848, 138; 1852, 163; 1861, 167–68; 1864, 110, 111, 132; 1868, 157; 1884, 158
Preston, Sally, 107, 108
Pryor, Roger, 165
Pulaski, Tennessee, 77

raids
at New Bern, North Carolina, 191; by David Hunter, 131; by Jeb Stuart, 65–66; by John Brown, 59; by John Hunt Morgan, 81–82, 83, 84–88; at Manassas, 47; by Nathan Bedford Forrest, 72, 76; by William T. Sherman, 181–82
Ramage, James A., 80
Rappahannock River, 26, 128–130
Ready, Mattie, 79, 83, 87
Richmond, Virginia, 33–34, 39–40
Richmond Academy, 183
Richmond Whig, 17
"Ride Around McClellan," 59–61
Ringgold Gap, 118
Rock of Chickamauga, 51, 117, 144
Ronayne, Mary Ann, 113
Roosevelt, Theodore, 54
Rosencrans, William S., *84*, 141, 180
Battle of Chickamauga and, 143–145; Morgan's raids and, 84, 85; Patrick Cleburne and, 116; Thomas J. Jackson and, 18, 45, 51
Rosser, Tom, 193
Round Tops, 130
Rumanian army, 172

Salem, Indiana, 86
Salineville, Ohio, 86
Salt Lake City, 94
San Juan Island, 184–85
Sanson, Emma, 73
Scheibert, A., 64
Schofield, John, 103, *111*
Scott, Winfield, 8, *9*, 18
Beauregard joining, 162; Braxton Bragg criticizing, 138; Joseph E. Johnston and, 31; Mexican War and, 45; Robert A. Toombs and, 151
secession
Jubal A. Early on, 127; Robert A. Toombs on, 150, 151; Robert E. Lee on, 7, 8
Second Calvary, 6, 104
Second Manassas
casualties, 25; James Longstreet and, 47–48; Jubal A. Early and, 129; Robert A. Toombs and, 155
Seddon, James A., 120, 145
Sedgwick, John, 126, 138
Seminary Ridge, 187

Seven Days Battles, 23, 104
Seven Pines, Battle of, 46–47, 186
Sharpsburg, Maryland, 155
Shenandoah Valley
burning in, 135; Jeb Stuart and, 59; Jubal A. Early and, 131–34; Thomas J. Jackson and, 21–23
Sheridan, Philip, *66*
George E. Pickett and, 192–93; Jeb Stuart and, 67–68; Jubal A. Early and, 134–35
Sherman, William T., 121
Albert Sidney Johnston and, 95–96, 99; death, 42; John Bell Hood and, 109–11; Joseph E. Johnston and, 37, 38–39, 40–41; Leonidas Polk's death and, 182; Nathan Bedford Forrest and, 76; Patrick Cleburne and, 117–18; raid in Mississippi, 181–82
Shiloh, Battle of, 98–100
Beauregard and, 168–69; Braxton Bragg and, 139; casualties, 99; Leonidas Polk and, 178; Nathan Bedford Forrest and, 71–72
Shiloh Church, 100
Shiloh National Military Park, 100
Sigel, Franz, 28
slavery
Albert Sidney Johnston and, 91; Jubal A. Early on, 136; Patrick Cleburne on, 119; Robert A. Toombs on, 148, 149–50, 151; Robert E. Lee on, 3, 7; Thomas J. Jackson on, 19
slave trading, 69, 70–71
Slidell, John, 163, 164
Smith, Edmund Kirby, 82, 115, 135, 140
Smith, William Sooy, 74
Sorrel, Gilbert Moxley, 46, 186
Southern Historical Society, 136
Spotsylvania, 67–68
Spotsylvania Court House, 67
Spring Hill, 111–12, 121
St. Bernard Parish, 162
Stephens, Alexander, 149, *151*, 152, 157
Stewart, Alexander, 110
St. John's Episcopal Church, 174
Stones River, Battle of, 84, 141–42, 179–80
"Stonewall." *See* Jackson, Thomas J.
Stonewall Brigade, 21
Stratford Hall, 3, 4, *5*
Streight, Abel D., 73
Stuart, Isabella, 113
Stuart, James Ewell Brown (Jeb), 57–68, *60*
Battle of Brandy Station, 64–65; Battle of Gettysburg and, 50, 57, 66–67; Beauregard and, 161; Chambersburg and, 63; criticism of, 63–64, 65; death, 68; Evelington Heights and, 61; gala shows by, 106; hat of,

62; invention by, 59; marriage, 58; personal/physical characteristics, 57–58, 62; raids for supplies by, 65–66; 'ride around McClellan' and, 59–61; Thomas J. Jackson and, 26, 62–63, 64; at West Point Academy, 6, 58; youth, 58
Stuart, John T., 184
Suffolk, Virginia, 49
Sumner, Edwin, 35
Sunken Road, 100
Symonds, Craig L., 30, 113

Taliaferro, Norborne, 126
Tarleton, Susan, 120, 122
Taylor, Zachary, 80, 92, 138
Tennessee River, 72
Theophilus Holmes, 154
Thibodaux, Louisiana, 139
Thomas, D. Y., 120
Thomas, George, 51, 93, 109–10, *118*, 141, 143, 180
Thompson, Jeff, 178
Thompson, Sarah, 88
Thompson, William Y., 151, 158
Tilghman, Lloyd, 96–97
"Tom Fool." *See* Jackson, Thomas J.
Toombs, Robert A., 148–158, *149, 152, 157*
as anti-government, 156–57; as attorney, 149; Battle of Antietam and, 155; death, 158; education, 148–49; in exile, 157; Fort Sumter and, 153; Hamilcar speech by, 150–51; Jefferson Davis and, 155–56; marriage, 149; personal characteristics, 148; in politics, 149, 151; presidency for Confederacy and, 151–52; resignation, 155–56; Second Manassas and, 155; as secretary of Confederate state, 152–53; on slavery, 148, 149–50, 151
Toombs, Sallie, 157
Toronto, Canada, 135
Tourgee, Albion, 143–44
Transylvania University, 80
Trimble, Isaac, 189
Tullahoma, Tennessee, 142, 143, 180
Tunnel Hill, 118
Turkey Island, 191
Twiggs, David, 162–63, 164

Union College, 148
United States Military Academy at West Point. *See* West Point Military Academy
University at Chapel Hill, 173
University of Georgia, 148
University of Mississippi, 44
University of North Carolina, 173
University of the South, 13, 175–76, 182
University of Virginia, 13
University of Virginia Law School, 148–49

Vandiver, Frank E., 23
Van Dorn, Earl, 8
Vaught's Hill, 84–85
Vera Cruz, Mexico, 31, 135
Verdiersville, Virginia, 62
Vicksburg, Mississippi, 36, 37
Villere, Marie Laure, 162, 163
Virginia Military Institute (VMI), 16, 18–19
Virginia Theological Seminary, 174

Walker, William H. G., 120
Wallace, Lew, 132, *132*
Walter Reed Hospital, 133
Warrenton, North Carolina, 137
Washington, George, 4, 13
Washington, Georgia, 148
Washington, Kentucky, 91
Washington and Lee University, 6
Washington College, 12–14
Washington, D.C., 125
Washington Territory, 184–85
Wayne, Anthony, 102
Waynesboro, 135
Webb, Thomas Gray, 83
Welles, Nancy Gideon, 157
West, Jessamyn, 86
West Point Military Academy
Albert Sidney Johnston at, 91; Beauregard as superintendent of, 164; Beauregard at, 162; Braxton Bragg at, 138; George E. Pickett at, 183, 184; James Longstreet at, 44–45; Jeb Stuart at, 6, 58; John Bell Hood at, 103; Joseph E. Johnston at, 30; Jubal A. Early at, 125–26; Leonidas Polk at, 173–74; Robert E. Lee as superintendent of, 6; Robert E. Lee at, 5
Wheeler, Joseph, viii, 73
Whigs, 126, 149
Whiskey Rebellion (1794), 4
Whitehorn, Joseph W. A., 135
White Sulphur Springs, 126
Whiting, William, 147
Wigfall, Louis T., 38
Wilder, J. T., 140
The Wilderness, 11, 27–28, 67
Will, George, 155
Williams, C. D., 88
Williamsburg, Battle of, 186
Wilmer McLean House, 12
The Wilmot Proviso, 149
Winchester, Virginia, 133
Wise, John, 128

Yellow Tavern, 68
Yell Rifles, 115
Yorktown, 34
Young, Brigham, 93

Zollicoffer, Felix, 96